The social context
of health

Health Psychology

Series editors:
Sheila Payne and Sandra Horn

Published titles

Psychology and Health Promotion
Paul Bennett and Simon Murphy

The Social Context of Health
Michael Hardey

Pain: Theory, Research and Intervention
Sandra Horn and Marcus Munafò

Stress
Dean Bartlett

Loss and Bereavement
Sheila Payne, Sandra Horn, Marilyn Relf

The social context of health

Michael Hardey

Open University Press
Buckingham · Philadelphia

Open University Press
Celtic Court
22 Ballmoor
Buckingham
MK18 1XW

email: enquiries@openup.co.uk
world wide web: http://www.openup.co.uk

and
325 Chestnut Street
Philadelphia, PA 19106, USA

First Published 1998
Reprinted 1999

A catalogue record of this book is available from the British Library

ISBN   0 335 19863 5 (pb)   0 335 19864 3 (hb)

Library of Congress Cataloging-in-Publication Data
Hardey, Michael.
    The social context of health / Michael Hardey.
       p.   cm. – (Health psychology)
    Includes bibliographical references and index.
    ISBN 0–335–19863–5 (pb.). – ISBN 0–335–19864–3 (hb.)
    1. Social medicine.   I. Title.   II. Series.
RA418.H33   1998
306'.4' 61–dc21   98–4843
                                                                                              CIP

Typeset by Graphicraft Limited, Hong Kong
Printed in Great Britain by Biddles Ltd, Guildford and King's Lynn

Contents

Series editors' foreword

This new series of books in health psychology is designed to support post-graduate and postqualification studies in psychology, nursing, medicine and paramedical sciences, as well as the establishment of health psychology within the undergraduate psychology curriculum. Health psychology is growing rapidly as a field of study. Concerned as it is with the application of psychological theories and models in the promotion and maintenance of health, and the individual and interpersonal aspects of adaptive behaviour in illness and disability, health psychology has a wide remit and a potentially important role to play in the future.

In this book, Hardey has set health psychology in its social, political and historical context. Inequalities in health and extended concepts of illness causation beyond biomedical factors have been increasingly highlighted in recent years, and it is no longer possible for health psychologists to ignore social influences on health or remain concerned with individual factors alone. Hardey's book provides a detailed and accessible account of social factors in health and health services provision. He has ranged widely in his consideration of the contextual factors surrounding health from the perspective of a medical sociologist, including the birth and development of the British National Health Service, professionalization in medicine and nursing, and gender issues. His insights are often challenging, and the material from which he draws may be unfamiliar to some psychologists, but we would argue that a thorough grasp of the social context on all aspects of our lives including health, will enrich our understanding of health psychology.

Sheila Payne and Sandra Horn

 # Introduction

Health is deeply embedded in the social world. It is also much abused as a concept. People are said to have a healthy attitude to life, some foods are supposedly good for your health and parents worry whether their child has a healthy interest in sex. International trade may be healthy, a business may make a healthy profit and a political party may have a healthy majority in parliament. The dark side of health is represented by the unhealthy and associated with the negative if not the immoral. Such vague and various usage of health comes more sharply into focus when we feel the need to visit a doctor. We anticipate a consultation that involves a process of diagnosis, treatment and cure. This reflects a faith in the ability of medicine to resolve problems that range from a cough to a feeling that a relationship may not be working. Health and its binary opposite therefore wields considerable ideological power which in part stems from its association with the apparent certainties of medicine. However, social scientists have shown how medical knowledge is itself social and reflects the culture and politics of its time. This does not mean that sociologists would contest, for example, that the heart pumps blood around the body, but they would seek to understand why, when and how this particular piece of knowledge became accepted as such. Furthermore, they are interested in how and to whom this knowledge is applied. While medicine and psychology are essentially based on the individual, sociology takes a more collective approach which blurs into some areas of social psychology, history, philosophy and other disciplines. This blurring of academic disciplines and uncertainty about boundaries is one of the challenges of what has been variously called late or high modernity, post-industrial or postmodern societies. Such labels are associated with particular writers or theoretical positions. However, while recognizing the significance of such distinctions where appropriate, they are largely used in this book in a more general sense. Given the breadth of work on health and illness, there are inevitably some aspects that receive greater emphasis than others in this book. Decisions about what to include and exclude have been driven by the desire to put together an account of the essential social nature of health and illness rather than provide a comprehensive survey of all the topics and literature that could be covered. Dimensions of social aspects of illness that include ageing and death are relatively neglected here but are represented in a growing literature (e.g. Clark 1993; Field *et al.* 1997). Health promotion has received attention from Bunton *et al.* (1995) and Bennett and Murphy (1997) while detailed consideration of the social aspects of mental health has found the space it deserves in Busfield (1996) and Pilgrim and Rogers (1993).

The relationship between health and the social world forms the central theme of this book. It opens with an examination of the development of modern medicine and shows how it was shaped by, and in turn shaped, social processes. Ideas about the human mind and body were central to the eventual success of medicine and remain significant in medical practice today. The political and ideological role of medicine is highlighted in the racialization of early medical knowledge. Alternative or complementary medicine is becoming increasingly popular and challenges both the scientific basis of medicine and how it is practised. It is suggested that a characteristic of postindustrial societies is increased choice and risk. This uncertainty can be linked to the evolving role of non-orthodox medicine and wider concerns about 'new plagues' that may threaten the existence of whole societies. It is also possible to discern a long-established tension between the natural and the unnatural at work here.

Chapter 2 moves on to consider lay understandings of health. Parsons' (1951) well-known formulation of the sick role provides a useful starting point from which to situate later sociological research. It is shown that studies about how people conceptualized health and illness emerged from a particular set of academic and policy concerns. The use or neglect of health services remains a significant policy problem and it is shown how factors that include social class, gender and race shape responses to illness. While all deviations from an individual's expectations about health can be threatening, the onset of chronic illness and disability may involve a reconstruction of self-identity. However, it is shown that identity and ideas about risk may be transformed by presence of conditions such as HIV which may have little immediate impact on physical capacity.

Chapter 3 examines the role of the National Health Service (NHS) in shaping the medical professions and the organization of the delivery of care. It is suggested that broad economic and social changes since the inception of the NHS have had a formative impact. This is reflected in the place of private healthcare in Britain which, despite a discourse about choice, may ironically provide its clients with only limited opportunities to be consumers. Tensions in the delivery of care are increasingly evident in the care of people with mental health problems. The role of drugs, surveillance and politics are examined and related to recent social and economic changes.

Increasing concern with the healthy population is manifest in recent public policy as well as health education and health promotion. The collective nature of these aspects of public policy are situated within wider debates about self-help groups and individual action.

The emergence and nature of the health professions are examined in Chapter 4. Political and ideological struggles around the creation and maintenance of boundaries between lay and professional domains as well as between the professions or occupations themselves show how they are a creation of the social world. The exclusion and later marginalization of women illustrates this well. Recent developments within nursing and midwifery are critically examined and related to the dominant position of medicine. Such gender and other inequalities can be seen in lay and professional encounters which can be conceptualized as encounters that reinforce and legitimate established boundaries. Consultations with non-orthodox practitioners are different in form and content and may indicate how traditional boundaries and power structures are being questioned if not undermined. The new technology of the Internet is examined as a potential way for lay people to access and challenge the expertise of professional medicine.

Social division and the impact they have on health and illness are examined in Chapter 5. The development of social class as an instrument of health research is explored and situated within nineteenth century debates about improving the health of the poor. The incorporation of race into studies of health has proved to be problematic, and like the conceptualization of poverty the boundaries around various categories used remain contested. The Black Report (Townsend and Davidson (1982, 1992)) has a formative impact on the debate about health and the social structure. Differences in mortality and morbidity are examined and various explanations for the links with social class are analysed. Associations between the unequal distribution of health are considered in relation to factors that include deprivation and social exclusion, race, gender and lifestyle.

Chapter 6 picks up the theme of gender and health and examines the distinction between biological sex and gender. This is linked to the gendered nature of the body and the relationship between it and personal identity. Bodies can be reshaped through diet, reconstructed through medical interventions and used to express a social and sexual position. The family is frequently seen as central to both identity and the health of its members. The problematization of women's health, which stems partly from their relationship to care work, has meant that men's health has been defined as relatively unproblematic. The changing nature of fatherhood is used to explore some of the ways men experience and seek to shape the behaviour of others. Developments in reproductive technology not only contribute to shaping the form of families but also highlight gender and social difference. These are also reflected in mental healthcare and debates about the use of psychotropic drugs.

The final chapter, Chapter 7, pulls together some of the issues considered previously and situates them within ideas about lifestyle, identity and choice. It is argued that environmental and social deprivation beyond the boundaries of any one country can have a major impact on individual experiences and concerns about health and illness. Health may not only be inherently social but also increasingly diverse and global in its scope.

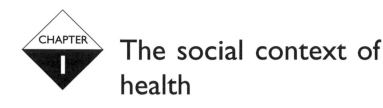

The social context of health

The emergence of modern medicine

Contemporary ideas about health and illness are embedded in the development of the biomedical model and the emergence of the natural sciences which can be traced back to the Renaissance. Following a general movement to recognize the rational capacity of humans to understand the world through non-religious means (Turner 1996), René Descartes provided the intellectual case for separating the thinking subject (the mind) from the passive object of thought (the body). This image of 'man the machine' helped to removed layers of superstitions, beliefs about the way sick people were in an intimate struggle with transcendent forces and the potency of divine intervention.

> The medical body comes to be viewed not primarily as purposive and ensouled; nor as the scene of moral dramas; nor as a place wherein cosmological and social forces gather; but simply as an intricate machine. It operates, so the model goes, according to a variety of physical forces: electrical, chemical, hydrodynamic, and the like.
>
> (Leder 1992: 3)

It is now possible to investigate the body using similar objective tools and processes that were used to study any other part of nature. People could intellectually disengage from the body and religion in a way that had not been possible previously. As Foucault (1976) argued, the 'medical gaze' is shorn of mysticism, magic and faith because the scientist or doctor is informed by nothing more than material facts. This is expressed through a discourse that rotates around notions of disease and pathology which are located within the body. The body becomes part of nature and thus part of the project to identify and classify the workings of nature. Like other aspects of nature, the body is self-contained, and while its workings may be opaque there are no inherently unobservable or spiritual factors to hinder scientific understanding. This leads to the 'epistemological primacy of the corpse' (Leder 1992: 7). The body is conceived of as more or less 'strange' territory which the scientist like the explorer of a new land can penetrate, observe and seek to understand. The boundaries between the living and the dead body break down as one comes to represent the working and the other the non-working mechanism. Frankenstein's determination to build a new working body out of various 'spare parts' reflects this conceptualization. The problem of the soul and other transcendent matters are not the province of science under Descartes' paradigm. As Turner (1992) has noted, this separation of mind and body has left a legacy whereby, until recently, the body was the province of natural science and the mind the focus of the humanities.

Medicine in the early eighteenth century has been described as 'library medicine', which places an emphasis on the classical learning and status of the doctor (Ackerhnecht 1967). By the late eighteenth century, the physician-botanist Françoise Bossier de Sauvages had developed a classificatory system that identified 2400 diseases that were grouped into ten classes (Longino and Murphy 1995). Reiser (1978) points out that until the eighteenth century, medical diagnosis was based largely on the patient's own observations and feelings, so that if necessary, diagnosis could be conducted through the exchange of letters. The knowledge held by the patient was therefore fundamental to comprehending illness (Rothman 1991). The wealthy, who could afford doctors, often acted as their patrons and had a close relationship with them. Although the importance of patronage has been contested (Pellign 1978), doctors generally visited patients in their homes to practise 'bedside medicine'. Diagnosis and treatment was largely based around the patient's own perceptions, which gave scope to negotiate with the patient (Jewson 1976). Foucault (1976) has described how, in the eighteenth century, attempts to understand disease moved away from the observation of the symptoms experienced by sufferers to the organic traces left in dead bodies.

> That which hides and envelops the curtain of night over truth, is, paradoxically, life; and death, on the contrary, opens up to the light of day the black coffer of the body.
>
> (Foucault 1976: 166)

The focus on cadavers remains an important part of contemporary medical education. In 1816, René Laennec used a piece of wood to listen to the internal workings of a patient (Starr 1982). The stethoscope enables doctors in a sense to 'see' inside the patient and make their own observations of the body without having to rely on the patient's observations or outward signs such as coughing. The stethoscope localized the site of pathology in a way not possible before and provided empirical data (Nuland 1988). This new 'clinical gaze' (Foucault 1976) produced new scientific data, which supported by evidence from autopsies, led to new models of chest infections.

Armstrong (1983) following Foucault, suggests that this technology gave rise to a 'new concept of the body'. Critically, doctors could 'look' inside the body and identify the site of infection without needing the active participation of the patient. Symbolizing the new relationship, the stethoscope could only be used if the patient remain silent and still. The examination often involved the patient in removing clothes, laying down and being still in a manner resembling that of a corpse. Involvement in the diagnostic process was confined to mechanical instructions like 'take a deep breath' or 'move a limb'. Later technological developments such as laryngoscopes for examining the throat and the microscope for identifying cellular pathology further marginalized the role of the patient as an active participant in diagnosis (Reiser 1978). Armstrong (1983) sums up the medical conceptualization of the body:

> This body appears to be discrete because it was recorded in separate case notes; it was accessible because at this time medicine began to use methods of physical examination; it was analysable because pathology became localisable to a distinct point within the body; it was passive because a patient's personal history was relegated from its primary position as the key to the diagnosis to a preliminary; and it was subjected to evaluation because patients were moved from the natural locus of the home to the neutral domain of the hospital.
>
> (Armstrong 1983. 6)

As Armstrong notes the new technology found its natural place in the hospitals that were being built in the nineteenth century. Foucault (1976) has traced the development of the clinic in France as centres for the practice and dissemination of the new medical practices of clinical observation, physical examination, pathological examination and bedside teaching. From the late eighteenth century, medical and biological science gradually developed the notion of specific aetiology. This conceptualized diseases as having particular causes which could be identified and treated. Jewson (1976) argues that 'hospital medicine' which replaced bedside medicine, changed the nature of the doctor–patient relationship by placing the former firmly in charge of the latter. However, the patients in the clinics were the poor who had access to 'modern' healthcare at the cost of their passive collaboration in the medical process. This process for Foucault (1976) involved the surveillance, regulation and discipline of bodies. The clinic provided an environment for a new form of consultation,

> . . . the medical encounter is a supreme example of surveillance, whereby the doctor investigates, questions, touches the exposed flesh of the patient, while the patient acquiesces, and confesses, with little knowledge of why the procedures are carried out.
>
> (Lupton 1994: 115)

This indicates the interaction between symptom, sign and pathology which replaced the earlier conceptualization of symptom and pathology. The symptom as experienced by the patient remained relevant but might not be as significant as the signs discovered and interpreted by the doctor through clinical examination. The medicalization of the body is reflected in the way it became common for people, and especially women to feel that parts of their bodies were 'revered for lovers and doctors' (The Boston Women's Health Collective 1984). As Zola (1983) has argued:

> If anything can be shown in some way to affect the working of the body and to a lesser extent the mind, then it can be labelled an 'illness' itself or jurisdictionally 'a medical problem'.
>
> (Zola 1983: 261)

Signs pointed to the disease that gave rise to symptoms. Foucault (1976) describes these changes as part of a 'spatialisation' of illness. Supported by the new medical technologies the body became three-dimensional in that the 'depth' of the body represented by its inner space could be examined for signs. Inspection, palpation (for example, feeling a 'painful' area with the fingers), percussion (for example, hitting the body to assess the condition of organs) and ausculation (listening to, for example, the heart via the stethoscope) make up the classic techniques of clinical examination used in the search for signs (Armstrong 1995). The resulting diagnosis can be confirmed by postmortem examination which in the initial development of the hospital provided an important contribution to the understanding of disease. The use of X-rays, analysis of the blood and other technological innovations in the late nineteenth century meant that diagnosis could take place in the absence of a sick body, so that the patient was further marginalized. Jewson (1976), following Ackerhnecht (1967), has referred to this as marking a shift to 'laboratory medicine'. It was laboratory evidence that divided the normal from the deviant and had a critical role in understanding disease. However, this represents a refinement of techniques and does not replace the centrality of the hospital or the processes in the identification or treatment of disease (Armstrong 1995). Recent new technologies combined with case notes and other representations of the patient can construct a 'virtual patient'. The 'virtual human' project has given a 'virtual life' to a dead man and woman, whose bodies can be manipulated in minute three-dimensional detail. Case notes represented an initial stage in the assimilation of patients (S. Epstein 1995) that is, moving on to virtual representations that can be dissected, discussed and reduced to taxonomies free of location and time. This also has implications for the nature of the work of the medical professions:

> . . . physicians came to believe that to know the disease and its treatment is to know the illness and the treatment of the ill person. This provided further basis for the idea that individual physicians count

for little *as individuals* [emphasis in original]; it is their knowledge of disease and medical science that cares for the patient. In this thinking, a disembodied knowledge connected to some sort of mechanical doctoring machine would do as well and so one should not be surprised at the numerous attempts to formulate computer diagnostics or therapies.

(Cassell 1991: 20)

The biomedical model includes the following elements:

◆ *Dualistic*. The Cartesian divide of mind and body is at the centre of how diseases are understood and treated. There are other dualistic divisions such as that between the observer and the subject, man and nature, diagnosis and treatment, health and illness, sex and gender, and so on, that underpin the biomedical project.
◆ *Mechanistic*. 'Man the machine' points to a causal chain that is governed by complex universal rules. These causes and rules are open to 'discovery', classification and understanding by scientific methods. For example, the use of the microscope made it possible to identify microorganisms.
◆ *Reductionist*. Biological explanations of disease are sought out from the observed behaviours of the body and the particles associated with the condition. The work in the nineteenth century of Louis Pasteur and Robert Koch identified the bacterial causes of diseases such as tuberculosis.
◆ *Empirical*. Knowledge is generated by observation and can be confirmed through a process of experimentation. This entails the objective role of the observer and the assumption that the material being observed is only subject to natural forces.
◆ *Interventionist*. Medical knowledge can be applied to 'repair' damage or sick biological systems. This frequently involves the direct use of instruments to make changes to the body.

Medical knowledge and the medical profession (see Chapter 6) are constructed through complex social processes that embrace the apparently neutral and objective sites of scientific endeavour such as the laboratory (Latour and Woolgar 1979). As the history of biomedicine suggests, the practice of medicine contains social and political dimensions that may be obscured by the faith invested in medical neutrality. This can be seen in the development of such basic categories as the sexed body, that is, the body defined by its sexual characteristics, as product of science and the development of biomedicine in particular. Laqueur (1990) argues that before the Enlightenment, the anatomies of men and women were thought to be basically the same. It was thought that one sex could turn into the other, there was no conceptualization of the modern category of homosexuality, and men could commonly lactate. Bodily differences did not provide a basis for explaining the social and economic differences between men and women. Therefore *'sex'* (or the body) must be understood as the epiphenomenon, while *gender*, what we would take to be a cultural category, was primarily 'real' (emphasis in original) (Laqueur 1990: 8). The development of the natural sciences from the eighteenth century transformed the understanding of human sexual difference by situating it with the different anatomies of men and women. These differences were seen not only in reproductive organs and functions but as science advanced in every aspect of women's bodies. Menstruation became identified in animals and women. Deviations in the menstrual cycle were thought to produce insanity and by the late nineteenth century this accounted for a significant number of admissions to the asylums (Busfield 1996). Attention was also paid to other features such as the size of the male and female pelvis and skull. The 'science' of phrenology was employed in the measuring and assessment of skulls and heads to identify sex, racial and other differences. The mapping of such sex differences is important, as they provided the basis for the exclusion of women from the public sphere. The male body became the paradigm and deviations from this norm, such as the female body, became a 'problem'. Furthermore, this paradigm was specifically 'white', so that women and people from the 'lesser races' compared unfavourably with it (Stephan and Gilman 1991). The political and cultural milieu in which medical and natural science was situated in the nineteenth century generated this new mode of thought which 'set up whites as absolute and distinct and considered all non-white races only in terms of how much they deviated from the illustrious Caucasian standard' (Young 1994: 167). Science provided the methods to measure and assess every part of the anatomy, with special attention being paid to the head as the seat of intelligence. Classifications soon became complex, contested and overlapping, as the European population alone was divided up into Nordic, Alpine, Mediterranean types and others. This project collapsed under the weight of its own internal contradictions (Stephan 1982), but the notion of intelligence being associated with a conceptualization of race remains culturally significant. For example, the book *The Bell Curve: Intelligence and Class Structure in American Life* (Herrnstein and Murray 1994) attempted to revisit the theme of inheritance and race (Fraser 1995). Like others who did not fit the paradigm of the male body, it was argued that women should not be accorded the rights of citizenship (e.g. to vote, be educated, etc.). As Busfield (1996: 107) notes, 'by the twentieth century the familiar polarization of male, scientific and rational with female, intuitive and emotional was well-established'.

The identification of 'illness' and the construction of 'treatment' are not therefore 'natural' scientifically based processes but profoundly social. Drapetomania provides a commonly cited and stark example of this social construction of disease that is related to the classification of 'lesser races'. In the mid-nineteenth century, Negro slaves displayed symptoms of drapetomania by persistently running away from their owners (Cartwright 1851; S. Epstein 1995). The cause of the condition was overindulgent treatment and lack of the discipline which it was thought they required.

As S. Epstein (1995) argues, these slaves in crossing the border could have simply been defined as criminals. However they also crossed an ideological border and by defining them as 'mad' rather than 'bad', the medical profession legitimated the ideological boundaries around slavery and highlighted the dangers of changing the treatment of Negro slaves. The late nineteenth century has been called the 'golden age' of hysteria, when this paradigmatic female condition was at its height (Goldstein 1987). Diagnosed in women, it helped legitimate their exclusion from education and other non-domestic settings for which it was thought their biology was 'naturally' unsuited. The identification and categorization of homosexuality as a treatable condition and more recent searches for a 'gay gene' or 'gay brain' reflect the continuity of this role in biomedicine. For J. Epstein (1995), diagnosis is the key to the surveillance of boundaries. She uses the example of hermaphrodites, birth defects and AIDS to illustrate the nature of 'provocative diagnosis'. Considerable resources were used to study hermaphroditism and other conditions because they challenged binary opposites upon which a gendered social hierarchy is established. Epstein refers to the 'new invisibility' that modern diagnosis and surgery make possible by correcting 'genital abnormalities'. 'You can change, albeit with great difficulty and at great cost, from one sex to the other, but you cannot straddle the two' (J. Epstein 1995: 116). Similarly, the social response to AIDS is centred on reinforcing the boundaries around 'normal' sexuality and family.

> HIV infection and AIDS pose a threat to systems of guarding not only the physical boundaries of the body, but also the borders of social and moral categories as they are fixed, in the West, in transgressive notions of sexuality and human desire.
>
> (J. Epstein 1995: 166)

Pluralistic approaches to health

While orthodox medicine has its roots in rationalism and the demystification of the body, non-orthodox approaches to health from the perspectives of contemporary practitioners and users marks a 're-enchantment' (Weston 1992). The label 'holistic' has recently become common in orthodox medicine and especially nursing (see Chapter 4). Although there is a wide diversity of meaning given to holism, it broadly indicates a critical distancing or break from the biomedical dualism of mind and body. The dominant position of orthodox medicine can make it hard to understand the role and nature of some non-orthodox approaches. The terminology used is in itself problematic in that non-orthodox implies a comparison with a more favoured orthodox view of health. In Britain, 'alternative' and 'complementary' medicine are common labels. They again indicate a relationship with the biomedical model and may further distinguish between approaches that more or less correspond to it. A number of therapies can 'complement' medicine in that they do not reject medical diagnosis and may provide techniques that can be used with conventional treatment. For example, chiropractic therapy utilizes conventional anatomy and physiology. In the United States, complementary medicine is more widely used and this reflects the more direct competition between practitioners in a market-led healthcare system. Sharma (1992), writing about Britain, also favours the complementary label because she argues it points to collaboration rather than conflict between the approaches. From his analysis of the struggles between the medical establishment and non-orthodox practitioners, Saks (1995) favours the alternative label as indicating inherent conflict (see Chapter 4). The 'orthodox' and 'non-orthodox' dualism will be used here as it recognizes differentials in power and prestige evident in postindustrial medical systems. This, like other descriptions, is also inadequate, especially as it fails to capture the diversity and complexity of non-orthodox approaches.

The dominance of orthodox medicine makes it easy to forget that it has a comparatively short history of little more than 150 years. Previously there was a great diversity of beliefs about illness and potential treatments that competed for customers (Stacey 1988). In the nineteenth century, the 'big four' more or less complex medical approaches of herbalism, hydropathy (associated with the use of spas), homoeopathy and mesmerism competed with medicine (Cooter 1988). Indeed, even after the Medical Registration Act it was often hard to distinguish between what became orthodox and non-orthodox practitioners. Table 1.1 indicates the range of non-orthodox approaches. Indigenous or culturally situated approaches are those which developed in a number of societies and often include religious, philosophical and health elements. Considerably older than biomedicine, these remain significant in many countries, despite attempts to establish the domination of Western medicines which was part of the colonizing process (Doyal 1979). Body focused therapies include those approaches that are centred on the manipulation of the body in order to restore what is considered to be a healthly balance. Mind-focused approaches concentrate on achieving changes in mental state or more generally orientation to life. Both are holistic in that they seek to understand and influence the mind and body. 'Natural' non-allopathic therapies seek to restore the bodies 'natural' healing processes and reject the use of, for example, antibiotics.

Indigenous or folk medicine remains important in many communities and countries where orthodox medicine may be of secondary importance for those living in rural areas or the poor (Doyal 1996). In such settings, orthodox medicine may be one of a number of therapeutic approaches, all of which are embedded in the history, religions and experiences of the community. Research on recent and later generations of immigrants in Britain shows that indigenous medical beliefs and practices remain significant despite the availability of orthodox medicine. Thorogood's (1990) research into the health beliefs and practices of the Caribbean community

Table 1.1   A classification of non-orthodox approaches to health

---

Indigenous or culturally situated
  Hindu or ayurvedic medicine
  Islamic or unani medicine
  Chinese medicine

Body-focused therapies
  Aromatherapy
  Dance therapy
  Osteopathy
  Chiropractic
  Reflexology

Mind-focused therapies
  Psychic healing
  Hypnotherapy

'Natural' non-allopathic therapies
  Herbalism
  Homoeopathy

---

in Britain revealed that women adopted a multifaceted approach to health
that incorporated indigenous and orthodox medical beliefs. This reflects
the way that indigenous medicine can be situated within religious beliefs
and a wider sense of community identity. Other research has pointed to
the complex interplay between approaches to health that are particularly
important in shaping the use of medical resources (Bhopal 1986; Nettleton
1993; Thorogood 1990).

Over the past two decades or so, an increase in the use of non-orthodox
therapies and an increase in the number and range of practitioners has been
identified in postindustrial societies (Pietroni 1991; Bakx 1991; Weston 1992,
Sharma 1992; British Medical Association 1993; Lupton 1994; Saks 1995).
It is difficult to assess the extent to which people visit non-orthodox practitioners because, unlike orthodox medicine, there is no monolithic structure
concerned with the utilization of such services. A Consumer's Association
survey cited by a British Medical Association (1993) report estimated that
one in four of the population have consulted non-orthodox practitioners.
A glance through any local paper will reveal advertisements for 'psychic
fairs' where non-orthodox practitioners along with 'spiritual traders' are
selling their services. A number of surveys based on specific conditions such
as irritable bowel syndrome have suggested that less than 20 per cent of
sufferers have sought non-orthodox therapies (Smart *et al.* 1986). However,
as this survey was based on patients using orthodox medicine, it is likely
to underestimate the number of sufferers who have used non-orthodox
therapies. Sharma (1992) cites a number of surveys carried out in Britain
and in other post-industrial societies that indicate that women are rather

more likely to use non-orthodox practitioners than men. Partly reflecting a rationing by price, middle-class clients are more common than working-class clients (Crawford 1980). People with high cultural capital such as teachers and social workers who work in the public sector and therefore have relatively low economic capital tend to follow 'ascetic' consumption patterns (Urry 1990). These include a preference for 'natural' pursuits such as climbing, yoga and outdoor activities. Their perceived 'expert' knowledge (Savage *et al.* 1992) contributes to the critical consumption of healthcare and a willingness to pursue 'natural' approaches. The identification of trends in the use of non-orthodox practitioners is even more difficult because of the lack of repeated survey data. Similarly, it is difficult to assess the degree to which there has been an increase in the number of people offering non-orthodox services. However, it is possible to identify an increase in the number of practitioners registered with various non-orthodox medical organizations (Saks 1995). The more conciliatory approach to non-orthodox practice, evident in the British Medical Association report (1993) (see Chapter 4), reflects the increasing number of references and papers about non-orthodox therapies in medical journals (Saks 1995).

A key tension between orthodox and non-orthodox medicine is the problem of the effectiveness of treatment. Indeed, the notion of a diagnosis and treatment cycle is alien to some non-orthodox practices that focus on lifestyle or 'attitude' rather than the duality of health and illness. The techniques of some non-orthodox therapies are more amenable to medical assessment and there is an increasing use in orthodox medicine of, for example, acupuncture and aromatherapy. Acupuncture can be subject to scientific measurements and its effect on the relief of pain can be clinically assessed. The Medical Acupuncture Society set up in 1980 has an exclusively medical membership which has campaigned to gain scientific recognition (Saks 1995). Unlike many non-orthodox approaches, explanations in terms of biology can be offered to help legitimate the techniques. Unlike acupuncture, aromatherapy does not involve the physical penetration of the body but uses fragrant oils to affect the physiological and emotional condition of the patient. Massage is commonly used to apply the oils and its use has been advocated by nurses, especially for chronically ill patients. The clinical effect of aromatherapy is hard to assess and although patients are usually satisfied with the treatment, this may reflect the impact of massage or the breaking of hospital ward routine. The gentle application of fragrant oils is in tune with both femininity and the orientation of nursing towards a holistic approach to care (see Chapter 4). In contrast to orthodox medicine, non-orthodox therapies rarely use technology and place an emphasis on empathy and sensitivity to clients' problems.

The major methodological dispute between orthodox and non-orthodox medicine remains the validity of the randomized controlled trial. For many, non-orthodox practitioners the question of scientific proof is irrelevant as they reject the scientific method.

They feel they know from experience that their treatments work. Scientific proof might appease others, but it is not necessary to their self-confidence. Nor is it necessary to ensure clientele, since for many patients the question of scientific proof is equally irrelevant. They have already tried orthodox remedies which are supposed to have been subjected to such rigorous testing but which have not worked for them.

(Sharma 1992: 206)

The conventional non-orthodox critique of the randomized controlled trial is that treatment is individually situated and therefore the same symptoms may be treated differently. Furthermore, double-blind trials cannot be devised where there is no direct intervention. For example, while acupuncture could be tested by randomly inserting needles and comparing the effects with the proper use at 'meridian points', the oils and application of aromatherapy are shaped by the overall status of individual patients. The apparent satisfaction with non-orthodox medicine displayed by consumers' increased use of therapies is often cited as sufficient 'proof' of effectiveness (Bakx 1991). Most patients have little understanding of the complexities of orthodox medicine and have to trust the diagnosis and treatment (Cassell 1991). For many people, their ideas about the 'proof' or otherwise of their orthodox or non-orthodox treatment will be shaped by popular culture and other lay people's experiences.

Giddens (1991) has argued that a feature of post-industrial or 'high modernity' is the lack of certainty provided by an 'overarching authority' such as Parsons' (1951) formulation of medicine. Combined with an emphasis on individual responsibilities and choices within a consumer-orientated society, non-orthodox medicine represents an extension of self-help and individual gratification. The growing availability of self-diagnostic kits and off-the-shelf non-orthodox remedies such as homoeopathic products in chemist shops indicates the increasing popularity of such products. Ironically, the consumers of such products, while making active choices, are doing so in a way that undermines much of the basic philosophy of holistic treatment. The majority of non-orthodox therapies require the active involvement of the 'client' (rather than 'patient', which indicates passivity). This is not only apparent in the need for clients to seek out practitioners (referrals via GPs are relatively scarce) but in the collaborative nature of the consultation process. Many therapies conceptualize individuals as having their own natural resistance to illness which the therapist seeks to encourage by the appropriate remedy. This may not involve the direct addressing of symptoms but rather an attempt to uncover 'underlying' dysfunctions or 'imbalances'. This can take a long process of ongoing treatment which may resemble the 'talking therapies' used in psychoanalysis. This process of negotiation provides clients with explanations of their condition that are situated in 'natural' and 'moral systems' that reward the right behaviours and attitudes (Crawford 1980; Coward 1989). Non-orthodox therapy attempts:

to recast the imagery of the body and disease by moving away from aggressive military metaphorical conceptualisations of the body . . . to depicting the body as 'natural', as self regulating and part of a wider ecological balance, with words 'balance', 'harmony', 'regulate', 'spirit' and 'energy' prevailing.

(Lupton 1994: 128)

In tune with the individualization and social reflexivity of post-industrial society (Featherstone 1991; Shilling 1993), the assessment and remedy applied to each client is unique as it is shaped by their biography and situation. Like orthodox medicine, the individual focus of practice tends to obscure the impact of collective problems such as poverty or environmental pollution (Coward 1989). However, the rhetoric of some non-orthodox therapies, especially 'New Age' approaches, has a romantic attachment to a more 'natural' past which involves a critique of the 'unnatural' present. Such Utopian visions are not uncommon but they are rarely translated into the political action manifest by 'New Age' protests against large-scale rural development projects. Instead, most non-orthodox approaches attempt to 'reclaim' a 'natural' mode of living for individual clients (Coward 1989).

Unlike orthodox medicine, there may be no clear end point of treatment or definition of 'wellness'. Indeed some indigenous therapies may involve following a particular philosophy that embraces all aspects of life. Sexual problems have become a significant area of non-orthodox practice and reflect the fusing of mind and body (Weston 1992). There is a blurring of boundaries here with the increasing number of 'counsellors' who provide varying degrees of advice and support to people suffering from psychological stress or disruptive life changes such as divorce (Rose 1990). Indeed 'personal problems' may be perceived as benefiting from non-orthodox intervention 'as a particular practice tends to adjust the individual to the society from which the pathology has arisen' (Berliner and Salmon 1980: 143). This is ironic as much of the discourse around non-orthodox approaches counterpoises 'nature' and the 'natural' with the urban life and 'artificial' drugs and food additives. There is also an interesting echo of Armstrong's (1983) claim that medicine has extended the clinical gaze beyond the realm of the body into the everyday activities of 'healthy' people. The potential for pathologizing areas of personal life that only engage with medicine in particularly acute forms is considerable (Lowenberg and Davies 1994). However non-orthodox medicine lacks both the cohesive professional power base and role in state policy to extend its gaze beyond the level of individual clients.

Medical success and the 'fearful other'

The Plague had swallowed up everything and everyone. No longer were there individual destinies, only a collective destiny, made of plague and the emotions shared by all. Strongest of these emotions was the sense of exile and of deprivation, with the cross-currents of revolt and fear set up by these.

(Camus 1971)

Albert Camus' classic description of an epidemic depicted a struggle between science and rationality and an irrational and mysterious 'Other'. In 1832, cholera killed around 15,000 people in four days in Paris (Delaport 1986). The medical establishment in France had not expected the disease that was spreading through eastern and Mediterranean countries to affect France. They thought it would be confined to those less civilized and weaker populations which experienced a poor and 'unhealthy' climate. Between 1838 and 1900, there was a 57 per cent decline in the death rate from tuberculosis (McKeown 1976). A similar marked decline in the death rate can be observed for previously prevalent infectious disease such as scarlet fever, cholera, diphtheria and typhoid. This appears to demonstrate the effectiveness of medical intervention and helps to account for the emergence of a general faith in medicine. It was expressed at both a policy level in the commitment of the state to the medical profession, and at the level of illness becoming synonymous with a visit to the doctor (Herzlich and Pierret 1987). However, as McKeown (1976) demonstrated in the case of tuberculosis, the main decline in mortality occurred before major medical interventions. He argues that causes outside the direct realm of medicine, such as the provision of clean water and sanitation, improved nutrition and better housing, were critical in the initial improvement in mortality rates. Such historical analysis highlights the significance of primary healthcare and health promotion. Illich's (1975) account of the harmful effects of medical intervention takes the criticism of biomedicine further. It becomes a threat to health because it has made people dependent on it and thus reduced their autonomy and freedom to cope with health and illness in a diversity of ways. The medicalization of death, which moved out of the community and home and into the hospital, as well as away from 'natural death' to a technological ending (e.g. decisions to 'turn off' assisted breathing) illustrate Illich's thesis. However, despite his and others' warnings about the iatrogenic effects of medicalization, faith in medicine and the expectation of improving health is one dimension of modernity.

During the 1950s and 1960s, optimism in medicine's ability to prevent and cure disease was at its height. This can be seen in the idea of a 'health transition' which held that as societies moved out of poverty and were able to feed and house their members, medical and pharmaceutical interventions would destroy the viruses, bacteria and parasites responsible for major diseases. The healthcare system would then be free to deal with chronic conditions that tended to affect the older section of the population. Evidence for this optimism could be found in successful programmes such as polio vaccination that effectively eliminated the disease in Western Europe and

North America. In the late 1950s, the World Health Organization launched a campaign to eradicate smallpox which had been a major scourge in Europe and had wiped out a third of the population in the Roman Empire (Fenner *et al.* 1988). The last sites of these diseases were located in the poorest parts of the developing world and Eastern Europe. Post-industrial countries were a long way from the struggles to eradicate such diseases, and people could read or watch reports of various epidemics that were often associated with natural disasters, war or stark poverty as they swept through distant lands. They were safe from such problems behind the barriers of their high standard of living, public health and healthcare systems.

The plague, cholera, typhoid and other diseases that at various times have threatened civilized society constitute a 'fearful Other' that became evident in the Renaissance and Enlightenment desire for a controlled and ordered world (Elias 1939 and 1978). 'The early modern suppression of uncontrollable, of grotesque, contained within it a defence against all that was considered irrational and excessive' (Mellor and Shilling 1997: 11). The response in the fifteenth century to the spread of syphilis is described by Sontag (1989: 47). 'It was the "French pox" to the English, morbus Germanicus to the Parisians, the Naples sickness to the Florentines, the Chinese disease to the Japanese'. By the nineteenth century syphilis had become linked to deviant sexual acts, black women and prostitutes (Gilman 1985). Immigrants from Ireland during the famine were linked to the typhus epidemics of 1847 and 1884 so that it became known as 'Irish fever' (Robins 1995). The Irish immigrant was depicted as:

> . . . the sorest evil that this country has to strive with. In his rags and his laughing savagery, he is there to undertake all work that can be done by mere strength of hand and back, for wages that will purchase him potatoes.
>
> (Carlyle 1839, cited in Robins 1995: 193)

'Otherness' is constructed around threatening diseases by associating them with alien countries, cultures and irrational and dangerous practices. AIDS was originally identified in the medical literature as Gay Related Immune Deficiency (GRID) and linked to both homosexual lifestyles and practices such as the communal bath houses in the United States and the use of 'poppers' (the inhalation of amyl nitrite) (Garrett 1994). The combination of homosexuality and promiscuity provided fertile ground for the generation of AIDS as a 'fearful Other' especially in the political climate of the 1980s when various attempts to reinforce 'family values' were made (see Chapter 6). The origins of AIDS became linked to Africa (the 'African disease'), the 'dark unknown continent' of past times and Haiti (the 'Haitian disease' as it was particularly prevalent among Haitian Americans in the 1980s) where it was associated with voodoo and sacrifice (Joffe 1997).

Ebola haemorrhagic fever (dramatically depicted as a 'flesh-eating virus') is another 'new' disease that emerged to threaten civilized society. It is very infectious and often fatal, with death occurring after eight or nine days. An outbreak in Zaire in 1995 killed 245 people, 70 per cent of those infected. Reports of the outbreak showed Western experts working in protective 'space suits' such was the apparent danger from the disease. Newspaper reports headlined 'The Plague worse than Aids turns bodies to water' (*The Daily Telegraph* 1995). Creutzfeldt–Jakob disease (CJD) has also been traced to a 'strange' and remote part of the world. Kuru was the commonest cause of death among the Fore people of New Guinea. In the past, they practised cannibalism and with the brains being given to children and women, the disease was less common among men. Once symptoms begin the disease runs a progressive and invariably fatal course. Kuru is similar to scrapie in sheep, bovine spongiform encephalopathy (BSE) and Creutzfeldt–Jakob disease (CJD) in humans. In 1986, the use of protein forage made from sheep carcasses was established, linking scrapie with BSE. 'Mad cow disease' provoked considerable alarm and resulted in people rejecting British beef and beefburgers (Lacey 1996). More recently a variant form of CJD in humans has been associated with BSE in cattle by the actions of an infectious particle or 'prion' (Prusiner *et al.* 1996). This made it highly likely that people who developed CJD contracted it by eating meat from cattle with BSE. Other threats to health related to food such as *Salmonella* poisoning, reflect modern food processing. The increased scale of food processing and the rapid delivery of food products to supermarkets across the country create the potential to enhance the spread of contaminated food. It is a mark of success of both public health measures and food processing that there are relatively few 'outbreaks' of *Salmonella* poisoning. However, the establishment of 'poisoned' food which is taken into the body symbolically and potentially materially undermines individuals' sense of control over their bodies. This is reflected in the increasing attention paid to allergies which are often thought to arise from contemporary methods of food production and processing as well as pollution.

Conclusion

Technology threatened to transport Ebola quickly into the heart of post-industrial societies and the demand for cheap food prompted the technology to feed sheep to herbivorous cows. A number of popular books such as *Virus X: Understanding the Real Threat of the New Pandemic Plagues* (Ryan 1996) argued that 'nature' was manifestly being distorted and was consequently threatening in new ways. The image is of a 'toxic society' which generates the seeds of its own destruction in a way similar to Marx's analysis of capitalism. This vision is equally romantic as Marx's in that it neglects the hazards of pre-industrial society. Sontag (1989) argues that such apocalyptic ideas are linked to the millennium. A general 'epidemic hegemony' has been identified in the discourse about 'epidemics' of teenage sex, child abuse, crime and so forth (Singer 1993). The erosion of traditional certainties such as the family and moral codes characterizes contemporary society according to Giddens (1991). He suggests that this confronts people with the never ending need to interpret meanings and make choices that involves risk and uncertainty. A sense of dread for Giddens (1990) is the opposite of trust which formed the basis for traditional social life. Apocalyptic visions of 'new epidemics' and biomedicine as an out-of-control and inexplicable leviathan on collision course with 'nature' therefore become part of late modern social life. The increasing number of health 'panics' reflect this sense of lack of control. If the body is the 'last retreat' where individuals feel they can exert control the 'Otherness' that threatens that autonomy takes on a renewed significance.

> To the death of oceans and lakes and forests, the unchecked growth of populations in poor parts of the world, nuclear accidents like Chernobyl, the puncturing and depletion of the ozone layer . . . to all these, now add AIDS . . . The taste for the worst-case scenarios reflects the need to master fear of what is felt to be uncontrollable.
>
> (Sontag 1989: 143)

Globalization fosters the rapid spread of disease and disasters. Infected people can move 'rapidly around the planet' (Garrett 1994). Lay understandings of health are often constructed around a notion of 'balance' and this has been transferred to a sense of the 'world out of balance' (part of the subtitle of Garrett's book). However, the number of deaths attributed to such 'new' diseases is insignificant when compared to deaths by heart disease, cancer and long-established and preventable diseases such as measles, whooping cough and diarrhoea that remain significant causes of death in the developing world. Ironically the very success of biomedicine in the form of antibiotics has produced increasing bacterial resistance to treatments such as penicillin.

Understanding health and constructing illness

CHAPTER 2

Introduction

Health and illness has been a main theme within sociology since the development of Parsons' theory of *The Social System* (1951). A search through the work of the 'founding fathers' of the discipline will find few references to health. Marx's concern for poverty and working conditions and Durkheim's treatment of suicide are representative of the way health was situated within wider theoretical concerns. This chapter begins with examining how the contemporary study of health emerged partly as a reaction to the biomedical model and partly as part of an all-embracing theoretical project. Initial social research was driven by problems defined by medicine and the healthcare system. This produced a flourish of studies focused on trying to explain why people did not always use health services in the way they had been intended to be used. There was also a general concern to define 'health' which took on international dimensions with the World Health Organization. Sociological interest in lay knowledge about health and illness is relatively recent (Gerhardt 1989) and was influenced by a number of qualitative and anthropological studies. The focus of these studies was initially on patients or other ill people and later shifted to the 'healthy' population. There remained a tendency to highlight the gap between lay beliefs and medical knowledge that is reflected in the terminology itself (Good 1994). The work of medical historians and anthropologists have reinforced this professional/lay duality by linking a decline in beliefs about magic, religion and illness as modern medicine becomes dominant (Glucklich 1997). There is a sense of the duality between the 'rational' and the 'irrational' that is sometimes evident in approaches to the analysis of lay understandings about health. Similarly chronic illness and disability have in the past had a rather uneasy place within health research. Classically in Parsons' original formulation of the sick role there was no conceptualization of how chronic illness fitted the model. Recent criticisms from disability movements have drawn attention to the tendency to make comparisons with 'healthy' people which may undervalue the autonomy of people who may regard themselves as 'healthy' despite lacking all the abilities taken for granted by the majority (Oliver 1990).

Health in the social system

In *The Social System* (1951), Parsons gave medicine a central role in maintaining the stability of society. Health appeared as a major element in social theory for the first time within this functionalist theoretical framework. Its place stemmed from Parsons' earlier empirical work on the profession of medicine which had impressed him with its diagnostic expertise and power over patients. A healthy population that could undertake the various tasks required to promote the smooth running of society has a fundamental place in functionalist theory. At a basic level Parsons viewed society as a system that contained mechanisms for shaping and controlling behaviour. In particular, behaviour that failed to contribute to or threatened the smooth running of society had to be identified and minimized. The nineteenth century writing of Auguste Comte that conceptualized the 'body social' as a sort of organism whose parts function in a way to maintain balance and stability influenced Parsons. The problem for Parsons was to identify the processes that ensured that the sick received care and the healthy fulfilled their roles as mothers, fathers, workers and so forth. From this perspective, illness was deviant in that sick people could not undertake their normal social roles. At a general level, an inappropriate amount of illness could threaten social stability by undermining people's willingness to maintain their social roles. Parsons' now classic formulation of the sick role was made up of two rights and two obligations:

Rights:

- The sick person is exempt from the normal expectations of their social role, e.g. employment, domestic work, etc.
- The sick person is exempt from responsibility for their sickness and has the right to expect professional and other help in order to recover.

Obligations:

- The sick person must seek appropriate treatment usually, from a doctor. He or she must also cooperate with whatever treatment is prescribed.
- The sick person must recover as soon as possible.

Rights are contingent on obligations and failure, for example to comply with treatment, will lead to withdrawal from the privileges of the sick role. The sick role is temporary in that people are expected to get better.

Although Parsons did not conduct any empirical work to verify the sick role, echoes of it can be found in lay discourse (e.g. Herzlich 1973). As critics pointed out, there was no provision for chronic illness in the original model. In a later reformulation of the sick role, Parsons (1975) argued that, although complete recovery was not possible for the chronically sick, it was medical practice to manage their condition in such a way that they could establish a relatively normal social role. The sick role was also universal in that anyone could enter it regardless of their social role or position. Reflecting his earlier work, it was the medical profession that gatekept legitimate entry and exit to the role. The doctor embodied the development of rational neutral science which could unproblematically define and treat patients. Essentially, as noted in Chapter 1, medicine was thought of as a mechanism of social control. Patients were conceived of as compliant and relatively powerless in the face of medical expertise. It was also anticipated that once people experienced symptoms, they would seek medical attention, however, as will be seen, there is a lot of evidence for the existence of a 'symptom iceberg' or a 'pool of unwellness'. This suggests that the relationship people had with healthcare was rather more complex than anticipated.

There has been widespread criticism of Parsons' conceptualization of the sick role and the functionalist project in general. Based on the assumption of social cohesiveness and consensus, the functionalist approach largely failed to find an adequate explanation for social conflict and change (Morgan et al. 1985). The complexities of lay health behaviours and the negotiation of illness do not have a place in the sick role model. It also fails to find a place for the unequal distribution of illness in the population which is partly created through social conditions such as deprivation (Gerhardt 1989). The sick role remains significant not just because it established a legitimate place for the examination of sickness outside the biomedical sphere but also because it proved a basis upon which later sociological theories about health could mark out the distinctiveness of their approach. Freidson (1976), for example, attempted to modify the sick role through labelling theory. He produced a scheme that argued that illness was a social state that was largely mediated by the reaction of people to symptoms or individuals who acted as though they were ill. Medical knowledge is reformulated so that it has a flexible social role in defining and 'creating' categories of illness (see Chapter 1).

Doing 'something' about illness

Following Parsons' functionalist theory, various forms of Marxist or conflict theories and interactionist or labelling theories entered into an academic debate about the virtues or deficiencies of the different approaches. Conflict theories broadly conceived of medicine as generated and supported by the economic and social system of market-based economies. It may reinforce unequal divisions in society by defining illness and disease as individual problems and drawing attention away from the association between, for example poverty or bad housing and health. However, until the 1970s, medical sociology was concerned with the problems identified by the medical professions and policy makers. The central problems from this perspective can be summarized as the underutilization of health services, the overutilization of health services and failure to comply with medical advice.

The underutilization of health services presented a puzzle to medical professions and policy makers once the NHS had been established. It had been assumed that once a 'free at the point of use' healthcare had been provided, there would be no barrier to people visiting their doctor or making use of other services. This was based on a model of what Mechanic (1962) called 'illness behaviour' that assumed the majority of normally healthy people would be able to perceive when they were ill and would therefore seek appropriate medical help. Writing in the United States, Zola captures the essence of this model:

> We postulate a time when the patient is asymptomatic or unaware that he has symptoms, then suddenly some clear objective symptoms appear, then perhaps he goes through a period of self-treatment and when either this treatment is unsuccessful or the symptoms in some way become too difficult to take, he decides to go to some practitioner (usually, we hope, a physician).

> (Zola 1972: 288)

Note the usage of 'patient' in the quotation that reflects the dominant place of the hospital medicine in the United States at this time. This is reinforced in the aside that recognizes the scope for seeking help from non-orthodox practitioners, but gives a clear indication what appropriate or 'successful' illness behaviour might be. However, doctors were becoming concerned about the number of patients who did not seek medical help until the late stages of an illness. In addition, a number of health surveys in Britain (e.g. Wadsworth *et al.* 1971; Hannay 1979; Townsend and Davidson 1982) and the United States identified what had become known as the 'symptom iceberg'. Later surveys have confirmed this picture and attempted to identify 'underutilizers' in terms of social class, 'race' and family form (see Chapter 5). A study undertaken in the 1960s and based in two London boroughs of 3153 respondents revealed that 95 per cent of them said that they had suffered one or episodes of ill health in the two weeks before they were interviewed (Wadsworth *et al.* 1971). The majority of those who reported that they had experienced some kind of illness had not sought any advice from medical professionals. Similarly a study in Glasgow (Hannay 1979) found that nearly a quarter of this sample had not sought any medical advice for a range of conditions from which they reported that they suffered pain or disability.

McKinlay (1972), in a review of the utilization literature, identified six approaches to the problem which ranged from the economic to organizational. This indicates the breadth of research that had developed in Britain and the United States by the 1970s. Attempts to understand the utilization problem can be broadly separated into those taking an individualistic approach and those which take a collectivist approach (Morgan, Calnan and Manning 1985). These approaches are underpinned by psychological and sociological theories. Individualistic approaches have developed various *socio psychological* models that explain and attempt to predict people's responses to symptoms. Developed by psychologists, the 'health belief model', which has evolved into many variations, represents an attempt to model individual health behaviours. Informed by a cost-benefit approach to human action, it has been used in health education and health promotion programmes. A related individualist approach to health is represented by the various forms of the 'health locus of control'. It is based in the assumption that people are able to perceive the degree to which certain behaviours will result in the outcome they wish to achieve. Again the health locus of control has been influential in health education and health promotion. However, both approaches have been criticized by psychologists (e.g. Bennett and Murphy 1997) and sociologists (e.g. Bunton and Macdonald 1992).

Collectivist approaches to understanding health behaviours focus the way people's actions are shaped by their social and cultural situation. Freidson (1970) attempted to capture this interplay between individual and social influences in what he called the 'lay referral system'. He identified these systems as social groups that 'enforced' particular interpretations of illness and treatment. The emphasis on 'enforce' indicates Freidson's view that individuals in relatively powerful positions in such networks could have an active role in defining illness and determining the response to it for less powerful members. An individual had to show 'evidence of symptoms . . . others believe to be illness' and these had to be interpreted in a 'way . . . others find plausible' (Freidson 1970) before sickness could be identified. The evidence of symptoms from, for example, a child or an elderly person, may be interpreted by a carer who may take them to a doctor. More generally, Freidson argued that decisions to seek medical, as opposed to non-orthodox or lay, help is partly determined by the degree to which the people belong to a culture that shares beliefs similar to that of biomedicine. This suggests, for example, that the Pathan mothers in Currer's study (1986) were likely to be primarily influenced by indigenous ideas about illness and treatments. Evidence to support Freidson's typology can be found in a study of maternity service utilization by working-class women in Aberdeen (McKinlay 1972). The 87 mothers in the study were identified as utilizers and non-utilizers on the basis of attendance at antenatal clinics before week 17 of pregnancy. The non-utilizers were found to live closer to relatives and visit them more often than the utilizers. When asked about who they would talk to about health problems they tended to say relatives who, as Blaxter and Patterson (1982) suggests, may be repositories of lay knowledge. They therefore had easy access to non-medical ideas and experiences about health. However, low utilization was also associated with the number of children a mother had. Some women may have been relying on their own knowledge from previous pregnancies rather than the lay referral system. A study of diaries kept by pregnant women over a six-week period revealed that married women talked to their husbands about their health problems, while single women sought help from their mothers (Scambler *et al.* 1981). Those women who talked to family and friends most frequently about their symptoms were more likely to seek medical advice. This would not have been predicted by Freidson's model and suggests the need to look at other factors that may influence utilization.

Other studies from this period were influenced by anthropology and examined the health of various communities. Zola (1973), in a well-known study of patients of Irish and Italian origin in New York, argued that each 'racial' group defined and communicated their symptoms in different ways. Typically, the Irish patients at the outpatient clinic in which the study was based gave fairly specific accounts of their health, in contrast to the more inclusive picture presented by Italian patients. Reflecting the use of lay referral systems, both groups had delayed some time before seeking any medical attention for their symptoms. From this Zola identified what he regarded as factors that 'triggered' the decision to seek medical help. He identified five conceptual triggers that ranged from an interpersonal crisis such as the death of a family member to a sense that the symptoms being experience should have ended. They included a recognition of pressure from family and friends to do something about symptoms. Therefore the symptoms themselves were less important than the social responses to them:

> For our patients the symptoms were 'really' there, but their perception differed considerably. There is a sense in which they sought help because they could not stand it any longer. But what they could not stand was more likely to be a situation or perceived implication of a symptom rather than any worsening of the symptom per se.
>
> (Zola 1983: 118)

It was suggested that the weight given to particular triggers varied across different ethnic communities. These triggers included the subjective and psychological as well as contextual factors such as social networks. However, there was a danger that this analysis was overly socially deterministic (cf. Dingwall 1976). Further evidence for the significance of contextual factors was provided by a study of the meanings people attach to the signs associated with a heart attack (Cowie 1976). Most participants in the study did not recognize the symptoms of their heart attack and instead had sought to explain the symptoms in the context in which they were experienced. For example, the pain might be explained as indigestion if it took place after a meal. There are clear links here with medical concern about when people seek advice about bodily changes and whether they make appropriate use of medical services. Such conceptualizations of, when, how and where services are utilized essentially try to situate 'the experience of illness is embedded in its social life and rhythms, that it is constrained by social structure, and that it is created in negotiation with others' (Pescosolido 1991: 166). They do so with varying degrees of success. The increasing desire of healthcare organization and the state to identify and measure the outcomes of primary care and other services creates a demand for survey instruments based on an instrumental view of human action.

The problem of the 'trivial' consultation and the overutilization of health services reflects lay and medical concerns. A person's desire not to be labelled as a 'difficult' patient may inhibit them from visiting their doctor. In the face of the decline of organized religions and increasing social fragmentation, it has been suggested that doctors represent a new 'priesthood' who should be consulted when any important decision is made (Zola 1972; cf. Illich 1976). The social control role of medicine may lead to the overutilization of, for example, psychotropic drugs. This not only makes 'inappropriate' use of health services but also fails to address the needs of the clients appropriately (see Chapter 4). The overuse, or rather, inappropriate use of Accident & Emergency departments was a focus for research in the 1970s. A number of studies (e.g. Calnan 1987) noted that what were clinically recognized as 'trivial' complaints were being dealt with in Accident & Emergency departments. Urban-based departments situated in poor areas of cities were found to be acting as the 'family doctor' for many people. This was a particular problem in the United States with its residual healthcare system. During the 1980s in Britain, with increasing social polarization and urban homelessness, similar concern about the substitute role of Accident & Emergency departments was expressed.

The problem of 'health' and 'illness'

The research noted above can be seen as broadly about the problem of people becoming 'appropriate' patients or users of health advice services. It was driven from a medical orientation that is reflected in Friedson's typology or the health belief model which underplayed the role of people as active agents. It also reflects the nature of medical progress and professional advancement which places an emphasis on 'interesting' cases. These may be diagnosed or treated in new ways which can later provide papers in medical journals and promote medical careers. Health problems rooted in, for example, social inequity are seen as beyond the scope of medicine or individual practitioners to address successfully. In addition, there is a tendency to research people who were already patients and therefore had sooner or later sought medical advice. People who never became patients or did so with great reluctance were largely ignored. In other words, if individuals believed that they were healthy or acted in a health way, they were not defined as a 'problem' worthy of attention.

During the 1970s, a greater recognition of the role of primary care and health education in preventing illness developed. This implied a need to pay greater attention to the 'healthy' population. Community medicine also had an interest in the general patterns of health and illness in communities which it was argued the medical establishment and the healthcare system was failing to address adequately (Jefferys 1991). Empirical research broadly followed the agenda and concerns of the healthcare system which was to focus on the hospital treatment of illness (Bury 1997). At a policy level, research that revealed that people undertook a high level of self-treatment and would use social networks or other resources such as pharmacists for advice was not unwelcome. It suggested that there may not be an ever increasing demand for more healthcare spending and provided a counter to calls from the medical profession to increase acute care provision. Theoretically and empirically, sociologists began to move away from an 'illness' perspective to a 'health' perspective (Stacey 1988). The influence of critical or conflict sociology and the 'social construction of reality' (Berger and Luckman 1971), together with existing research on people's ideas about illness, prepared the ground for taking lay ideas about health seriously. Zola's initial study was influential (Morgan *et al.* 1985) and its location of 'social factors' with an analytical framework made them less easy to dismiss as 'irrational'. The setting for research began to move away from the hospital or surgery and into the 'natural' settings of home and work where everyday life is acted out. This transition brought the problem of 'health' to the fore and a debate rapidly sprang up over what might constitute 'health'.

Attempts to define health can broadly be divided into 'top-down' or 'bottom-up' approaches. The most widely cited 'top-down' definition of health is that presented in the World Health Organization constitution: 'Health is a state of complete physical, mental and social well-being, not merely the absence of disease or infirmity' (WHO 1948). The definition is often cited by health professionals and finds its way into many official documents. This is curious, as a closer reading of the quotation will reveal that it is hard for very many people to be categorized as 'healthy'. It is an idealistic if not Utopian (Seedhouse 1986) definition that is significant because it embraces a definition of health that includes social, psychological and subjective dimensions. It also contains two views of health in that it refers to 'absence' that is a negative view of health and as well as a positive view of health as 'well-being'. Both approaches find support in lay ideas about their health (e.g. Herzlich 1973; Blaxter 1990) although the latter view may be overlaid with a moral association of 'goodness' with health.

Eisenberg's (1977) distinction between illness and disease attempts to separate out a number of dimensions of health:

. . . patients suffer 'illnesses'; physicians diagnose and treat 'disease' . . . illnesses are experiences of disvalued changes in states of being and social function: diseases are abnormalities in the structure and function of body organs and systems.

(Eisenberg 1977: 22)

In this definition, the term 'disease' takes on an 'objective'- or 'thing'-like quality. It refers to a malfunctioning in, or maladaptation of, biological, physiological or chemical processes in the body. Thus, disease is seen as a pathological condition identified on the basis of the appearance of certain signs and symptoms. Consequently, each disease acquires an abstract quality, a 'thing-like' status and in some cases is perceived as a condition which is 'independent of social behaviour'. This reflects the biomedical, biomechanical or medical model of disease noted in Chapter 1. 'Illness' therefore refers to the experience of disease and as such deals with the subjective experiences of bodily disorder and feelings of pain and discomfort. It is shaped by 'cultural factors governing perception, labelling and explanations of discomforting experience' (Kleinman *et al.* 1978: 252). Distinguishing between the illness and disease helps to establish a place for lay health knowledge. Dingwall (1976) usefully notes that health and illness are a 'contrasting pair' and that the recognition of one depends upon a knowledge of the other. As will be seen, people tend to follow this dichotomy although their discourses about health and illness are complex, inconsistent, dynamic and fragmentary.

From a more experiential approach, Blaxter (1987) has argued that it is possible to experience illness without the presence of disease and have a disease without feeling ill:

If 'disease' is defined as biological or clinically identified abnormality, and 'illness' as the subjective experience of symptoms of ill-health, then it is obviously possible to have disease without illness, and to have illness without disease.

(Blaxter 1987: 5)

In other words, it is possible that an individual may have an undiagnosed organic disorder and not experience any symptoms, or if they do experience symptoms, these may not be recognized as such and explained away. The tensions between 'top-down' and 'bottom-up' approaches to defining health reflect broader theoretical and methodological debates. As we saw earlier, functionalist concepts such as Parsons' sick role had little difficulty with definitions. In contrast, interactionist and anthropologically informed studies into lay knowledge prioritized concepts of health and illness which became apparent from the social groups that were studied.

One of the first studies to explore the way in which people define health and illness was undertaken by Herzlich (1973). The study has had a lasting influence and was based on interviews with a sample of 80 middle-aged subjects, drawn mainly from middle-class backgrounds and living in Paris or Normandy. Participation in the study was not confined to people who had defined themselves as ill by being patients but was based on a wider apparently 'healthy' section of the population. From what amounts to long conversations with the participants in her study, Herzlich (1973) identified three distinct dimensions of health embedded in their accounts of health and illness:

- 'Health in a vacuum'. The view of health as simply the absence of illness and a lack of awareness of the body.
- 'Reserve of health' approach. The view that health is defined within relation to the capacity of the individual or constitution to maintain good health and resist illness. Health is like a capital asset which can be spent or renewed.
- 'Equilibrium'. The view that health is embedded in positive feelings and good relationships with others. Herzlich refers to this as 'real' health and it contains the notion of health as an advantageous balance. There are similarities here with Maslow's (1954) ideas about 'self-actualisation' or 'becoming what one is capable of becoming'.

Herzlich's informants perceived illness in a number of ways which she distilled down into three 'metaphors'. Firstly, there was what she termed illness as an 'occupation', often associated with chronic illness. Individuals spent much of their time fighting or dealing with their health problems to the degree that it required all their energy and became like a new occupation. Secondly, illness could be regarded as a 'destroyer'; sometimes associated with the onset of chronic illness, people saw their health problems negatively or would seek to deny the symptoms. Illness could mark the end to a 'normal' life. Lastly, illness could be conceived of as a 'liberator', in that people could escape the problems of their 'normal' life, or what Parsons would regard as taking up the sick role. To quote one of the participants 'when I'm very tired, I often wish I were ill . . . illness is a kind of rest . . . it's being set free' (Parsons 1957: 114). Herzlich stressed that people frequently were not consistent in the metaphors they used and would often produce complex and sometimes contradictory explanations. In other words, people had many conceptualizations of health that were more complex than a simple opposition of 'health' with 'illness' (see Blaxter 1990).

One significant strand in these explanations was ideas about 'natural' (rural, traditional) and 'unnatural' (urban and modern) lifestyles. Similar feelings about the 'unhealthiness' of modern urban life were found by Blaxter (1990) in an extensive survey of health and lifestyles in Britain. Seldom given any definite meaning, such ideas owed much to media and cultural representations which in Herzlich's study were seen as related to changes to French society. Herzlich, influenced by the work of Foucault, investigated cultural representations of health in a later historical study. It was argued that cultural representations were 'woven into the collective pattern of thought that form social reality of illness and the sick' (Herzlich and Pierret 1987: xi). This French study had an influence on other researchers and found support among the funders of research who recognized the potential of qualitative research with people who were apparently 'healthy' (e.g. Williams 1981, 1983; Pill and Stott 1982, 1985; Calnan 1987; Blaxter 1990). As Bury (1997) notes, the 1976 government report *Prevention and Health: Everybody's Business* (DHSS), which emphasized the role of healthy lifestyles and individual responsibility provided momentum from state agencies to understand health and responsibility. Sociologically, 'lifestyle' tends to refer to a broad concept that involves people's material ability to access consumer goods and services (see Chapter 7). Clearly, people have different opportunities to develop lifestyles and for some groups such as the poor urban dwellers there may be little opportunity to, for example, purchase fresh food as part of a healthy diet. Although published under a Labour Government, the report set the tone for the Conservative Government's approach to health policy in the 1980s (see Chapter 5). In a study of elderly people in Aberdeen, Williams (1981, 1983) followed Herzlich's categories of illness as an 'occupation' and as a 'liberator'. Williams' informants were all living at home and drawn from both middle-class and working-class backgrounds. He argued that it was possible to break down categories such as 'illness as a destroyer' into logical premises and consequences. He identified three premises

◆ If I am active, then I am not ill.
◆ If I am myself, then I am active.
◆ I have something to offer if and only if I am active.

Through this analysis, Williams suggested that the logical consequences of an individual believing that he or she was ill was that they were not themselves, had nothing to offer and were 'fading away'. In contrast, those who related to the 'occupational' metaphor were likely to feel they were 'keeping going' and 'fighting'. This is significant because it helps to explain why older people may regard themselves as 'healthy' despite suffering from chronic conditions such as arthritis (see Herzlich 1973; Williams 1981, 1983; Blaxter 1990). In commenting on the similarity between his findings and those of Herzlich (1973), Williams (1983: 201) stated that: 'These resemblances, in groups which are divergent in age, class composition and nationality, suggest that cultural conceptions of a relatively fundamental kind are involved here.'

A study of 41 mothers, aged between 30 and 35 years, who lived on a suburban estate in South Wales and whose husbands were skilled manual workers provided further support for Herzlich's analysis (Pill and Stott 1982). The main focus of the study was the interplay between ideas about individual responsibility and conceptualizations of the causes of illness. Pill and Stott found that it was possible to identify two main differences in how the women they interviewed understood health. Those women who tended to have more formal education than other participants, and were buying their own homes, were identified as lifestylists. They saw a dynamic relationship between the individual and their environment that gave them the ability to influence their health. The majority of women who generally lived in council housing were classified as 'fatalists' in that they believed that 'germs' over which they had no control were the main cause of illness. Blaxter (1983) similarly found that poorer working-class women regarded the causes of illness as beyond their control. Although in later work the stark division between the 'fatalists' and the ' lifestylists' was reduced (Pill and Stott 1985) there is a relationship between the structural and material circumstances of the women that can be glimpsed in the following response to a question about becoming ill:

> I think it boils down to money every time as far as I am concerned because people like, you know, my husband has to work so many hours to make it worthwhile for your family and your everyday life to go right . . . so far as food and that goes. There's a lot of worry attached to it. I think it is this that makes people ill, mainly nerves and you know the rush!
>
> (Pill and Stott 1985: 989)

Working-class fatalism finds echoes in Blaxter and Paterson's (1982) study of women in three-generation working-class families in Scotland. They found that health was primarily defined in negative terms, that is as the absence of illness, rather than in positive terms of physical fitness or a sense of well-being. Both mothers and daughters considered themselves healthy if they were able to carry out 'normal' daily activities and could go out to work. One of the interviewees expressed it thus:

> After I was sterilized I had a lot of cystitis, and backache, because of the fibroids. Then when I had a hysterectomy I had bother wi' my water works because my bladder lived a life of its own and I had to have a repair . . . Healthwise I would say I'm OK. I did hurt my shoulder – I mean, this is nothing to do with health but I actually now have a disability, I get a gratuity payment every six months . . . I wear a collar and take Valium . . . then, just the headaches – but I'm not really off work a lot with it.
>
> (Blaxter and Paterson 1982: 29)

This not only represents a functional definition of health but also illustrates the low expectations of health and physical well-being held by the women. Essentially, they felt they were healthy if their bodies would function sufficiently well not to have a negative impact on their daily lives. The women also made a distinction between 'normal' and 'serious' illnesses. The former were common ailments that were viewed as an inevitable part of life. The latter disrupted everyday life and were commonly experienced as tuberculosis, cancer and heart disease. Some conditions such as the menopause were considered to be part of the ageing process and not 'illnesses' or bodily changes that were worth seeking medical help for. There was a tendency for respondents to 'normalize' some health conditions and not view them as illnesses. If the condition in question was seen as due to the 'wear and tear' associated with growing old or 'women's troubles', then they were accepted as normal and something they just had to learn to live with (Blaxter and Paterson 1982: 31). While common ailments were accepted as part of everyday life, respondents reserved the label 'illness' for serious conditions such as cancer and heart disease. There is a moral dimension in these views of health (Blaxter and Paterson 1982: 32) in that: 'People were not ill if they did not "lie down to it," "dwell on it" or "let it get them down." Illness was not so much the experience of symptoms as the reaction to symptoms.' Furthermore, some people were seen as 'weaker' than others with a greater risk of illness. This may suggest an underlying religious conviction about the virtues of self-control. Williams' (1990) study in Scotland attempted to link involvement in the Protestant Church with health beliefs. He suggested that religious belief tended to reinforce ideas about self-reliance and helped coming to terms with chronic illness. In line with other studies of working-class women, the material and structural factors of the women interacts with their own and their families' experiences of health, their perceptions of their bodies and their own identity.

Other studies have attempted to compare the perceptions of working- and middle-class women (Calnan and Johnson 1985; Calnan 1987). A qualitative study of 60 women from social classes I, II, IV and V living in Outer London found that all the women felt that individuals were mainly responsible for their own health. Questions concentrating on the state of the individual's own health elicited more 'negative' definitions (i.e. absence of illness) than positive ones. Working- and middle-class women felt that they were healthy if they could 'get through the day'. However, women from working-class backgrounds tended to talk about health in negative and functional ways when asked in abstract terms about health. Middle-class women had a multidimensional view of health which included ideas about well-being and fitness. A middle-class woman illustrates these views as follows [Healthy people]

> are very spontaneous and flexible, and I think they have more opinions that they experience . . . They are feeling connected to a larger purpose and connected with people . . . I would also say that being in power, feeling powerful in your life, feeling responsible for your life is a very important part of it.
>
> (Quoted in McGuire 1988)

A cross-class study of 4000 people from Lorraine in France and who were taking part in a health examination also found that those situated at the lower end of the social class scale tended to define health negatively

(d'Houtaud and Field 1984). There is some evidence that social class differences are maintained across racial differences. Currer (1986) undertook
a study of Pathan mothers who originated in the Northwest frontier of
Pakistan and lived in Britain. The women were strict Muslims and
practised purdah. Currer found that they shared a functional concept of
health, 'the women's value, in their own eyes and those of their community'
lay in their ability to care for their husbands and children and manage the
home' (Currer 1986: 189). However, Calnan concluded from his data that,
on the whole, his respondents did not view health in terms of ability to carry
out daily tasks. Only a minority of his interviewees found this concept
of health familiar and they all came from working-class backgrounds.
Thus, Calnan questions the assertion that it is the experience of material
deprivation and adverse social conditions which leads to people subscrib-
ing to functional definitions of health. He suggested a possible alternative
explanation in which social class differences in concepts of health are
products of the social context of the research interview. The more elaborate
responses to questions about health elicited from middle-class respondents
could be a consequence of the nature of the interaction between interviewer
and interviewee. Middle-class interviewers may be more successful in
developing rapport with interviewees from similar social backgrounds
(Calnan 1987: 35). Calnan does not deny that economic circumstances and
social background influence the way health is perceived and notes that: '. . .
in spite of this denial of the functional definition of health, the state of health
in which many carried out their daily tasks was quite low' (Calnan 1987: 39).

Most of the research considered so far reflects theoretical approaches that
favour small-scale in-depth qualitative studies. This enables researchers to
'get close' to the participants (a term favoured over 'subjects' in this area).
Blaxter (1990) undertook one of the few large-scale quantitative studies
that have attempted to explore the complexities of health and people's
wider social context. The research was based on a random sample of 9000
men and women in England, Scotland and Wales. The Health and Lifestyle Survey (HALS) found that in old age, functional definitions of health
predominated, with men in particular focusing on their ability to perform
common tasks and carry out normal daily routines. In contrast, young
male respondents viewed health in terms of physical fitness, strength and
associated it with sport. While physical fitness appeared in the definitions
given by young women, they placed emphasis on such aspects of health as
vitality and the ability to cope as well as physical appearance. With the
approach of middle age, concepts of health become broader and more
complex with the emphasis shifting to notions of total physical and
mental well-being. Women in higher social class categories or with higher
educational qualifications frequently expressed multidimensional concepts
of health. It was also found that women, unlike men, were more likely to
define health in terms of their social relationships with other people. For
example, young women referred to health in terms of being able to 'cope

with the family'. In general women provided more expansive answers to the questions on health than men.

> Participants were asked to define health in another person and then in relation to themselves. Many subjects described health in others differently from health in themselves. Health in another person was described as 'positive fitness', as 'the ability to work or perform . . . normal roles' or as 'not being ill'. In contrast, with reference to oneself health was seen in psychological terms, . . . respondents were less likely to emphasise physical fitness or lack of disease, but rather to say that health is defined as being unstressed and unworried, able to cope with life, in tune with the world and happy.
>
> (Blaxter 1987: 141)

This emphasis on the physical ability to 'cope' or 'work' has been revealed in a number of studies (e.g. Cornwell 1984; Calnan and Johnson 1985; Mullen 1993). Again, there is a gender difference here in that the focus on work and physical activity tends to be a male concern while women tend to stress relationships and the ability to cope (Cornwell 1984).

Although race was not considered in the original report a secondary analysis of the HALS data suggested that Asians tended to have a functional view of health compared to the white subjects (Howlett *et al.* 1992). Afro-Caribbeans described health in terms of energy and strength and often held fatalistic views about the causes of illness. The relative lack of power is a common aspect of the lives of those groups who are identified in various surveys as having a fatalistic approach to health.

The importance of adopting the right 'attitude of mind' in order to avoid illness, maintain good health or cope with life has been noted in a number of studies. Cornwell (1984) studied working-class men and women living in Bethnal Green in East London and observed how they offered 'public' and 'private' accounts of their illnesses. Public accounts tended to make moral judgements about 'good health' and reflect lay interpretations of medical opinions. Private accounts emphasized the practical difficulties and material concerns associated with being ill. Cornwell describes how the attitude respondents adopted to employment was reflected in the attitude taken towards health. Although they had very little control over their working lives, they adopted a positive attitude to hard work and approached it with fortitude. As far as health is concerned:

> They experience themselves as having very little control over whether or not they are healthy, and yet they take seriously the idea that having the 'right attitude' is the passport, if not to good health, at least to a life that is tolerable. The moral prescription for a healthy life is in fact a kind of cheerful stoicism, evident in the refusal to worry, or to complain, or to be morbid.
>
> (Cornwell 1984: 129)

There are echoes here of the Health Locus of Control (HLC) model. As with the respondents in Blaxter and Paterson's study, the men and women interviewed by Cornwell believed in the power of 'mind over matter', expressing the view that a great deal of illness was due to a lack of strength of character on the part of the individual. As this indicates, perceptions about health are closely connected with ideas about the causes of illness.

The causes of illness

The HALS study reported that stress and worry as well as a poor diet were regarded as the main causes of illness. In Blaxter's earlier work (1983), she found that infections were seen as the commonest cause of illness, followed by heredity, environmental factors and stress. Her respondents talked about viruses as causes of colds and influenza. Although cancer and tuberculosis were the most frequently mentioned diseases, these were referred to through synonyms and causes were not discussed. This reflects Sontag's (1988) assertion that some diseases take on a metaphorical significance that represents death and the unknown. Relatively few of Blaxter's respondents mentioned causes related to lifestyle choices. In producing these causal accounts, the women linked together their health experiences and situated them with their current bodily and mental states. A similar prioritizing of germs and infections was noted by Pill and Stott (1985). In a review of a range of studies from different cultures, Christman (1977) identified the following models or 'logics' of causation:

- ◆ A logic of invasion which includes germs, cancer and other incursions into the body.
- ◆ A logic of degeneration which relates to 'being run down'.
- ◆ A mechanical logic in which illness is the result of blockages to the gastrointestinal track or other bodily structures.
- ◆ A logic of balance whereby illness follows a lack of harmony within the body or between an individual and the environment.

These 'logics' are embedded in cultural beliefs about health and may therefore vary in significance and form across different cultures. The connection between understandings of health and wider social beliefs and structures has been seen as a 'system' of beliefs by a number of anthropologists.

In a classic study of the ideas about colds and flu among patients of a North London general practice, Helman (1978) argued that a folk classification ('folk' rather than 'lay' reflects the discourse of anthropology) of cause could be identified: '. . . chills and colds are due to a by-product of one's personal battle with the natural environment – particularly with areas of lowered temperature'. In this view, damp or rain ('cold/wet' conditions) or cold winds or draughts ('cold/dry') can penetrate the boundary of the skin and cause similar conditions within the body. Thus colds are caused mainly by individual behaviour in contrast to fevers which are caused by germs that travel through the air and 'originate in other people rather than the natural environment'. Patients classified their illness according to whether they felt hot or cold rather than any medical definition of colds and fevers. People often talked about clouds of tiny particles from which an individual could catch a cold. This depiction of the causes of illness was often reinforced by general practitioners who gave diagnosis in terms of 'You've picked up a germ, You've got a flu bug.' There are parallels here with the 'logic of invasion'.

Explanations of the causes of illness can be divided into those which regard the cause of illness as external to the individual and those which locate the cause with the individual. Individuals who subscribe to the view that illness is caused by external factors are unlikely to accept responsibility for their condition. As Locker (1981) has argued if the major cause of illness is believed to be outside the individual's control then they are not held responsible for their actions. The onset of illness is attributed to bad luck or misfortune and the individual is seen as being blameless and therefore not morally accountable for becoming ill. This suggests a view of the individual as subject to greater or less degrees of exposure to the risk of illness over which they are perceived as having a greater or lesser degree of control. Davison *et al.* (1991, 1992), in an anthropological study linked to a health promotion campaign in Wales, found an association between lifestyles and risk. They broke factors influencing health into the following categories:

- 'self-evident personal differences' (e.g. hereditary factors);
- 'social environment' (e.g. loneliness, occupational risks);
- 'physical environment' (e.g. climate, pollution);
- 'fatalism' (e.g. bad luck, personal destiny).

As in other studies (e.g. Blaxter and Paterson 1982), ideas about personal destiny or fate were common explanations of illness. An apocryphal 'Uncle Norman' was identified who has many 'unhealthy' behaviours such as persistent heavy smoking and drinking. He is consequently overweight and 'red in the face' but lives into old age with few illnesses (Davison *et al.* 1992: 682). Many participants in the study had an 'Uncle Norman' somewhere in their family. 'Uncle Norman' suggests a 'luck' factor that operates in an unpredictable and apparently irrational way so that 'fat smokers really do live till advanced old age, and some svelte joggers really do "fall down dead"' (ibid. 683). As in Williams' (1990) research, a sense that of a 'timely' illness, or death was noted. 'Risk factors' related to, for example, smoking, diet and exercise that are routinely identified in epidemiological studies and underpin health promotion campaigns. Notions of fate and luck, which are seen as beyond any individual's control, do provide less fertile ground for established ways of changing health behaviours. In order to make sense of illness, people draw on the 'knowledge and lore received from the wider society' (Davison *et al.* 1991: 5). As noted earlier, a number of studies show (e.g. Blaxter 1990) how this knowledge is shared across generations and may be situated within communities (e.g. Helman 1978). In other words, like an epidemiologist, people seek to explain occurrences of illness through their own experiences and the 'lore' they share with others. Davison *et al.* (1991) calls this a 'lay epidemiology' to highlight the different knowledge bases of the lay and scientific approaches. However, 'lay epidemiology' may use ideas from medical and other scientific explanations. In particular, Davison *et al.* (1991) note the influence of the health promotion campaign 'Heartbeat Wales' on the explanations offered by their informants.

'Uncle Norman' and others who appear to contradict medical expectations about illness and mortality may be statistically insignificant in epidemiological study. They are important as 'stories' (Plummer 1995) or cultural knowledge which provide social explanations for illness and health. Stereotypes of the kind of people who are prone to illness can be significant. 'Thin and nervous' women have for example been identified by lay people as more likely to get breast cancer (Calnan and Johnson 1983). Interactions between biological, medical and lay explanations are reflected in stories and metaphors. 'Fate' or 'luck' may provide an adequate explanation for observations about ill health that appear to contradict official or scientific evidence. It also may reflect individual experiences of social disadvantage or as Stainton-Rogers (1991: 93) put it: 'Are "fatalists" fatalistic because life has given them a raw deal, or do they get a raw deal because their fatalism leads them to make no effort to help themselves?'

The context in which explanations about health are offered is significant. Calnan's (1986) concern about an interviewer is effect on his data and Cornwell's (1984) distinguish between 'public' and 'private' accounts was noted earlier. The latter tend to be provided during initial interviews and draw on what the interviewee perceives as the normative views about health. These accounts are often in accordance with medical ideas and people are keen to represent themselves as healthy. 'Private' accounts may emerge after a number of interviews have taken place and a degree of trust has developed between participants. The recognition of the interview or other data-collecting strategy as a social process becomes more important the more sensitive the subject is (e.g. sexual or mental health matters) to the informant (O'Connell *et al.* 1994). Furthermore, in an interview situation people often tend to want to provide what they anticipate the interviewer will see as the 'right' or 'expected' responses. As Blaxter (1990) notes

> there is a high level of agreement within the population that health is, to a considerable extent, dependent on behaviour and in one's own hands . . . at the least it is recognized that these are the 'correct or expected' answers to give.
>
> (Blaxter 1990: 81)

When talking about health, people may qualify their statements by phrases such as 'I suppose' and indicate that they are 'unsure of themselves and less articulate' when discussing medical and health topics (Pill and Stott 1982: 46). An example from Cornwell's (1984) research of a woman who initially said that she was lucky to have good health illustrates the nature of these layered depictions of health:

> Kathleen's medical history included having such bad eyesight as a child that she was expected to be blind by the age of twenty, lung disease including tuberculosis in her late teens, a miscarriage, a thyroid deficiency which requires permanent medication, and six years prior to interviews, a hysterectomy.
>
> (Cornwell 1984: 124)

This also reflects what Calnan (1987) calls a 'surface view'. He suggests that people tend to provide accounts that 'fit' what they perceive to be the generally accepted explanations when asked general questions about health. This may change when they are asked about personal experiences although again the linkage between 'good health' and 'goodness' in a moral sense may result in an underreporting of poor health or illness related to socially deviant behaviours. A qualitative study undertaken in the United States of men and women who had cancer reported that they said they were in 'good health' (Kayawa-Singer 1993). In a dichotomy based on a sense of 'I am still me' despite cancer, the informants sought an identity based on the positive values of health. This was based on 'their ability to maintain a sense of integrity as productive, able, and valued individuals'. As we noted earlier, 'in health' is therefore more than the 'absence of illness'.

Persistent ill health and disability

While good health is valued, poor health and especially persistent and visible poor health may be feared and hidden. It also represents for most people a fracturing of reality as the '. . . fidelity of our bodies is so basic that we never think of it – it is the certain grounds of our daily experience. Chronic illness is a 'betrayal of the fundamental trust' (Kleinman 1988: 45). The first national survey of the number of handicapped and impaired people in Britain was undertaken in 1968–9 (Harris *et al.* 1970). The survey was intended to provide data on people's need for assistance from the state and involved assessments of individual self-care abilities. Nearly 4 per cent of the 16–64 age group in Britain were found to have an impairment. This figure increased to just under 28 per cent of the over-65 population. Five per cent of all handicapped people had very severe handicaps with over 11 per cent being severely handicapped. Overall, women experienced a higher rate of handicap than men. However, the definitions used in this survey have been criticized for being imprecise. The World Health Organization (1980) provided what has become a commonly used set of categories:

- Impairment: any loss or deviation in the functioning or form of an individual's body or mind. This may involve a disease or trauma.
- Disability: any restriction of the ability to perform normal daily tasks. This tends to be linked to the ability to self-care.
- Handicap: any social disadvantage resulting from impairment or disability. This highlights the significance of material and social exclusion.

These categories have been generated out of complex processes involving health professions, researchers, policymakers and disability groups. However, many people who have a disability object to the word 'handicap'. Furthermore, as Zola (1983: 2) suggests, people with disabilities should not be characterized as 'nouns', that is 'the disabled'. 'No matter what label is used it cannot help but equate the person totally with his/her disability.'

The WHO model is important because it has informed later health surveys, and in linking the social and material consequences of chronic illness, shaped social and health policy. The material disadvantage of the elderly and the disabled was highlighted in the rediscovery of poverty in the 1960s (Townsend 1979; also Chapter 5). However, the distinctions between the WHO categories are blurred (Bury 1997) and often involve professional or lay judgements. This was recognized in later surveys of disability that used a combination of medical, social and self-assessment to estimate the demands made on social security (Martin 1988). It was estimated that there were over six million disabled adults in Britain with about 70 per cent being aged over 70 years. This reflects the incidence of chronic illnesses that tend to be experienced at older ages such as arthritis. It is also evident from this survey that older women experience a higher incident of disability than older men. This may partly reflect a higher death rate among those with disabling conditions. The definition of 'low severity' was inclusive and covered such problems as difficulty with dexterity that may have had a small impact on daily living. People with long-term managed disabilities may make relatively few demands on health services (Longsdale 1992).

Chronic illness involves a disruption of normal taken-for-granted routines of everyday life. It also frequently involves bodily changes that may be easily observed (e.g. loss of a limb or paralysis) or are visible through interaction (e.g. hearing or speech difficulties). The experience of chronic illness has an impact on the bodies of people and affects their identity and sense of self. As Goffman has put it:

> people expect . . . the cripple to be crippled; to be disabled and helpless; to be inferior to themselves, and they will become suspicious and insecure if the cripple falls short of these expectations . . . [the] cripple has to play the part of the cripple.
>
> (Goffman 1968: 47)

This symbolic interactionist perspective draws attention to the way identity is the product of interactions between people. Chronic illness disrupts the sense of self and leads to the negotiating of new social and personal identities (Kelly and Field 1996; Gerhardt 1989). Bury (1988, 1991, 1997) suggests that there are two types of meaning related to the onset of chronic illness. Firstly, there are 'consequences' affecting everyday life at a practical level, such as problems associated with carrying out domestic tasks. A number of studies have drawn attention to how particular conditions disrupt and eventually redefine previously taken-for-granted activities. Secondly, the 'significance' of the condition relates to an individual sense of self that is shaped by the reaction of others and the cultural significance of the disability. Chronic illness has a varying degree of cultural significance. Sontag (1977), in her book *Illness as Metaphor*, argues that diseases like cancer (for which she was receiving treatment) and tuberculosis have an important cultural role. She suggests that they can be understood by the use of metaphor. For example, tuberculosis was often described as 'leading to a noble often lyrical death'. By contrast cancer is a disease of uncontrolled, abnormal growth that invades the body, 'a demonic pregnancy' (Sontag 1989: 14). Until the rise of AIDS, cancer was the dreaded disease and often mentioned only by its initial 'C'. As with other conditions such as epilepsy, people understand the illness through a historical screen based on fear and apprehension. Less dramatically, people with diabetes (Rajaram 1997) or arthritis (Singer 1974) may attempt to hide or minimize their symptoms because they do not want to be regarded as 'disabled' or unable to take part in everyday activities.

People negotiate a new identity and make sense of their illness through their lived experiences. Bury (1982) has identified this as 'biographical disruption' to draw attention to the impact of the onset of disability at a particular moment of an individual life course. This disruption takes place at a number of levels:

> First there is the disruption of taken-for-granted assumptions and behaviours. Second there are more profound disruptions in explanatory systems normally used by people such that a fundamental re-thinking of a person's biography and self concept is involved. Third, there is a response to disruption involving the mobilisation of resources in facing an altered situation.
>
> (Bury 1982: 166)

This biographical disruption has been described as a rupture in the connections between an individual's 'biographical time', 'conceptions of the body' and 'conceptions of self' (Corbin and Strauss 1988). This 'BBC' chain is defined as 'conceptions of self, arising directly or indirectly through body, as they evolve over the course of biographical time' (p. 253). Thus, the onset of disability involves a reassessment and renegotiating of people's lives.

Coping with chronic illness inevitably involves dealing with the bodily problems the conditions generate. Tasks such as going to the toilet, eating or bathing can become the focus for the renegotiating of identity that is shaped by the symbolic meaning of these activities. For example, being able to go to the toilet without adult intervention is a symbolic marker of the transition from infant to child. The need for help with intimate personal activities places considerable demands of the person concerned and their immediate family who are frequently informal carers. The relationship of husband and wife, for example, can be disrupted when one becomes more or less dependent on the other for such daily physical tasks (Parker 1993). This dependence can generate 'hypervigilance' of a kind familiar to new parents. To quote from the husband of a woman who suffers from insulin dependent diabetes;

> . . . I'll wake up in the middle of the night, she'd be having a dream or something, tossing or turning or something and I'd just think she is just having a reaction and I'll wake her up, 'You're OK?' Yes, that makes her mad too. I do worry about her.
>
> (Rajaram 1997: 290)

Considerable social value is placed on independence and self-control. Furthermore, as we have seen, 'health' can take on a moral element which makes it difficult for those with disabilities to present a positive image. The process of constructing and maintaining such an identity in the face of illness has been referred to as the 'pursuit of virtue' (Williams 1993). Within a culture that emphasizes 'wellness' expressed through independence, self-reliance and the body, conditions that visibly 'mark' or disfigure the body may make it hard to establish a positive identity (Longsdale 1990). Thus 'the body is not merely the location of the disease, but is that through which one continues to apprehend the world and oneself in it' (Radley 1989: 232). Shilling (1993) and others, have also argued that in a rapidly changing society with few certainties, the cultivation and maintenance of the body represents one of the few arenas of stability and control. This recognizes the centrality of the body in contemporary society and reflects the challenge made from the perspective of the politics of disability, that bodily difficulties have been understated in medical and social research (Oliver 1990).

The notion of 'coping' is commonly used by health professionals as well as lay people who often say they are 'coping' with their chronic illness. Bury (1991: 460) defines coping as 'the cognitive processes whereby the individual learns how to tolerate or put up with the effects of illness . . .'. However as Bury (1997) notes, this contains a normative sense which suggests a 'successful' response to health problems. Sociological approaches to coping are more collective in orientation than the individualistic model (Marks 1996) used in psychology which are characterized in Lazarfield and Folkman's model of stress and coping. A process of 'comeback' (Corbin and Strauss 1991) has been identified whereby people adapt to their changed circumstances in a way that enables them to 'tolerate' the consequences of their condition. Overlapping with coping, Bury (1991: 461) identifies 'strategy' as 'the actions people take or what people do in the face of illness'. The opportunities for people to develop strategies depend to a large extent on the availability of material and social resources. Family and social networks are important although trends in divorce and family form mean that an increasing number of people are living alone (Burghes *et al.* 1997). However, changes in people's circumstances can mean the loss of social networks (Morgan 1989) and place considerable strain on the immediate family (Pruchno and Potashnik 1989; Rajaram 1997). Material resources can be equally problematic given that chronic illness is associated with ageing which in turn is frequently associated with poverty. Furthermore, a disproportionate number of the poor elderly are represented by women who have disabilities (Townsend 1979). Finally, and again overlapping with the other two categories, Bury (1991: 462) identifies 'style' as the way people respond to, and present, important features of their illnesses or treatment regimens'.

Following Goffman's concept of 'performance', people have to represent themselves in social interactions in a way that reconciles the 'competing demands of their bodily symptoms and those of society' (Radley 1994). The development of a style is easier when the symptoms or bodily difference are less obvious. Longsdale (1990) notes the problems of overcoming negative responses to visible metallic appliances or uncontrollable bodily functions. In contrast, people with epilepsy may be able to conceal their condition (Schneider and Conrad 1983). The degree to which the person with disabilities is able to control information (in both the verbal and bodily forms) partly defines the styles they can adopt. For example, a wheelchair is highly visible and communicates a set of messages about disabilities while epilepsy may be invisible. Artefacts associated with disability such as wheelchairs or dark glasses may take on a symbolic meaning that emphasizes 'negative difference' (Phillips 1990). As we noted earlier, some people may withdraw into the home, 'give in to illness' while others will see a virtue in 'fighting' the problems they have. If a political element is added to the concept of style, the boundaries around 'normal' and 'abnormality' in health come into question as disability movements emphasize a notion of 'difference'. This brings to the fore the problems of unequal access to education, employment, leisure and housing experienced by people with disabilities (Oliver 1996) which indicates the interrelationship between 'style' and 'strategies'. This came to a head in Britain in the debate surrounding the Disability Discrimination Act 1995 and continues in demands for autonomy and individual rights (Shakespeare 1993).

HIV/AIDS has not only had important social implication but also challenges some of the established ideas about chronic illness. The general trend of chronic or life-threatening illness to be associated with increasing age and often confined to very old age is thrown into reverse by the incidents of HIV/AIDS. AIDS (acquired immunodeficiency syndrome) causes the collapse of the body's immune system which leaves it unprotected from a range of fatal illnesses. HIV (human immunodeficiency virus) is linked to AIDS and acquired through the exchange of blood or bodily fluids. HIV infection is closely associated with AIDS and death although there can be a long period when few symptoms are experienced. Since the 1980s there has been an increasing recognition of the problems associated with AIDS and a consequent expansion in medical and social research into the condition. Those infected with HIV live at the boundaries between wellness and unwellness. They are apparently healthy but are subject to an 'unknown' higher degree of risk. They are not chronically ill but feel that they face the inevitability of becoming so sooner or later, more or less disabled or incapacitated. There is some evidence that once diagnosed with HIV people attempt to come to terms with it by a process that involves biographical reflection similar to that discussed above (Carricaburu and Pierret 1995). Gay HIV-positive men were able to construct positive identities that were legitimated and supported by gay culture. However, haemophiliac men who had coped with their illness found it difficult to come to terms with HIV and tended to withdraw from social contact. This suggests that there is an acceptance of HIV/AIDS within the gay community and a recognized 'style' that the newly infected person can adopt. Furthermore, unlike the majority of people with chronic illnesses, the gay community is relatively young and has greater access to material resources (Winn and Skelton 1992).

Sontag (1990) identified an 'epidemic psychology' based on a social fear and panic that surrounded the appearance of AIDS. Not only was AIDS a new disease, its main means of transmission was through sexual contact. This goes to the heart of human society and behaviour which in recent years has seen an apparent proliferation of dangers over which people feel they have little control. The late twentieth century has be characterized by a 'politics of anxiety' that has been fostered by the creation of hazards such as environmental pollution, BSE and 'food scares'. These threats to health are largely a product of human action. Armstrong (1993a) contrasts this with the 'natural' threats present in the environment in the past. Thus God, nature and fate, which are all beyond individual control, were seen as the source for such hazards. It is argued that diseases such as AIDS, threats to health such as BSE and the increasing immunity of bacteria to antibiotics, are conceptualized within a social framework. It is human action which, despite the biological nature of AIDS, is seen as causal: 'The victims who could reasonably be deemed guilty are those – homosexual, or heterosexual or drug abusing who have refused to adjust their behaviour' (*Independent* 1988). Furthermore, with no medical cure, it is social behaviour that has become the main site for intervention. The role of health promotion and education has done much to promote research into risks related to AIDS and sexual health. Epidemiological research has attempted to identify risk factors across a whole range of human activities based on survey research and official statistics of morbidity and mortality. Probability theory under-pins assessments risks. This gives risk factors the appearance of scientific validity and helps legitimate public health interventions (Lupton 1995). The 'holy trinity' of risks – smoking, diet and exercise – inform and shape lay ideas about health. However, the way people assess risk is obscure and difficult in the face of '. . . nuclear, chemical, genetic and ecological mega-hazards [which] abolish the . . . calculations of risk (Beck 1992: 99). Such risks are ever present threats to individuals who have become increasingly responsible for their own health. Although there is no marked transition to Beck's model of a 'risk society' it is usually associated with the spread of HIV and AIDS and a number of disasters in the 1980s for example, Bhopal in India and Chernobyl in the Ukraine (Giddens 1990).

Conclusion

This chapter has considered the various ways health and illness have been studied and the range of ideas people have about health. There has been a move from the absolutism of the sick role which accepted biomedical definitions of illness, to a range of approaches that prioritize lay people's understanding and experiences of health and illness. This shift is reflected in empirical research which was preoccupied with problems identified by medical professionals. The influence of medical anthropology is important because it helped create the space to study healthy people as well as those who, because they were attending a clinic or were part of a health educa-tion programme, had a particular concern with health. This is reflected in the shift from studies about 'illness behaviour' to studies about 'health behaviour'. Research on 'lay beliefs' which embraces the examination of the causes of illness has more recently emerged as a concern with 'lay knowledge'. This represents an attempt to recognize the complexity and depth of lay knowledge and draw attention to 'lay' and 'medical' knowledge as a contrasting pair.

There is a significant bias running through the research considered in this chapter, in that most studies are focused on women's health. Although the studies cited here do not constitute a representative sample of research on lay knowledge, the focus on women's health is typical. Calnan and Johnson (1985: 57) explain why their research focused on women: '. . . because they tend to be the lay carers in the family and bear the major responsibility for the families' health.' It is this social role of women that make them the 'natural' focus for research. Furthermore, women are often assumed to be more willing to talk about health issues and to be more accessible to researchers (Stacey 1988; Mullen 1993). However, as women experience a higher incidence of chronic illness than men, there is some justification for the gender bias. Research is now far more eclectic theoretically, methodo-logically and in the substantive problems that are studied. However, it should not be forgotten that most empirical research is dependent on funding and that the state and medically orientated charities have a large role to play in shaping the research agenda (Hardey and Mulhall 1994; Bury 1997).

At the beginning of the chapter, Parsons' model of the sick role was examined and situated within his wider theoretical project. Although this made the social aspects of illness a legitimate area of concern, it did so in a way that reflected the problems identified by medicine. The chapter ended with an exploration of the cultural significance of disease and a concern for how lay people related their knowledge to the risks and uncertainties of contemporary society. This represents the shift from narrow 'top-down' ideas about health to a wider 'bottom-up' focus on lay knowledge and finally to general issues about the nature of society.

The health services and the delivery of care

Introduction

The National Health Service (NHS) came into being on 5 July 1948. It was unique in that it provided a universal 'free at the point of use' service. The hospitals owned by various voluntary organizations were nationalized and placed under the Ministry of Health. Under the National Insurance Act 1911, some 21 million people had access to free general practitioner care and this was extended to the entire population and not made dependent on an insurance contribution. The new NHS was based on the principles of comprehensiveness, universality and collectivism; the additional principle of professional autonomy had been conceded by the Labour Government after a long struggle with the medical profession (Stacey 1988). This indicates how important it is to situate the creation and development of the NHS within a wider political and social context. For example, changes in how work is organized in industrial and post-industrial societies helps to unravel some of the developments in the healthcare system. It is also important to examine the private sector of healthcare in order to see some of the tensions between a social and market model of care provision. Despite rhetoric in the 1980s about the 'privatization' of the NHS, healthcare in Britain remains under state control. However, there has been a restructuring 'revolution', the effects of which are still reverberating through the system. The nature of these structural changes and the impact of them on the delivery of care can be seen in the emphasis on community care. Within the NHS there has long been a tension between prevention and secondary care that has recently been manifest in the changing role of health promotion and what has been called the 'new public health'. The wider social implications of this trend towards prevention have been described as part of the development of a 'new regime of total health' (Armstrong 1993b).

Creating the NHS

In the new NHS, the consultants in teaching hospitals retained their privileged position at the top of their profession as well as the ability to retain the practice of private medicine. Bevan later claimed he had 'stuffed their mouths with gold' (Stacey 1988). General practitioners did better than nurses, who had little input into the debate that surrounded the setting up of the NHS (Stacey 1988; Dingwall *et al.* 1988; Baly 1995). Ancillary workers were not considered in any of the negotiations. The establishment medical hierarchy was therefore reproduced and confirmed in its dominance over other health occupations. This was reflected in the tripartite organizational structure that was set up in 1948, which has since been seen as a classic example of political and administrative expediency (Willcocks 1967). With hindsight, a logical structure would have been regionally based with one financial centre and built-in accountability (Morgan *et al.*1985). However, in practice, hospital services, general medical and dental services and local authority health services retained or created their own spheres of influence with divergent funding arrangements. Under this system, general practitioners were largely independent of local council control and therefore retained what they saw as their professional autonomy. Community and environmental services which included health visiting, aftercare for the mentally ill and maternal health, became the responsibility of the local authority health services. Hospitals had their own administrative system which was regionally based around the locality of teaching hospitals rather than any conceptualization of geography or the distribution of patients. This stored up trouble for the future when inequalities between different parts of the country in everything from the provision of acute beds to the general practitioner : patient ratio became recognized as a major health problem. Overall, there was no association between the various services and the areas they drew clients from. This made coordination at an everyday level difficult in that the hospital ward, primary care services and welfare agencies which may be involved in patient discharge had their own structures and systems. Baly (1995) depicts the intricacies of the system:

> The mental hospitals were separate from the general, the chronic from the acute, the teaching from the non-teaching and within the substructure itself there was a three-tiered system of administration. It was devolution of authority downwards on almost Napoleonic Code lines, and bewildering to the average citizen whose needs the system had been set up to serve.
>
> Baly (1995: 188)

The tripartite structure gave consultants control over expenditure and policy within the hospitals. General practitioners remained self-employed and became subcontractors rather than salaried civil servants. The power of the medical profession ensured that it was well represented in all the key decision-making forums of the NHS.

The NHS replicated the medical hierarchy which not surprisingly was reflected in the financing of healthcare. Effectively, overall spending was based on the previous year's figure plus a growth factor. This money trickled down the hierarchy so that the main teaching hospitals (especially in London) received funds that were disproportionate compared to the needs of other institutions such as mental health hospitals. Inequalities in the healthcare system were therefore set to increase rather than decline. Between 1950 and 1981, the proportion of spending on hospital services increased from 55 to 62 per cent. Over the same period, the proportion of spending on general practice declined from 10 to 6.5 per cent and that on health authority community services from 8 to 6.5 per cent (Ashton and Seymour 1988). As these figures suggest the hospitals dominated the NHS to the extent that it has been called 'the national sickness service'.

Those who anticipated that there would be a decline in the demand for health services forgot that patients who were treated successfully would eventually become ill again in the future. Even without any form of free health service, improved diet and public health measures would have led to an increasing elderly population. The NHS enabled older people to live more healthy lives and deal with chronic illness in ways that had not been thought possible before the Second World War. The other major problem that confronted the policy makers and planners was the dilemma of 'need'. As we have seen, a number of studies indicated that people could be suffering from all kinds of conditions without making any demands on the health-care system (see Chapter 2). For those concerned with containing spending on health, this suggests that there is potential for making everybody more self-reliant and encouraging self-treatment. The opposite case can also be made, which focuses on 'unmet need' and suggests that more effort needs to be spent to encourage the 'underutilizers' to make use of the health services. There is a level of uncertainty here in that it is not possible to quantify the costs equation of the late referral of symptoms that call for expensive interventions.

Klein (1989: 58) notes that the main success of the 1950s was to 'make the NHS work' but that the cost was a 'bias towards inertia' and consensus. This involved the work of a new administrative layer in the hierarchy of groups employed by the NHS. Until relatively recently, this group was confined by the dominance of medicine to enabling the 'service to run rather than run it' (Cox 1991). This inability of the administration to 'manage' has been a major cause of state intervention into the NHS as various governments have attempted to gain control over spending and more generally the delivery of services. By the 1970s there was the increasing evidence that the NHS was failing to provide a geographically universal service. There was also a growing economic crisis promoted in 1973 by a massive increase in oil prices and a recession that resulted in cash limits on public spending in 1976. In addition, Hart (1971: 405) identified what he called the 'inverse care law' under which 'the availability of good quality medical care varies inversely with the need for it in the population itself'. Various schemes for the control of planning, budgeting and organization were developed (e.g. the Hospital Plan 1962, NHS Planning System 1976) and only the more significant can be referred to here. The Resource Allocation Working Party (RAWP) set up in 1976 was an attempt to shift resources in line with the demand for health services. It devised a formula based on various demographic data (e.g. perinatal mortality rate, standard mortality ratio) to allocate money and in so doing made visible the sometime glaring disparities between various parts of the country (Klein 1989). A reorganization of the NHS structure was introduced in 1974 which attempted to improve the effectiveness of management and simplify the decision-making structure. The reorganization also sought to increase democracy by creating various committees with lay representation and for the first time nursing was given a place on regional and local level boards. Preventative medicine, represented by local authority medical officers of health, was brought into the NHS and placed under health authorities. Despite a number of changes of government there was a broad degree of consensus over the reforms that needed to be made to the NHS (Klein 1989). However, the power of the medical profession remained to the fore during various attempts to reform the system in the 1970s. They used the notion of responsibility to the patient to protect them from attempts to make doctors responsible for management decisions (Stacey 1988). The argument was that doctors must have the unquestioned right to decide any treatment they thought fit. The same case was made in the struggle over the restriction of prescription drugs in the 1980s, which the profession effectively lost. The management style of the time has been depicted as a 'diplomacy model' under which managers were reactive and had little scope to change the organization (Harrison et al. 1990). There is a resemblance to the doctor–nurse game here in that administrators were often engaged in a similar manipulative exercise although the dimension of gender was usually absent.

The Griffiths Report (DHSS 1983) was in fact a statement of proposed action rather than a paper for debate (Flynn 1992). It marked a clear break from the political consensus over the NHS and represented an attempt to introduce 'management' rather than 'administration' into the system. This is captured in the commonly cited comment that 'if Florence Nightingale were to carry her lamp through the corridors of the NHS today she would almost certainly be searching for the people in charge' (DHSS 1983: 12). Griffiths argued that the NHS could – and should – be managed like a business with clearly defined objectives, lines of accountability and measurable outcomes. Both the British Medical Association and the Royal College of Nursing opposed some of the reforms proposed by Griffiths but neither could stop the momentum of the push for efficiency. Introduced in 1983, the Griffiths restructuring provided for the 'first time in the history of the NHS, a direct and explicit hierarchical chain of command in which managers at each level assumed personal responsibility for the execution of bureaucratic control' (Flynn 1992: 65). This involved the replacement of the representative management teams introduced in 1974 with clearly defined 'line managers'. The medical professions were brought under the managerial control through a series of measures which included making them responsible for budgets and achieving targets.

These changes in the NHS have been characterized as amounting to a 'moral crusade' (Strong and Robinson 1988). This indicates that the restructuring of the 1980s went beyond changing the organization of the NHS and marked a transformation of the culture and values of the organization. Strong and Robinson (1990), in an ethnographic account of the impact of reorganization, observe that this 'crusade' has done little to change the relationships between the various occupations engaged in delivering healthcare. In particular, the inequalities of power between nursing and other occupations 'allied to medicine' (e.g. social work) remained largely untouched by the managerial changes. The management changes that followed in the wake of Griffiths reflect this and have been referred to as 'new managerialism' which some commentators have linked to the emergence of post-Fordist organizations (Reed and Hughes 1992).

Post-Fordism and the rise of the consumer

The late 1970s were a period of economic and political crisis that are characterized in the 'winter of discontent' and the election of the Conservative Government of 1979. It was committed to 'roll back the welfare state' and reduce government intervention. Influenced by right-wing academics such as Hayek and Friedman, the Conservatives wanted to move the state away from the collective provision of services. They placed the individual at the core of this approach and wanted to provide people with the ability to make choices expressed through the market. It was argued that the provision of services through the state bureaucracies encouraged dependence on them and the professions which provided the services. The professions therefore had an interest in fostering this 'dependency culture' under which they controlled the supply and shaped the demand for services. The solution was to restore (some advocates of the 'New Right' pointed to the *laissez-faire* policies of the past) responsibility and control to the individual. The demand and nature of professional services would be determined by the working of the market, which it was argued represented at least as much a democratic expression of consumer preferences as the ballot box (Culyer 1976; Flynn 1989; King 1989). These ideas were initially implemented through changes in local government and trade union law, followed by the introduction of subcontracting and competitive tendering for a wide range of services provided by low-skilled workers. Professional groups remained largely untouched until the late 1980s when less powerful professions such as opticians were 'deregulated' and placed fully in the market (Higgins 1988). This reflected a hostility in some important parts of the Conservative Administrations to the status and influence of the professions. There was, for example, continued sniping about the status of social workers as a professional group for which there was no private sector equivalent and which represented a key aspect of the 'dependent culture'. In the climate of uncertainty and disruption of the 1980s, the previously politically unacceptable ideas such as the 'demolition' or 'privatization' of the welfare state were raised.

Pahl (1988: 4) argues that 'we are living through a period of change that is qualitatively and quantitatively different from that typical of most of the twentieth century'. Changes in the NHS do not happen in isolation and are part of general social and economic changes that have been conceptualized as a broad movement from modernism to late or postmodernity. The origins of modernism are commonly traced to the end of the eighteenth century and the 'Age of Enlightenment' in the West. This period is associated with the emergence of the 'sciences' and a philosophical commitment to rationality. Human beings rather than transcendental entities (e.g. God) became recognized as creating knowledge and an understanding of the universe through scientific endeavour (Foucault 1976). Society therefore becomes secularized and the division of labour in modern societies becomes increasingly organized on rational as opposed to traditional or ritualized lines. There is an accompanying optimistic belief in the progress of human thought and organization. This profound social, cultural and philosophical transformation is reflected in all aspects of human life from the arts to employment. Scientific management or Taylorism is a high point in the modernization of work. Developed in the United States, it involved the detailed scientific study of production processes that were analysed and broken down into simple tasks that could be timed and organized. This, as Adam Smith in the *Wealth of Nations* had previously predicted, increased productivity and reduced costs. It was Henry Ford who put these ideas into practice and saw how they could create a mass market for new products like the Model T car. Fordism is therefore linked to the development of specialist tools and technologies that enable complex processes to be undertaken by relatively unskilled labour. This involved a division between 'doers' and 'thinkers' who were needed to monitor and develop the organization. It was not until after 1945 that Fordism became fully developed in most industrial countries. It was characterized by attempts to centralize control over an area of work, the development of less-skilled occupations based on creating specialist subdivisions, and within a simple hierarchy. It was also capital intensive, relatively inflexible to change and tended to produce a uniform product as manifest in the classic black Model T car. The creation of the NHS can be seen to follow this Fordist logic (Stacey 1988; Klein 1989). The welfare state itself has been situated with a Fordist framework as it follows the logic of centralization, hierarchy and specialization. The organization of nursing provides a good example of Fordism in healthcare (see Chapter 4). Nurses were trained to be subservient to doctors and worked within a bureaucratic hierarchy that allocated work on the basis of specialist tasks. Although the more senior nurses did have some degree of freedom to make decisions about their work, it was doctors who diagnosed and prescribed treatment. Braverman (1974), writing about patterns of work, made a similar distinction between 'conception' and 'execution' in marking out the difference between 'doers' and 'thinkers'. Their pay and conditions were negotiated at national level and there was rigid demarcation of different nursing specialisms and levels of nurses. From this perspective, the introduction of general management following the Griffiths report can be seen as the high point of Fordism in the NHS (Owens and Glennerster 1990; Flynn 1992). It attempted in Fordist fashion to reduce the autonomy of various professional groups and centralize control over the use of resources.

Fordism is synonymous with a time of economic growth, mass consumption and large corporations profiting from the economies of scale. However, the rigid structure of these enterprises caused tensions and contradictions that resulted in low morale in employees and labour unrest. A 'sea change in the surface appearance of capitalism' (Harvey 1989: 189) has been traced to the early 1970s. This included a deindustrialization of manufacturing, the rapid rise of new technologies based on the microprocessor, the growth of the service sector (especially financial services) and the development of international competitiveness for goods and services (Harvey 1989; Lash and Urry 1987). There was a consequent restructuring of the labour market which involved considerable levels of unemployment as well as the emergence of women as a significant source of full- and part-time labour (Pascall 1995). These changes have been seen as producing a more flexible workforce that can be divided into 'core' and peripheral groups (Hakim 1979). This encouraged a polarization between those in full-time skilled employment and those who were unemployed or situated on the periphery in low paid and insecure jobs. At the same time, following the logic of its philosophy, the Conservative Administrations of the 1980s fostered deregulation and non-intervention into the economy and what some have referred to as a 'crisis' of the welfare state (Offe 1984).

Post-Fordism is associated with 'disorganized capitalism' (Lash and Urry 1987) and is characterized by flexibility, uncertainty and the priority given to consumers. There is a considerable literature on post-Fordism and some divergence of opinion on its scope, causes and effects (Piore and Sable 1984; Aglietta 1987). However, it is possible to tease out some general themes and apply them to the analysis of the NHS. The flexibility of the NHS workforce has been increased through subcontracting and the professionalization of nursing. From the mid-1980s, it became necessary for employers such as hospitals to seek competitive tendering for ancillary work like domestic cleaning and catering (Pulkingham 1992). These sub-contracted workers are largely women who are employed on a part-time basis on relatively low wages. Like other peripheral workers they can be quickly taken in or out of employment in line with the demand for their labour. The increased flexibility of professional nurses is considered in Chapter 4. Their greater expertise and autonomy (e.g. the expanded role) are characteristic of post-Fordist work. The introduction of primary nursing and the use of individualized care packages reflect the central place of the individual consumer in post-Fordist organizations. Driven by the demands of the internal market the 'skill-mix' of qualified to less-qualified care assistants became an important source of cost saving. Ranade (1994) shows how the ratio between the core of qualified and the periphery of less-qualified nurses changed from 61 : 23 to 58 : 28 between 1990 and 1991. The elevation of the consumer has been identified as one of the major changes that took place in the 1980s. As Nettleton notes, the NHS Management Executive (1993) cited 'Ford motor company's present-day marketing slogan EVERYTHING WE DO IS DRIVEN BY YOU as providing the rationale for the way forward in the NHS' (Nettleton 1995: 217). This neatly marks the transformation of the place of the consumer in both Ford's marketing and the NHS.

Ironically, a Fordist project of centralizing bureaucratic control over doctors can be seen in the emergence of the post-Fordist NHS. The introduction of medical audit provided a greater degree of surveillance over doctors by opening their decisions to a process of peer review. The 1989 White Paper, in classic Fordist fashion, sought to specify the working practices of consultants more closely. It is debatable whether the autonomous working practices of doctors in general could have been described as strictly Fordist in the first place. However, we are more concerned with the general changes within the NHS at this stage. The rise of health economists as a occupational group (Nettleton 1995) is associated with the new managerialism. It is argued that they can provide a 'rational' analysis that will reduce the influence of political factors in making decisions and 'replace ad hoc and politically motivated decision making, as far as possible with an impersonal means–end calculus' (Ashmore 1989: 36). In order to place the consumer at the centre of the restructured NHS through the mechanism of an internal market, it was necessary to provide basic information about costs, outcome and demands. The development of the internal market led to further demands for new forms of information and surveillance over the delivery of health. In the past, 'consumer satisfaction' had been manifest in the doctor–patient relationship. It now had to be incorporated as a central plank of the internal market and various quality assurance schemes have developed to do this. Performance indicators (PIs) were introduced as an important part of the attempt to measure efficiency and enable comparisons to be made across sections of the healthcare system. This was essential if managers were to be able to plan and encourage effective practices. PIs included norms and averages for patient turnover, inpatient days and other data which 'provided a technique for enhanced internal managerial control, and a mechanism for external inspection and evaluation' (Flynn 1992: 35). Information technology promised increased levels of surveillance and made an appearance at all levels of the health service. A new bureaucracy was established under the new managerialism within the NHS to provide and manage this information. Thus the move to a post-Fordist organization of healthcare required a 'catching-up' of the system with some aspects of Fordism. In effect, the proliferation of quality indicators provided part of a panoptic system of surveillance hitherto absent from all but the lower echelons of the healthcare system (Foucault 1979; Clegg 1989).

The markets – or more appropriately the quasimarkets – that were introduced into the NHS are very complex and inherently artificial in that it is hard to identify either the 'market' or the 'producer' or 'customers'. Despite the rhetoric, the patient was not the customer in that general practitioner (GP) fundholders and health authorities acted as the consumer and purchased care from separate 'provider' units such as hospitals and the ambulance services. At a basic level, patients are able to choose their general practitioner but in reality this choice is constrained. GPs do not encourage the free movement of patients across practices and there is pressure on individual patients to express choice within large group practices rather than between different practices (Thompson 1989). It is instructive that the Government, keen to encourage private healthcare and the privatization of the state's services, separated the purchasers of health services from the recipients. The core of the Government's argument was that patients did not have sufficient knowledge to make appropriate decisions about their healthcare. Quite what this implies about the consumers of private healthcare is not clear. However, a pool of pent-up consumer demand might be anticipated based on the United States' experience (Abel-Smith 1994) and this may have concentrated minds on the problem of containing costs rather than inventing consumers.

The private sector

Since the NHS was established, GPs and hospital consultants have been able to have private fee-paying patients. There was also a small number of independent non-profit hospitals, commercially led institutions and clinics that operated completely within a private health sector. However, many of these hospitals were poorly equipped and only able to undertake minor surgery. As in the United States, private healthcare offers to deliver a 'personalized' level of care with short waiting times for treatment and a high standard of hotel-like hospital amenities. Critics have argued that private provision is parasitic on the NHS as it does not train any of its staff and insurance companies carefully exclude the more costly and chronic conditions from their cover (Watkins 1987). The tensions between the private and public practice of hospital-based doctors came to the fore in the 1970s with Labour Government's attempt to restrict the use of 'pay-beds' in the NHS. A sometimes bitter dispute, between consultants on one side and the Government and trade unions representing the less-skilled healthcare workers on the other, rumbled through the late 1970s until a compromise was agreed in 1979. This was an early victim of the incoming Conservative administration which cancelled the agreed phasing out of pay-beds and gave tax relief to employer-based health insurance schemes (Klein 1989). The new Government sponsored a series of measures to encourage the private sector including building greater flexibility into consultants' contracts. Health authorities were encouraged to collaborate with the private sector and make provision for it in any future planning. There was a rapid although sporadic growth in health insurance until the late 1980s. Much of the initial growth was due to employer-based schemes which used health insurance as an employment benefit mainly for senior staff. Marketing strategies and worries about the 'decline' of the NHS and waiting lists encouraged a small minority of individuals to take out insurance.

Following the anticipated reduction of pay-beds, a number of private commercial hospitals had been built in the late 1970s. This programme was given added impetus by the Conservative Government and a number of US hospital corporations moved into what they hoped would be a growing market. From owning only 5 per cent of all private hospitals in 1979, British and US commercial groups owned nearly 40 per cent by 1989 (Independent Hospital Association 1989). During the same period, the number of hospitals controlled by charitable religious organizations also declined from 32 in 1979 to only 10 in 1989. Most of the hospitals were sold to the profit-based sector. This broad picture of growth was followed by a relative decline marked by the withdrawal of two major US groups from the British market in 1989 (Higgins 1992). There are also regional disparities in private provision, with most of the industry being centred on London and the south of England. The extent of work undertaken in the private sector has always been difficult to estimate due to the lack of records (Higgins 1992). The White Paper *Working for Patients* (Department of Health 1989a) claimed that 9 per cent of the population was covered by healthcare insurance. It expressed the Government's view that the private sector was complementary to the NHS and other policies were to enable the sector to compete in competitive tenders for health work (Flynn 1992). This was a two-way process in that NHS providers could also compete for the business of the private sector. In broad terms, the private sector is biased towards particular forms of treatment such as cosmetic surgery, hip replacements, cholecystectomies and abortions. About half the annual number of abortions have consistently been carried out in the private sector, but an unknown number of these are undertaken for patients from abroad. It is generally held that individuals use the private sector to have

treatments that are not available under the NHS (e.g. routine breast enlargement), treatments for which they believe there is a long NHS waiting
list and in order to have a higher level of hotel services. At one level, this is
an expression of choice in line with the Conservative Party's expectations
but in the majority of cases such choice can only be exercised through insurance schemes. There is an incentive for healthcare insurance schemes
to acquire the least potentially expensive clients. Once claims are made, as a
medical director of a private clinic quoted by Samson (1995: 264) indicates,
there is pressure to restrain treatment 'we know what their insurance
policies will pay for, so we make sure we come within that'. Busfield
(1990) has argued that in practice the schemes provided little choice because
the private sector is dominated by a few corporations and insurance companies place severe restrictions on individual choice.

Hospital and community care

Modern medicine developed around the hospital and it remains the seat of
power and status within the healthcare system. Community based healthcare
has often been seen by health authorities in a negative way as care outside
the hospital. Like 'care' 'community' is hard to define and has a romantic
'rose-tinted' association that has often been placed at the core of political
discourses about health policy. It tends to be associated with a place where
people have a 'sense of belonging' with established family ties and strong
social networks. Tonnies' (1887 and 1957) classic distinction between this
'Gemeinschaft' society and a 'Gesellschaft' society which is dominated by
self-interest and loose relationships remains relevant in the representations
of community. References to community often reflect a nostalgia for an
imagined earlier period where people had a direct participation in decisions
and all spheres of life were tightly intertwined (Plant 1974). A distinction is
commonly made between 'care in' the community which includes NHS
and local authority provision and 'care by' the community that covers the
efforts of families and the voluntary sector. While community implies a
locality, it is ironic that in healthcare terms there is a tradition of overlap
and gaps between the various community services. For example, general
practitioners do not often cover the same area as health visitors, who work
in different areas from social workers. The establishment of the NHS in
the short term led to a decline in community based hospitals as they were
closed under the policy to take advantage of economies of scale and concentrate resources on large district general hospitals.

There is a blurring of health and social care in the community at both the
level of practice and policy. Until the 1974 reorganization of the NHS,
health and social services had links through the medical officer of health.
The Seebohm Report (DHSS 1968) called for a new model of social work
practice that emphasized collaboration with families and communities. It

also led to social services being put under a director of social services within local authorities. Meanwhile, health services were reorganized into area health authorities and district authorities so that the boundaries between social and health services were often different. Furthermore, general practitioners operated independently from both services.

In 1948, there was a large number of people who were being cared for in what was defined as the community in the old workhouse system that by then tended to care for the elderly who lacked families or the mentally ill. The first day hospitals were also opened in 1948. Community care is clearly not a product of the 1980s. In 1956, the Guillebaud Committee had recommended community-based care for some people (Baggott 1994). Enoch Powell, the Health Minister in 1959, introduced the Mental Health Act and predicted the closure of mental hospitals in the following fifteen years. The Act allowed some patients to choose the place of their treatment which included the community. The 1962 Hospital Plan emphasized the need to expand community care at the expense of hospital-based care (Ham 1992). However, while there was a broad political consensus about the desirability of fostering community provision, there was little change in the delivery of services until the 1980s outside the area of mental health (Walker 1989).

The early mental hospital in both its architecture and its locality is a dramatically different institution from the general hospital. The asylum was located in the countryside, often remote from the nearest town. This originally provided a contrast to disorganized privately run asylums in the cities that were often a source of tuberculosis and other diseases. Some historians have emphasized the humanitarian motivations behind the development of the asylum and the belief that the countryside would help cure problems that may have been caused by the alienating ('Gesellschaft') urban environment (e.g. Jones 1960). Other accounts have linked the asylum with the rise of industrial capitalism (e.g. Scull 1977, 1993). It is suggested that from the beginning of the nineteenth century the poor, who acted as a vital source of cheap flexible labour, were segregated into the able-bodied and those who could not work. The workhouse acted as a threat to the poor and helped to contain the behaviour of the masses. Ideas about the nature of madness were changing and it became broadly recognized as a loss of self-control rather than a fundamental loss of humanity and a return to an animal-like state. Scull argues that this created the space for the medical profession to expand into treating mental problems. Early attempts such as the York Retreat, which attempted to provide a 'moral' treatment, set the precedent for the later medical treatment of the insane. The 'mad' were separated from the able-bodied and incarcerated in the new asylum away from the cities and the public view. Foucault (1976, 1979) provides a more complex analysis in which he traces the origins of the asylum to the Enlightenment which established the modern roles of surveillance, discipline and rationality. This necessitated a redefinition of unreason so that in the new social order lunatics replaced lepers as the 'race apart' that must be identified and excluded from disciplined rational society. About 1 per cent of the Paris population who were 'incapable' of useful work were incarcerated in the general hospital of the late seventeenth century. The asylum rapidly became a repository for the social deviants who it was felt were not capable of useful work and potentially disrupted everyday life. Ironically, the labour of patients was an important source of income to the institutions which saw their costs climb when such unpaid work declined after the Second World War (Scull 1977). In Britain, the asylum population reached a peak after the First World War. Treatment of any kind was threatened by the numbers that had to be cared for and the institutions soon became more concerned with containment than cure. The asylum system contained a contradiction between treatment and containment that was to be a factor in the decline of asylum.

Busfield (1989) identifies three explanations for the move from institutional to community care: therapeutic or pharmacological explanations, economic explanations and explanations that are based on a reconceptualization of medical knowledge. Firstly, therapeutic or pharmacological explanations highlight the development of neuroleptic drugs since the Second World War. Major tranquillizers helped to alleviate symptoms of patients and evolving ideas about psychiatric rehabilitation helped them to leave institutional care (Pilling 1991). The pharmaceutical industry heavily advertised the use of drugs in the 1980s as creating a route from hospital to community care (Samson 1995). The retention of drugs as the basis for mental healthcare was central to the continued involvement and status of psychiatry as only doctors could prescribe. The decline of the institutions posed a threat to the profession's established power base, although during the 1980s, physical treatments and biomedical theories of mental health remained significant in medical care. It has also been argued that the effectiveness of the new drug treatments was overstated by psychiatrists as part of this professional strategy to retain control over this area of medicine (Treacher and Baruch 1981). In any case, the existence of new drugs that help modify behaviours does not necessarily account for the move to the community on its own. Empirically, a number of studies have established that the pattern of discharge from hospitals was established before the general use of tranquillizers and that their widespread adoption did not speed up the rate of discharge (Busfield 1989). The therapeutic or pharmacological explanation also cannot explain why people with severe learning difficulties who were not generally able to benefit from the new drug treatments were increasingly cared for in the community.

Secondly, economic explanations point to the cost of institutional care. Scull (1977) writing from a Marxist perspective about the United States argued that the cost of institutional care grew rapidly in the 1950s and the development of welfare systems provided a relatively cheap alternative. He argues graphically that the segregation provided by the institutions is retained for the majority of ex-inmates in the community:

the alternative to the institution has been to be herded into newly emerging 'deviant ghettos', sewers of human misery . . . within which (largely hidden from outside inspection or even notice) society's refuse may be repressively tolerated.

(Scull 1977: 153)

Scull's conception of community care may be cost efficient but its implementation in Britain may not prove to be a cheap alternative to institutional care. In addition, the deinstitutionalization policies in the United States were implemented at a time of economic growth and increased public spending (Busfield 1989). Rose (1986), in a cross-national study, found that there was no association of the decline of institutional care with economic crisis. In Britain, the capital costs of the neglected and largely Victorian buildings were seen as an important factor in the debate over community care.

A third set of explanations focus on a reconceptualization of medical knowledge. Prior (1991) argues that psychiatric knowledge has changed over time and the object and form of its interventions have also changed. He suggests that in the nineteenth century the brain and degeneracy were seen as the source of madness. The appropriate intervention was exclusion to the asylum where the madness could be contained and controlled. Freudian theory developed concepts related to the mind and situated the source of problems in individuals' experiences. Psychoanalytical approaches to mental health increased in popularity after the Second World War and involved the collaboration of patients (Rose 1986). In the late 1950s and 1960s, institutional coercive treatment came under attack by a group of US psychiatrists (Laing, Szasz and Cooper) who collectively became known as the 'antipsychiatrists'. They broadly argued that the roots of, for example schizophrenia can be found in the family and therefore rejected the medical model of mental health which locates the problem as being 'inside' the patient. Mental illness is seen as having a social origin and is firmly linked to the modern industrial lifestyle. Goffman (1968), in his work based on observations of an asylum in the United States, offered further criticism of institutional care. His depiction of 'degradation ceremonies' and the way the system promoted what, in work, would be seen as 'unhealthy' behaviours was widely influential. Research in Britain that was critical of Goffman's methodology and accepted the validity of institutional psychiatric treatment found that patients became overpassive and withdrawn. In some cases, a more stimulating 'natural' environment could improve behaviour (Wing 1962). A widespread pessimism was identified among all levels of staff who had little indication of what might be seen as good practice (Brown 1973). Goffman's and other research had a particular influence on psychiatric nurse training which later, as part of the professionalization of nursing, embraced holistic forms of care and the nurse–patient relationship. In Prior's observational study of a long-stay psychiatric hospital, he found that behaviour was the central focus of nursing attention. Individual care plans were mainly concerned with patients' behaviour and 'activities for daily living' such as personal care were used to assess progress. Nurses were attempting to 'normalize' patients' behaviour by encouraging the formation of relationships and the involvement of their family. However, they were doing this in a setting which clearly was not 'normal'. Prior (1991: 487) argues that 'in choosing behaviour as an object of therapeutic focus psychiatry and psychiatric nursing have lost their rationale they once had for confining themselves within the grounds of a psychiatric hospital'. This suggests that the move to the community was a logical development of professional practice. The increasing popularity of counselling and the use of therapeutic techniques to address behaviours that range from anorexia to smoking and 'aggressive driving' adds further support to the idea of a shift in the form and nature of psychological concern.

The disjuncture between theory and practice noted by Prior (1991), the overcrowding and lack of resources in mental health care, contributed to a number of scandals and subsequent enquiries. Ely (1996), Whittingham (1972), Napsbury (1973), Warlingham Park (1976), Darlington Memorial (1976), St Augustine's (1976), Winterton (1979), Brookwood (1980), Rampton (1980) and others were all the sites of institutional abuse and were seen as an indictment of institutional care (Martin 1984). In 1988, the publication of *Community Care: Agenda for Action* and the later White Paper *Caring for People* put the final seal on the move from the hospital into the community. *Community Care* attempted to establish coordination between local authorities and health and welfare agencies by introducing care managers. This move into the community was not uncontested and as in the hospital sector there were soon some well-publicized scandals associated with community care. A former inpatient, Sharon Campbell, killed her social worker in a knife attack in 1984. The following enquiry highlighted the need for the various agencies concerned with patients to communicate effectively with each other. In 1994, the enquiry in the case of Christopher Clunnis produced similar recommendations for improvements in monitoring and assessing patients in the community.

A thread that runs through the story of mental health care is the way the social context of mental health shapes both the definitions of 'good' mental health, the cause of 'bad' mental health and the consequent treatment. Foucault (1976) described the exercise of panoptic power and surveillance in the hospitals and Goffman exposed some of the results of this power. The problem of surveillance and control which was seen to be breaking down in the institutions was also evidently difficult in the community. Armstrong (1983: 100), from a Foucauldian perspective, links the universal provision of health provided by the NHS and the increasing concern with health in the community with 'a new paradigm of power which spreads its gaze throughout society'. In the community, the patient is no longer subject to a regime that encourages passivity. Patients (or 'clients' in the language of community care) are encouraged to participate in the generation of their own good health. Active social engagement is also encouraged and seen as an indicator of good health. Armstrong (1983) traces the origin of community care to the dispensary that developed in the nineteenth century to screen, diagnose and treat people with tuberculosis. These dispensaries acted as a bridge between the hospital and the community and provided a new way of interpreting illness. They also provided a way of monitoring and treating disease beyond the walls of the hospital. Tuberculosis and other conditions were spread through human contact, so medicine became concerned with social relationships in order to determine the origins of disease. In seeking out pathology, the medical gaze was directed away from the interior of the body to the dynamic social spaces between bodies. Therefore, it was not just people who had been defined as ill who became subject to surveillance, but also those who were potentially ill because they might have been in contact with a sick person. This involves both a reorganization of care and a reconceptualization of illness which breaks down the distinction between the 'sick' and the 'healthy'. The concern with apparently healthy people reflects the diversity of lay understandings of health and the rise of consumer culture with the emphasis in individual responsibility for health. Armstrong (1993b) refers to this as the 'new regime of total health' under which people are expected to maintain and monitor their own health as well as acting as active consumers of healthcare. At an individual level, this is reflected in 'lifestyle' concerns about diet, exercise and the cultivation of the body. At policy level, 'total health' reflected the shift of emphasis from cure to prevention that is expressed in policies directed at health promotion and public health.

Health education, promotion and community health

Klein (1989: 171) notes that 'in the 1970s Britain, like the rest of the world, rediscovered prevention'. This was partly out of a realization that medicine had limited capacity to deliver health in the form of interventions such as vaccines that prevented illness. The 1970s' economic crisis raised an alarm at the apparently ever increasing costs of medical care. The 1976 Labour Government's report *Prevention and Health: Everybody's Business* (DHSS) (see Chapter 2) sought to encourage people to take responsibility for their own health. Health promotion developed from health education and was shaped by public health. In the nineteenth century, medical officers of health and sanitary inspectors attempted to deal with epidemics related to overcrowding, urbanization and poor sanitation through the National Public Health Acts of 1848 and 1875 (Ashton and Seymour 1988). Public health at this time emphasized the importance of sanitation, safe food supplies. By the 1870s, public health attention had shifted to individuals and measures such as encouraging the provision of public baths to help improve basic hygiene. Ashton and Seymour identify the 1930s as the 'therapeutic era' which coincided with the decline of infectious diseases and a weakening of public health as resources flowed into hospital-based therapies. Health promotion first emerged as a concept in a Canadian report in 1974 that introduced into public policy the idea that there were four distinct elements to the causes of disease. These were inadequacies in healthcare provision; lifestyle or behavioural factors; environmental pollution and biophysical characteristics (Bunton and Macdonald 1992). It was argued that improvements in the environment or structure and lifestyle could lead to significant reductions in illness and premature death. The Canadian Government shifted the emphasis of its public policy towards prevention and subsequently the WHO took up the theme in the Alma Ata declaration of 1977. This created what Ashton and Seymour call the 'New Public Health' which

> goes beyond an understanding of human biology and recognises the importance of those social aspects of health problems which are caused by life-styles . . . In the New Public Health the environment is social and psychological as well as physical.
>
> (Ashton and Seymour 1988: 21)

The new public health inverts the nineteenth-century focus on intrusions of 'nature' into bodies with a focus on bodies intrusions into the natural environment (Armstrong 1993a).

Traditional health education has been criticized for taking a simplistic behavioural view of human action which assumed that if people were provided with suitable information they would change their behaviour in the desired way. An analogy can be made with the biomedical model in which experts diagnose and mass prescriptions are provided in a one-sided consultation process. This model not only fails to take account of any structural factors but also tends to 'blame the victim' in that inappropriate behaviour is seen to cause illness (Bunton and Macdonald 1992; Crawford 1977). Research on the smoking behaviour of pregnant women reveals the flaws in this approach. Despite agreeing that smoking is bad for their own and their baby's health, Graham (1987b) found that many mothers continued to smoke. She found that the mothers who were dependent on benefits and lived in poor housing experienced great stress. Smoking for the women was a way of coping with their situation and so they could not risk giving it up in case they would no longer be able to cope. Another study of pregnant women who smoked found that they rejected health education advice because they thought that a low birthweight baby was desirable (Oakley 1989). Structural factors like poor housing, poverty and lack of social support are all factors that individuals may have little immediate control over and which clearly shape their response to messages about healthy behaviours. Lack of appreciation of social class and cultural difference has been highlighted as a major problem in a number of health education projects (Pearson 1986). This points to a broadly 'top-down' approach that is informed by dominant white, middle-class values. Health promotion influenced by the new public health, holds that people should be encouraged to take control of their lives so that they can make healthy choices. 'Empowerment' is a key concept that recognizes the problem of structural constraints that may have to be overcome. Thorogood (1992) sums up the division between health education and promotion as follows:

> . . . health education has been criticised for too narrow an approach, focusing on individual behavioural change in a socio-economic vacuum. Health promotion has acknowledged that good health is not achieved by a series of individually located changes but by situating them in a wider context which both actively promotes and facilitates these choices. What health promotion has perhaps failed to recognise is that 'the healthy choice' is not a unitary concept and that there are many social, cultural, and symbolic meanings which need to be taken into account.
> (Thorogood 1992: 59)

Taking account of such factors can be a problem for a government that may have a political or ideological interest in messages about behaviour that is being promoted. The AIDS campaign of the 1980s has been criticized for a reluctance to promote safe sex in a range of sexual practices and relationships in the face of a desire to foster 'family values' and monogamy (Watney 1988).

The health promotion perspective is represented in the various WHO strategies such as 'Health For All' (1985) and the 'Healthy Cities' project (1986) which involves community development, empowerment and participation. Proponents of the 'Healthy Cities' initiative distanced the approach from paternalistic town planning manifest in nineteenth century sanitary reforms by emphasizing 'citizen control' 'citizen participation' or 'active citizenship' (Ashton and Seymour 1988). Conceptualizations of 'citizen control', 'community empowerment' and so on, range from spontaneous citizenship action (self-help groups and social movements) to various forms of citizen participation in decision making (policy forums and planning groups). Significantly, while the Ottawa Charter for Health Promotion (1986) refers to the communities 'ownership and control' of its destiny, it provides no strategies for effecting empowerment (Stevenson and Burke 1991). The community health movement which developed in the 1970s offered a challenge to medical dominance. Self-help groups offer alternative sources of support and advice while some community groups developed political campaigns against road developments that were seen to threaten health or for better housing (Watt and Rodmell 1993). The involvement of the community became a plank of Conservative Government policy from the mid-1980s. The volunteers, charities and self-help groups were regarded as a way to encourage informal care in the community that complemented a self-help ideology and was economically attractive. This posed a dilemma for community groups because, although funding and various other support became available, it would be unlikely to be given to groups seen as being undesirable or subversive of the Government's aims (Farrant 1991). There is also a tension in the notion of 'empowerment' in these circumstances since the provision of 'expert' advice to community groups may reinterpret their needs (Grace 1991). Schemes that have involved 'partnerships' between 'experts' and residents to improve the environmental conditions of run down council estates have to work out the tensions between residents' desires and expert opinion that may advise against particular courses of action. People may refuse to be involved in projects when problems are imposed on them by experts (Hunt 1993). Empowerment is problematic in that the more the state or its agencies become involved, the less the scope is for the 'wrong' decisions to be made.

Conclusion

While the extension of state involvement directly into community health may be characterized as one of constrained self-interest, the development of health promotion and the new public health fits Armstrong's (1993b) model of the new regime of 'total health'. Nettleton (1995) notes that:

> It is possible to identify a shift in the form of social regulation in relation to health from an external to an internal approach . . . people are being increasingly induced to monitor their own health and are being instilled with healthy attitudes. The control of health must therefore come from within the person.
>
> (Nettleton 1995: 240)

Health and identity are therefore reinforced and the surveillance of one (e.g. sexual behaviour) may be inseparable from the other (e.g. sexual orientation or desires). Middle-class distaste for 'junk food' or smoking is not just a simple response to health advice but a way of distinguishing their lifestyle from that of the working class. This involves seeking out activities and artefacts that display their distinctiveness such as the membership of executive health clubs and the buying of expensive wines and imported beers (Ehrenreich 1990). The European Charter on Environment and Health states that, not only is the individual entitled to an environment that facilitates health and well-being, but also that they have 'a responsibility to contribute to the protection of the environment, in the interests of his or her own health and the health of others' (WHO 1990: 4). In the face of concerns about the 'environmental crisis', the individual is pressed by the state and the advertising industry to curb and change their own unhealthy, risky and ecologically damaging consumption (Roche 1992). The boundaries around identity, health and politics become increasingly blurred and individuals struggle to make sense of competing advice and apparently increasing risks.

CHAPTER 4

Caring and curing: the health professions

Introduction

The provision of a privileged status for the practice of medicine in Britain can be traced back to the early sixteenth century when the Royal College of Physicians was granted a charter to practise within seven miles of the City of London. However, the most significant piece of legislation that laid the foundation for the contemporary organization of medicine was the Medical Registration Act 1858. The Act set up the General Medical Council (GMC) which remains responsible for the monitoring of educational and professional standards. Before the passing of the Act physicians, surgeons and apothecaries had their own corporations which controlled entry into the occupations through various educational and training programmes. Physicians, surgeons and apothecaries competed for clients within a status-based hierarchical framework that reflected wider social divisions. Physicians were a small élite mainly educated at Oxford or Edinburgh. They took a leading role in the various scientific societies that sprang up at this time and were involved in the early medical journals. Reflecting their position in the social structure, clients often spent considerable sums on their services. As befitted their status, they prescribed drugs in Latin which were dispensed by those working in 'trade'. Surgeons and apothecaries undertook a period of apprenticeship and often made and dispensed their own drugs. However, despite such distinctions the treatments and drugs were broadly similar. Surgeons were originally represented by the Royal College of Barber Surgeons which indicates the root of their trade. Apothecaries were more or less regarded as 'shopkeepers'. Both faced competition for clients who ranged from wise women and various healers to chemists and druggists who also catered to the general population. What the 1858 Act now defined as 'unorthodox' practitioners remained a threat to conventional practitioners partly because of the relative scarcity and expense of medical care. Until the end of the century, a great diversity of therapeutic practices remained available. Offering contrasting conceptualization of illness as well as cures, they presented what for many people was a viable alternative to the biomedical model that was evolving in the new hospitals and clinics. After 1858, there was still direct competition between doctors and unorthodox practitioners for posts supported by commercial enterprise or the various insurance schemes that existed before 1911. Non-medically qualified practitioners also represented an indirect threat in that they challenged the claim of exclusive expertise based on equally exclusive education made by orthodox medicine (Stacey 1988). The struggle between medical and non-medical practitioners was characterized by a series of campaigns against 'quacks' (Porter 1990). Almost as significant as the 1858 Act, the National Insurance Act 1911 substantially improved the position of doctors in the health market and reflected the close association between the state and the British Medical Association. By the end of the First World War, the competition from clients from non-orthodox practitioners was declining in the face of the perceived successes of medical treatment.

The Medical Registration Act 1858 marked the establishment in Britain of the modern divisions of labour in medicine. The GMC was dominated by practitioners so that the profession was self-regulating. While the Act defined who could be a licensed doctor, there were significant differences within the new profession. It was largely controlled by a privileged London elite who exercised considerable influence on the developing medical schools. GPs ranged from those who had sufficient resources to gain consultant posts and high-status clients to those with few resources working in areas remote from the big cities. Family and marriage effectively determined the career of the early doctors. A 'good' wife was considered essential and most practices were set up in family homes (Davidoff and Hall 1987). A suitable wife was an important asset to any doctor because it enabled him to cultivate women who were the main target for gaining patients. This reflected the Victorian division of domestic labour which made the home, domestic life and health the concern of women. Significantly, GPs had no representatives on the GMC until 1886.

Medicine as a profession

We have previously noted the formative role of Parsons (1951) in the sociology of health. His initial interest in health developed in examining the nature of the medical profession in the United States. Professions were to have a central place within his theoretic system. Influenced by Weber, professions were seen to be a new form of authority that was based on rational scientific knowledge. In contrast to Weber's approach under which professions were expected to give way in significance to bureaucratic forms of authority, the functionalism model of society regarded professions as fundamental to the development of stable industrial societies. Within the complex series of checks and balances that underpin functionalist theory, the professions provided a collegial and altruistic contrast to the imperatives of business. For Parsons, the doctor–patient relationship characterized the wider social role of professions. He argued that these macrostructural features could be witnessed in such everyday interaction. The theories of Freud and other psychoanalysts allowed Parsons to see parallels in the therapeutic relationship with the doctor–patient relationship. In particular, the encounter between expert and lay client was also an encounter of the powerful with the relatively powerless. It was this acknowledged inequality that allowed medical examinations and other interventions that would in different circumstances be seen as assault and abuse. As we noted in the sick role, the role of the patient was essentially as passive receiver of expert knowledge that the doctor used to diagnose and treat. Both people involved in the encounter were fitting into prescribed social roles that were underpinned by more or less overt checks and balances. The role of the doctor (physician in the original formulation) is partly defined by professional bodies (e.g. the GMC in Britain) which had sanctions to ensure that members adhered to a code of conduct that ensures a proper doctor–patient relationship. Parsons had in mind the way psychoanalysis dealt with the problem of transference which could lead to the client wanting to become emotionally involved with the practitioner. The role of the patient was defined by the sick role that provided rewards and sanctions to ensure compliance with treatment and the proper performance of the role. From this perspective, it is not surprising that the under- or overutilization of health services, or put it another way, the failure of some people to perform the role of patient adequately were important concerns in social research (see Chapter 2).

Before Parsons' major work the nature of the professions was a significant theme in sociology and there were a number of schemes that attempted to define their nature and role (e.g. Carr-Sauders and Wilson 1933). Like Parsons' approach, these and later studies identified various 'traits' that characterized professions (e.g. Goode 1960). A typical list of professional traits are shown below:

◆ A knowledge base that informs professional practice.
◆ The control of entry to the profession through a long period of training and examinations.
◆ A self-regulating code of ethics.
◆ A professional statutory body that is relatively free of lay involvement.
◆ A professional culture that is orientated to public service and which members usually belong to for their lifetime.

Such professional traits appear to fit the medical profession particularly well, which is only to be expected as medicine was the benchmark for much of the research in this area. At one level, the trait approach works quite well as it enables professions and occupations to be distinguished. However, this descriptive project reveals little about the processes involved within professions or why some occupations achieve status and others do not. Some areas of health work are problematic in that, while nursing may now be able to identify with the various professional characteristics, it clearly remains less powerful than medicine. There is an assumption that professions develop 'naturally' with the growth of expert, scientific knowledge and that this knowledge is used for the general good.

As Parsons (1951) observed, the doctor-patient relationship characterizes the wider social role of the two groups. An alternative interpretation of this encounter regards it as the site of a struggle between the powerful and the relatively powerless. As we have seen (see Chapter 2) lay understanding of health may often be at considerable variance with medical knowledge. Freidson (1970), from a theoretical base that combined conflict and interactionist theory, argued that this unequal relationship stemmed from the different social worlds typically occupied by doctors and their patients. What marked out a profession and enabled its members to maintain a social distance between themselves and people in other occupations was the autonomy granted it by the state: 'Unlike other occupations, professions are deliberately granted autonomy, including the exclusive right to determine who can legitimately do its work and how the work should be done' (p. 56). This autonomy is established as a result of a struggle with other competing occupations. As Freidson (1970) noted, there is something of a contradiction in this state–professional relationship, in that it is difficult to see how a profession can be regarded as autonomous when at the same time it is dependent on the state for its social position. He argues that the state in practice leaves 'technical' or clinical matters to the jurisdiction of the profession. In Britain, the GMC performs this role and provides medicine with considerable scope to organize and set its own work and standards. The state in Freidson's terms retains ultimate power over professions; this enables it to act as a 'shelter' in helping to prevent any attempts to lessen the role of recognized professions. Once established, professions continue to patrol the boundaries of the work and develop strategies to retain or further exert their 'professional dominance'. In Britain the National Health Service (NHS) has played a significant role in consolidating the dominance of medicine by placing the profession at the centre of public policy so that 'authority has been both state sustained and circumscribed' (Larkin 1983: 121). Thus medicine in Britain, unlike the United States, is constrained by the minor place of private medical care. Freidson referred to nursing and allied areas of medical work as 'paramedical professions' rather than professions in their own right because they operated on the border of medicine and were largely dependent on medicine. There is a shift of emphasis here in that under Parsons' scheme which emphasized the altruism of doctors the answer to the question, 'In whose interest does the profession's work?' would be their clients and the general social good. Freidson, in a study of medical students, found that there is 'little evidence that those aspiring to medicine have a stronger service orientation than those aspiring to other occupations' (Freidson 1975: 174). From his perspective, the answer to the question would be: 'In their own interests.'

An alternative Marxist explanation associates the rise of the medical and other professions with the emergence of capitalism (Johnson 1977; Navarro 1978). This approach also questions the altruism of professions and raises other questions about the nature of their power. Johnson (1972) suggests that the key to professional autonomy and power is its ability as a monopoly producer to define and satisfy the needs of the consumer in a manner that appears altruistic. This ability increases the greater the distance is between the provider and the consumer in terms of resources and knowledge. Patients have no organized and universal knowledge base, or outside pressure groups, any collective forum which they can use to counter the power of doctors. The uncertainty of lay knowledge compared to the coherence of medical expertise compounds the inequalities of power between them. Medicine, like any other producer, is able to foster its monopoly by controlling the supply of new doctors into the profession which in turn helps to legitimate relatively high status and salaries. Again the powerlessness of the patient is highlighted as a problem which symbolizes wider inequalities in the social structure. This has been referred to as the 'competence gap' (Waitzkin 1979) which, it is suggested, leads to the potential for an exploitative relationship. From this Marxist perspective, it is argued that professional dominance is reinforced by the unequal access to medical knowledge. Based on research in US hospitals, Waitzkin, like Parsons, sought to make links between the medical encounter and the general distribution of power in society. Adopting a similar analytical framework, Navarro (1978) argues that it is the social position of members of professions that enables them to exercise power rather than their access to knowledge. He goes on to make the point that medicine within a capitalist system helps to make problems that arise due to inequalities (i.e. disparities in the pattern of illness) appear to be the result of individual action. For example, an increased incidence of illness may result from pollution from a chemical plant, but due to the individualist nature of medicine, it may be hidden as individual problems.

Until the 1970s, the question of gender in the literature relating to professions was largely ignored and the established divisions of labour between, for example, medicine and nursing were not questioned. Etzioni (1969), in an echo of Freidson's model, described nursing and other occupations that included many women as 'semiprofessions'. These were conceived of as less objective, neutral and bureaucratic than the male-dominated professions. Reflecting the domestic division of labour, the semiprofessions mediated between the emotional and subjective work of caring for people and the scientific and rational professional work of diagnosis. Professional men were therefore protected from emotional labour involved in caring for the sick. Looking back over her own work, Oakley captures the way that such divisions of labour appeared 'invisible':

> . . . over a period of some months spent observing health-care in a large London hospital, I hardly noticed nurses at all . . . I took their presence for granted (much as I imagine, the doctors and patients did) . . . If this sounds a bit like Florence Nightingale's definition of a good nurse – an invisible, good woman – then perhaps we should not be too surprised. In many ways, history has defined a good nurse as a good woman, and this can be counted as both the weakness and the strength of nursing as a profession.
>
> (Oakley 1986: 56)

Under the impetus of 'second-wave' feminism, medicine was identified as a key example of the patriarchal exclusion of women. The 1885 Act did not explicitly prevent women from practising medicine but they were excluded from the universities. Elizabeth Blackwell, who had qualified in the United States and had a diploma from Dublin, was able to enter the medical register despite great opposition. The rise of medicine as a profession 'sounded the death knell for women's participation in healing practices' (Witz 1992: 75). Although more women than men remained working in healthcare, they did so under the control of men. Previously women had been instrumental in healthcare and some activities such as those surrounding reproduction were almost exclusively female concerns. Feminists argued that the gendered division of labour was not the result of some 'natural progress' associated with the inevitable rise of science but the result of a series of political gender-based power struggles (e.g. Ehrenreich and English 1979; Oakley 1976; Stacey 1988). Witz (1992) notes that the struggles to form professions or 'professional projects' draw on established patriarchal structures where women had markedly less resources to resist the development of male medicine. She identifies four strategies involved in the process.

Strategies employed by the dominant groups:
- ◆ Exclusionary. Mechanism that forces certain groups from the profession.
- ◆ Demarcationary. The separation of an occupational group into a separate area of practice while control is retained by the dominant group.

Strategies available to the subordinate group:
- ◆ Inclusionary. Strategies to gain admission to the profession, e.g. legal action.
- ◆ Dual closure. The acceptance of a separate, lower status and the creation of barriers to prevent others from entering it.

The treatment of Elizabeth Blackwell illustrates the exclusionary methods used by the medical profession against women who attempted to subvert the educational barriers to registration. The shelter of the state helped to maintain male domination because it underwrote the educational discrimination against women in the universities. It was, therefore, education around which the struggle for women's inclusion in medicine formed. The story of the first women who tried to gain a medical education is a dramatic one that has provided fertile ground for novels and films (Stacey 1988; Witz 1992; Roberts 1993). It should be remembered that this was also an ideological struggle in that the prevailing medical view at the time was that women were innately unsuited to the rigours of university education. The biology and the 'innocence' that constituted femininity, it was thought, would be destroyed by exposure to higher education and abstract ideas (see Chapter 1). A study of pioneering women in medicine and other professions in the United States at the turn of the century described the women as 'objective, competent, individualistic and predictable' as well as 'scornful of nurturing, expressive and familial styles of personal interaction' (Glazer and Slater 1987: 14). This suggests that in order to compete with men women had to do so on their terms and take on 'male' values.

The struggle over midwifery and obstetrics

Knowledge passed down generations of women enabled some to become 'handywomen' and act as midwives (Leap and Hunter 1993). Birth was traditionally very much women's business, although a few men began to practise midwifery as early as the seventeenth century. The development of scientific knowledge and the consequent invention of various instruments such as forceps to aid the process of birth provided an impetus for more men to become involved in midwifery. In the year that the GMC was established, men who were practising midwifery set up the Obstetrical Society. Significantly, the Latin-based title reflected the élite educational base of the male physicians compared to the more experiential knowledge of female midwives. While obstetrics was associated with birth and motherhood, the related but distinct discipline of gynaecology became associated with 'impurity' and disease (Hearn 1992). Gynaecology originally claimed to be concerned with the scientific treatment of all women's medical problems. However, because of the way such problems were thought to be linked to female sexual organs, these became the main site for gynaecological intervention. The Contagious Diseases Acts of the 1860s gave a boost to the activities of gynaecologists. These Acts were intended to control the spread of venereal disease among troops in garrison and port towns. Under the Acts, prostitutes were subject to compulsory inspections that involved the use of speculums in gynaecological examinations. Opposition to the Acts came from many quarters, including the early feminists who argued that the Acts used coercion against women for the pleasure of men (Walkowitz 1982). Not only did gynaecology become associated with disease and 'women of low class', it was also represented in nineteenth-century pornography. Images of the gynaecological examination were common in pornography and the activities of Jack the Ripper had similar overtones (Walkowitz, 1982). There were therefore several layers in the tensions between gynaecologists and midwives that ranged from competition over clients to cultural views about femininity and sexuality.

Midwives, in their attempt to retain their autonomy and identity, were confronted by a medical profession that followed a number of strategies to extend its power that reflected the divisions within the profession (Witz 1992). General practitioners pursued a campaign to gain formal control over all aspects of pregnancy and to redefine midwives as obstetric nurses. Hospital-based doctors and gynaecologists broadly supported the midwives but sought to confine their activities to 'normal' births. This tactic represented the economic interests of medical men in that it was mostly poor women who used midwives and their custom was of little interest to doctors. In any case, there the demand for midwifery services far exceeded the supply of doctors so the relegation of midwives to 'normal' births was a pragmatic solution. Male power and science was exercised through the control of 'abnormal' births, and from the Midwives Act 1902 the supervision of midwives and their education. Midwives therefore emerged into the twentieth century as deskilled in the sense that they now had to have formal training (controlled and largely delivered by doctors) but their sphere of practice and knowledge was constrained (Oakley 1986; Witz 1992). In addition, the midwives' relationship with the state was mediated through the medical profession (Witz 1992) and their practice was carefully confined to 'normal' births.

The home was the place for normal births until the 1930s and the majority of midwives attended births in the community. The growth in hospitals between the wars created the space for doctors to legitimize their argument that home births were subject to greater risk. In particular, in an echo of the earlier debate over spheres of influence, they noted that hospital births had the specialist knowledge of obstetrics on hand if they were needed. Although the risk of cross-infection may have been greater in the hospital (Tew 1995), the idea of safer hospital births spread through the popular media and was encouraged by many GPs. The alleviation of pain in childbirth had spread from the United States and before the NHS, women who could afford it were enthusiastic about its use. Interestingly a government report in the late 1930s suggested that modern women were becoming more sensitive to pain! (Symonds and Hunt 1996). Pain relief was confined to the hospital or clinic because, until 1934, midwives could not administer any analgesics. The unwieldy nature of the equipment and the requirement to have two midwives present before it could be used militated against the routine use of anaesthetics in the home. In general, the hospital had become the site for technology and so it is not surprising that anaesthetics, despite increasingly manageable portable equipment becoming available after the Second World War, became situated within them. More recently, a whole battery of technology has been developed to monitor the progress of the foetus. Since the 1970s, electronic foetal monitoring has become routine.

Despite claims by gynaecologists that such technology reduced the risk of foetal distress and consequent brain damage resulting in cerebral palsy, a *Lancet* editorial concluded that 'the continued willingness of doctors to reinforce the fable that intrapartum care is an important determinate of cerebral palsy can only be regarded as shooting the speciality in the foot' (*Lancet* 1989: 1252). There is also evidence that electronic foetal monitoring is instrumental in increasing the rate of caesarean births (Barrett *et al.* 1990). The nature of such surveillance remains contentious with gynaecologists arguing that it benefits high-risk mothers, while others argue it exposes women to unnecessary risks (Tew 1995). Sociologically, this role of technology has been linked to the association between it and patriarchy. It is argued that the largely male profession of medicine helped to ensure its power over women by retaining an expertise over the use of technology. More generally, it is suggested that men have carefully rationed women's access to technology to their structural disadvantage. For example, the typewriter or word processor was seen as 'women's' work while the computer remains largely an area of male expertise (Cockburn 1990). Thus, male-dominated gynaecology and hospital medicine that encourages the use of technological interventions from forceps to electronic foetal monitoring has the effect of reasserting medical dominance over midwifery.

The NHS provided a boost to the hospitalization of childbirth as it gave all women free access to it. What amounted to a further medicalization of childbirth had taken place so that by the 1960s the majority of births took place in the hospital. Consequently, midwives followed the move and became themselves confined largely to the hospital where they were under greater medical control (Robinson 1989). The hospitalization of childbirth brought in various rituals such as the 'prepping' of women by shaving them and giving them an enema which was unpleasant, raised anxiety levels and was of doubtful clinical value (Phillips and Rakusen 1989). There was a sharp decline in 'normal' births and an increase in the range of technological interventions. The majority of births became 'abnormal' partly under the influence of a system called the 'active management of labour' which defined the normal labour as lasting no more than 12 hours (Hunt and Symonds 1996). This resulted in a considerable increase in induced births which rose from less than 10 per cent of deliveries in the 1960s to a peak of nearly 40 per cent in the 1970s (Foster 1995). Episiotomies, forceps deliveries and caesarean sections also increased (Kitzinger 1979). A number of studies found that women found such procedures difficult and that their use supported the efficient running of maternity units rather than the needs of the women (Oakley 1993).

The Winterton Report of 1992 highlighted what it saw as the inappropriate medicalization of birth and echoed the feeling of a number of pressure groups such as The National Childbirth Trust as well as researchers such as Oakley (1986) that childbirth had been rendered 'unnatural'. *Changing Childbirth* (DoH 1993) is widely seen as a 'women centred' report that built on an earlier select committee's criticism of medicalized hospital maternity services. It encouraged a move to community services at a policy level and an emphasis on the continuity of care for clients. Reflecting wider changes in nursing for a holistic approach to care, this gave midwives an opportunity to reassert the sphere of their autonomy by identifying the midwife–client relationship as central to their expertise. Continuity of care demanded an ongoing relationship between an individual midwife and her client so the midwife mediated the client's access to childbirth services. Conceived of as a 'partnership', decisions about the place and form of the birth as well as pain relief could in theory be planned from an early stage. GPs and obstetricians did not have the time for such procedures and they were a revision rather than a threat to the hierarchy between medicine and midwifery. However, the boundaries between the professions remain contested especially over the definition of 'low-risk' pregnancies which is the key to home birth. The increasing fear of litigation may, as in the United States, encourage 'defensive medicine' which promotes the use of surveillance technology. The inequalities of power between gynaecologists and midwives is manifest at this point as it is the former who define 'low risk'. This may be done with a degree of caution that makes it possible for only a minority of women to put the care fully in the hands of midwives (Tew 1995).

Nursing as a profession

Florence Nightingale wrote that 'every woman was a nurse' and that as this made best use of women's 'natural abilities' they should not aspire to be doctors (Stacey 1988; Abel-Smith 1960). Early hospital nurses worked in poor conditions for poor rewards that were little different from those of domestic servants. Indeed, many of the first hospitals were located in large houses where the domestic division of labour was mimicked. Doctors represented the father and head of the household, nurses the mother and patients the submissive children (Gamarnikow 1988). By the middle of the nineteenth century, the reforms initiated by Nightingale had had an impact on the voluntary hospitals. Nursing found a pool of upper working-class and middle-class 'distressed gentlewomen' for whom nursing represented a new employment opportunity that exploited their domestic skills in the role of matrons (Dingwall *et al.* 1988). The hierarchical divisions within nursing emerged from its early history and reflected the social divisions of the period. The nursing of the poor largely took place in the workhouse where older paupers cared for the sick without any formal training. Developments in workhouses during the century meant that some became asylums where the male custodians were also nurses in that they cared for the inmates. Essentially, a male working-class occupation developed that was involved in the trade union movement. This social division of nursing has been remarkably persistent and remains reflected in the gender divisions within the profession. As in medicine, the class structure was reproduced in nursing with a few upper-class women becoming the leaders of the professions followed by the middle-class matrons and a mass of working-class nurses. The development of the Nightingale ward which gave nurses a particular physical space, also placed them firmly under the surveillance and control of doctors. This can been interpreted as signifying the confirmation of gender oppression (Gamarnikow 1988) or as a progressive stand marking a distinctive area of control for women in an age characterized by patriarchy (Abel-Smith 1960; Williams 1980).

The role of women and nurses in the Great War meant that in the post-war period, women had to be 'taken seriously' (Dingwall *et al.* 1988). The war had also highlighted the need for a uniform system of credentials and training for nurses. Nurses themselves were variously involved in trade unions, movements for women's rights and campaigns to professionalize nursing. A new Ministry of Health was established in 1919 to develop national health policies in the face of the growing social discontent and economic disruption of the 1920s. The Nurses' Registration Act 1919 reflected this growing state intervention into health and provided the registration of nurses based on a broad set of training experiences. Driven essentially by cost considerations, nursing remained diverse in the range of skills possessed by registered nurses and was typified as a relatively low-paid 'women's occupation' (Beardshaw and Robinson 1990). The lack of involvement of nursing in the debate about the creation of the NHS indicates the expectations about its role (Klein 1989). Significant divisions between the various specialisms such as midwifery, health visiting and mental health nursing prevented any cohesive professionalizing strategy (Witz 1992). It is important to recognize the divide between the unregistered nursing auxiliaries and registered nurses that in various forms runs through the history of nursing. The establishment of the NHS can be viewed as the effective nationalization of nursing and it did provide the basis for making nursing a more cohesive occupation.

In the family metaphor noted above, nurses were mothers. Such ideas about femininity are reproduced in nursing work which ranged from dealing with 'dirty' laborious work to intimate emotional caring. Graham (1984) makes a distinction between 'caring for' and 'caring about'. The former denotes the process of tending while 'caring for' indicates a relationship. In domestic settings, women are expected to express caring in birth sense as a mother cares about and for her child. Significantly, those women who deviate from these cultural expectations and, for example, seek adoption for their infant may be open to stigma or at least social work interventions. Leaving the domestic domain to enter the caring professions marks a rein-forcement of caring for. Nurses followed an apprenticeship-like training that emphasized practical skills, many of which were the same as those needed in domestic service or motherhood. As part of their training nurses learnt to practise role distance so that they did not 'care about' their patients in an over-emotional way. 'Caring for' in nursing orientated nurses to undertaking 'body work', especially the surveillance of patients (Foucault 1976) and dealing with their physical needs as defined by doctors. This reflected the medical view that parents 'will abide by instructions and will co-operate in carrying out the treatment' (Armstrong 1993b). This echoes Parsons' (1951) conceptualization of the role of the patient under the 'sick role' (see Chapter 2). Nursing work was arranged in a Fordist manner so that nurses tended to specialize in particular tasks. Not only did this prevent nurses becoming too close to patients, it also made the management of nurses relatively simple. For doctors, the domestic division of labour appeared to flow into their relationship with nurses. As in the home, women undertook the management of dependent bodies (cf. role of mothers) and domestic work like bedmaking. This stark reproduction of gender roles was viewed by nurses rather differently in that they emphasized differences in knowledge and training manifest in the diagnosis and treatment divide. However: 'At the interpersonal level, nurses gendered professional subordination to encompass the traditional power resource available – manipulating the powerful to internalise the outlook and perspective of the powerless' (Gamarnikow 1987). This notion that nurses influence and manipulate doctors rather than engage in direct debate with them remains evident in what has been called the 'doctor–nurse' game (Mackay 1989).

Although nurses have probably always asked about 'caring' for their patients and the public imagery of nursing is commonly associated with images of femininity and 'caring', the term is largely missing from the nursing literature until comparatively recently (Abel-Smith 1960; Davies 1980; Dingwall *et al.* 1988). Reflecting the recognition of the therapeutic role of doctor–patient communication, nursing research and theory in the United States examined the nature of nurse–patient communication. This reflected the differences in nursing in the United States as well as the importance of 'customer relations' in private healthcare. By the end of the 1970s, nursing theorists were emphasizing the importance of 'helping' the patient to communicate and this work found its way into training (e.g. Kratz 1979; Roper *et al.* 1980). 'Trust', 'emotions' 'empathy' and 'intimacy', which had always been an unrecognized part of female labour, became recognized and incorporated into new conceptualizations of the patient as a 'whole person' or as it is sometimes referred to in nursing as a 'bio-psych-social system'. This approach draws attention to nursing as 'emotional labour' which is captured in Hochschild's (1983) term 'the managed heart', (Lewin and Olesen 1985; James 1992). In common with other people-centred service sector jobs, nursing involves formalized intimacy that is shaped by the context of the 'customer–provider' interaction. Patients expect nurses to be pleasant, caring and cheerful and nurses are educated to engage with their patients in a 'professional' manner. A study of a hospice showed how dealing with emotions (e.g. telling patients and relatives about dying) was largely the work of women while the senior male staff played an organizational role in arranging the work of others (Mackay 1989). The presentation of self in the form of a 'pleasing personality' that is rapidly adapted to different situations can place considerable strain on individuals who may feel unhappy, stressed or angry. Through contemporary systems of mentoring, students are socialized into the appropriate behaviours which are reinforced through 'reflection'. This can be seen as a form of emotional surveillance that reinforces prevailing ideological values within nursing. The process of nurse–patient communication socially constructs not just the identity of the nurse but also the patient. Nurses, through their behaviour and interaction, manage the expectations of their patients. Overdemanding patients may be labelled 'difficult patients' and their calls for attention may not receive a rapid response. Conformist patients may be seen as 'sweeties' which indicates their child-like passivity. Emotional work can then be a strategy that empowers nurses and care assistants, as it provides a way to control their patients. A study of a residential home for the elderly found that care assistants 'utilised emotional bonds to evoke the idea that the "good" residents should do what the assistants demanded'. Through emotional work, assistants had created an effective means of controlling the home (Treweek 1996: 130).

It was the recombination of the two forms of 'caring' under the 'nursing process' in the 1970s that marked a major step in the professionalization of nursing. 'The nursing process could be used to impose a common occupational culture, dominated by general nursing, an aspiration which certainly went back to the original registration debate' (Dingwall *et al.* 1988: 217). Developed originally by a doctor in the private-orientated medical care system in the United States, the nursing process emphasized the need for a 'holistic' approach to care that recognized the patient as a 'whole person' (De la Cuesta 1983). In a commercially dominated healthcare system, such concerns with 'customers' should not be surprising. This differentiated nursing from the biomedical model and thus provided it, for the first time, with a philosophy based on holistic care and a theoretical model around which to generate the organizing principles of nursing work. It also enabled nurses to argue that there was a distinct – although rather undefined – nursing 'knowledge base' that demanded its own programme of nursing research. This was a vital element that had hitherto been missing in the struggle to establish the characteristics of a profession (Hardey and Mulhall 1991). Like medicine, nursing needed to identify and define scientific knowledge on which patient care could be based. The nursing élite who were instrumental in the nursing professional project had been disappointed that the Briggs Report (1972) failed to deliver their hope for recognition of increased status and income for nurses. Situated in nursing schools, the nursing process provided the rationale to shift from a training model to an educational model. The holistic approach demanded that all qualified nurses should be able to cope with all the nursing needs of individual patients as well as take on the new formal responsibility of catering to their psychosocial needs. The break with past nursing practices was indicated by the label 'new nursing' (Mackay 1994). In effect, nurses expanded the scope of their surveillance over patients' bodies to their minds: 'from a simple concern with the care of the patient's bodily functions, nursing has started to become a surveillance apparatus which both monitors and evinces the patient's personal identity: in doing so it helps fabricate and sustain that very identity' (Armstrong 1983: 459). This required the inclusion of social science in the nursing curriculum and the integration of academic work with practical skills. The new *Project 2000* education package introduced in the late 1980s embodied these changes within an academically orientated programme. Significantly, concern was expressed that the products of these courses would threaten established nurses with their new academic knowledge, while at the same time being less skilled in the traditional nursing crafts (Mackay 1989). On the ward, the 'care plan' which may have been drawn up with the collaboration of the patient, became the central organizing principle of nursing work. Under later schemes, such as 'primary nursing' which evolved from the nursing process, a nurse looked after a small group of patients enabling them to receive a more individual and sensitive package of care (Salvage 1992). Some aspects of the approach have been incorporated at policy level within *The Patient's Charter* (DoH 1991).

The widespread acceptance of 'new nursing' was not unopposed by the medical profession, some of whom argued that it relegated doctors to a residual role. These oppositions became focused on the nursing development units and the Oxford unit in particular. Between 1986 and 1989, this unit contained 16 nursing beds to which patients were admitted by a senior nurse. Nurses acted autonomously within the unit and were responsible for discharging patients and administering drugs. A practical attempt was made to operationalize the new nursing philosophy of sharing care with patients, by focusing on improving patients' knowledge and skills in order to maximize their independence. Each primary nurse worked with a team of associate nurses and care assistants who undertook domestic and basic nursing tasks (Salvage 1992). In effect, the primary nurse–team relationship was similar to the traditional doctor–nurse relationship. The exclusive primary nurse–patient relationship is similar to the traditional doctor–patient relationship and thus challenges the view that all patients require the full-time attention of doctors as well as redefining the nurse–doctor power relationships. Nurses had captured 'care' and established an exclusive knowledge of patients' holistic needs. This potentially relegated doctors to 'cure' under the guidance of nurses as representatives of the patient's interests. Partly due to opposition from doctors, the Oxford unit was closed in 1989 (Pembrey and Punton 1990).

The shift from a 'semiprofession' or an 'occupation' to a 'profession' was finally marked by the Judge Report (1985) that heralded the transfer of nurse education to higher education. However, the conduct of nurses remained rule bound and situated within an inflexible bureaucratic hierarchy.

This reflects the history of nursing which, despite organizational strategies such as team nursing, casts a shadow over how nurses view the profession. The introduction in the 1980s of a more highly differentiated system of nurse grades reinforced hierarchies and further differentiated the profession. In 1992 the United Kingdom Central Council for Nursing, Midwifery and Health Visiting (usually referred to as the UKCC) (the nursing professional body) changed the code of practice so that qualified nurses are trusted to act within their professional competency. This largely ended the previous system of tightly specified and minutely certificated specialist training. In addition, the UKCC accepted that holistic nursing care was preferable to one that was based on activities. This involved replacing 'certificates for tasks' with 'principles for practice' as the bias for changing the delivery of care.

The impact of this change in the work of nursing can be seen in the insertion of intravenous drips ('IVs') which had long been a source of friction between doctors and nurses (Mackay 1989). IVs are used to administer drugs and fluids through a fixed needle that is attached by a tube to a plastic bag. This equipment has to be checked every few hours. Qualified nurses have been seen as well able to do this, but in the past they required a special certificate to undertake this 'extended role'. The extended role amounts to a subcontracting of specific tasks to a subordinate professional group which remains under the control of the medical profession. This relationship is manifest in the way that consultants define the nature of the extended role within their specialism (Harvey 1995). Significantly, junior doctors who usually receive no specific IV training, are supposed to do insertions if no certified nurse is available. At night and weekends, in particular, junior doctors have placed pressure on nurses to monitor IVs. Combined with a concern over the long hours of junior doctors, it was generally regarded as in the patient's interest for nurses to undertake the task as they were always available on the ward. The end of 'extended role' certification helps legitimate nursing's claim on professional status and brought it closer to the medical profession by replacing a rule bound approach to the delivery of care with one orientated to individual judgement.

At one level, the story of nursing is that of a successful female professional project (Witz 1992). However, it remains unequal in its relationship with medicine. While an increasing number of medical students are women relatively few men enter nurse training and those that do are overrepresented in the mental health area. The gendered relationship between medicine and nursing remains and the higher numbers of female junior doctors can pose difficulties for nurses used to playing a gendered doctor–patient game (Mackay 1989, 1994). Gender is also significant within the nursing profession itself:

> In some respects, nurses are their own *worst enemies*. Many nurses seem to collude in maintaining the traditional subservient attitude towards the medical profession . . . On analysis it emerges that nurses

do not appear to sufficiently value the work and skills of their nursing colleagues.

(Mackay 1989: 180–1, original emphasis)

This analysis is important because it suggests that the views frequently held by managers and doctors, that nurses lack the expertise and commitment to a 'professional career', are reinforced in their daily encounter with nurses. It is debatable whether the 'bitchiness' identified by Mackay would in other professions be seen as part of the adversarial, combative masculine culture (Walby 1990; Davies 1992). What is significant is that nursing is viewed by more powerful groups through the screen of gender so that the status of nurses, nursing and women is reduced.

The success of registered nurses has been bought at the expense of other women who have become 'care assistants' to fill the gap left by nursing students who are formally 'supernumerary'. Often working part-time, the pay and conditions of care assistants are negotiated with individual Trusts. This holds out the prospect for a cleavage within nursing along a 'core and periphery' model. The 'core' of registered professional nurses may increasingly take on the supervision of 'peripheral' care assistants who deliver the majority of 'hands-on care' to patients (Walby *et al.* 1994). Such skill-mix arrangements are economically efficient for hospital Trusts but they are constrained to those areas of nursing where there is a significant amount of routine bodily care. The boundaries of nursing are being challenged by social workers who have made some incursions as 'key workers' into what health visitors have regarded as their province. However, within the hospital social workers remain marginalized (Mcleod 1995).

The micropolitics of lay and professional encounters

Parsons had assumed a consensual, if not deferential, relationship between doctors and patients. Both parties involved in the encounter learned what their appropriate role was and a wider system of rewards and sanctions encouraged the proper performance of lay and professional roles. This simple functional relationship based on consensus has, as we saw earlier, been widely criticized. The problem of utilization was noted in Chapter 2 and this work highlighted the importance of social class in the use of medical services. Alternative theoretical approaches based on assumptions about conflicts of interests also highlight the doctor–patient relationship as representing structural differences. Social differences therefore may be played out in encounters and the professionals involved should not be regarded as neutral almost scientific observers but active agents in the encounter. Studies of GPs' attitudes have found that they have distinct beliefs about patients they disliked such as patients with emotional problems and women with children (Stimson 1974; Stimson and Webb 1975; Roberts 1985). In the hospital setting, Waitzkin (1979) has argued that routine medical encounters serve to reinforce the general social structure. Influenced by Marxist theory, he saw the medical encounter as part of a process that made patients passive and unaware of the links between the capitalist order and their illness (e.g. employment in dangerous conditions, diseases related to poverty). Therefore, within this theoretical framework, the macro role of the professions in the capitalist order is manifest at the micro level of the medical encounter.

Feminist analysis has also highlighted conflict, but conflict mediated through gender. In medical encounters, assumptions about gender and behaviours that reinforce gender differences that reflected wider inequalities, are again played out. Four significant themes have been identified in feminist critiques of medical encounters (Foster 1989). Firstly, it is suggested that doctors' diagnoses of women's problems are overinfluenced by the stereotypes they hold that are reinforced through medical textbooks and education. Doyal (1994), for example, noted that a number of studies found that there is a bias towards regarding heart disease as a male problem, resulting in the late diagnosis of women. Secondly, traditional expectations about women's roles (e.g. mother and home-maker) are reinforced in the medical encounter so that deviations from convention are discouraged. Macintyre (1977) found that doctors categorized women who asked about abortion as 'good' and 'bad' girls. 'Good girls' were thought to have been 'taken advantage of' while 'bad girls' were seen as 'easy-going'. Thirdly, doctors may exert male values over female patients, so that for example, they will recommend sterilization for mothers with 'over-large' numbers of children. Finally, when women challenge these aspects of the encounter or medical diagnosis, they are met with defensive if not hostile responses. It might be thought that these gender differences would disappear or be largely modified when the encounter is between lay and professional women. However, the gendered nature of the medical profession and the nature of biomedical knowledge appear to socialize women practitioners to hold similar values to male practitioners (Porter 1990).

A number of studies of medical encounters emphasize 'negotiation', the symbolic nature of the encounter and the 'discourses' used (Heath 1984). Clearly, conflict is implied by negotiation but the role of wider structural differences is less significant in these studies than the micropolitics of the situation. From this perspective, the medical encounter may be asymmetrical but patients do have knowledge and are able to influence the nature of the encounter and the results. In addition the encounter, especially with GP, can in itself be seen as therapeutic. This was an important aspect of GPs' claim to status in the face of hospital medicine and was instrumental in the setting up of the Royal College of General Practitioners. The influence of psychoanalysis is again evident and in the 1950s it was accepted that:

> . . . by far the most frequently used drug in general practice was the
> doctor . . . it was not only the bottle of medicine or the box of pills

that mattered but the whole way the doctor gave them to his patient –
in fact, the whole atmosphere in which the drug was given and taken.

(Balint 1957: 1)

Stimson and Webb (1975), in a well-known study based in South Wales,
identified a number of strategies whereby patients attempted to shape the
encounter. These strategies included rehearsing the encounter, selectively
choosing which symptoms to present and simply ignoring the doctor's
advice. Doctors have greater scope to manipulate the encounter which
usually takes place within space that they 'own', such as the surgery. Non-
verbal communication is important and doctors can, for example, discourage
patients talking by reading notes, or signal the close of a consultation by
writing a prescription (Heath 1984). Time is also controlled by the doctor
and there is evidence to suggest that the average time of a general practice
consultation is declining (Tuckett et al. 1985). There is a ritual or ceremonial
element to medical encounters in that both parties usually have expectations
about the nature and outcome of the encounter. Strong (1979: 129), in his
study of consultations in Scotland and the United States, found that the
'medical control of the consultation was systematic, all pervasive and almost
unquestioned'. The provision of a prescription, especially for minor illness
such as 'flu' (see Chapter 2), is seen to mark a successful outcome while
the lack of a diagnosis or referral to a specialist is viewed as unsatisfactory.
However, GPs have a sense that changing policies and changing attitudes
since Balint's (1957) study have transformed the relationship of doctor and
patient. A study of GPs in Liverpool produced the following view which
appears to associate consumerism with a threat to the traditional relationship
of trust and compliance.

. . . both of my partners have had very stressful (formal) complaints
made against them, and it's only a matter of time before it happens to
me. It didn't used to be like this, and though both of them were dealt
with informally in the end, I think that there probably is a sense in
which people are told, 'This is how you complain, and so forth, and if
you want to complain about the doctor this is what you do'. It can get
a bit much to tell you the truth. But if people are taking responsibility
for their own care, and you're working with them and helping them
to find their way, it needn't be like that; there's too much confrontation
being built into the system, and it is the result of a deliberate policy.

(May et al. 1996: 195)

Challenges to professional power

As the Liverpool doctor above knows, the dominance of the medical
profession is expressed and reinforced through the micro level of medical
encounters. In the hospital, the 'consultant's round' has long been an

expression of power over medical students, nurses and patients. An Audit Commission (1993) report found that patients often felt insecure in asking questions and that they often did not get sufficiently good quality information from medical encounters. However, the 1990 contract for general practitioners (DoH 1989b), the White Paper *Working for Patients* (DoH 1989a) and *The Patient's Charter* (DoH 1991) indicate that patients are customers with implicit purchasing power. Family health service authorities and other bodies increasingly use various measures of patient satisfaction as a proxy measure for the quality of care (Williams and Calnan 1991). At a policy level, this represents a challenge by the state to overt medical domination that results in patient dissatisfaction. This has been referred to a process of 'proletarianization' (Oppenheimer 1973; McKinlay and Stoeckle 1988) by commentators who argue that the doctors are increasingly losing control over the context and content of medical work due to the bureaucratization and corporatization of healthcare. The related concept of 'deprofessionalization' also developed in the United States (Haug 1988) argues that the educational and cultural gap between doctors and patients is declining, thus undermining an important factor in maintaining medical power and control. Freidson (1994: 9) rejects the view that medical domination is declining and argues that instead the internal changes within the healthcare system are creating new hierarchies within medicine through which medical élites still exercise 'the considerable technical, administrative and cultural authority that professions have had in the past'. He claims that, despite attempts to introduce bureaucratic control over medicine, the profession is well represented within the strategic levels of these bureaucracies. It is unclear how applicable such theses are to the British healthcare system (Elston 1991) but they highlight that medical dominance is being questioned in a country that has a radically different healthcare structure. In Britain and the United States, the therapeutic nature of the encounter is being re-emphasized and patients are therefore being defined as experienced subjects who can contribute knowledge and take an active part in decisions. Significantly, this echoes the rhetoric on nurse–patient encounters which claims a similar privileged access to the 'whole person'. The macropolitics of the professions and lay people as well as that of the state and healthcare, are therefore clearly played out in the micropolitics of medical encounters.

> The medical profession, at best, denies women power; at worse, it reduces us to the state of passive victims. Feeling this loss of control, this passivity and powerlessness in men's hands, and desperate to 'do something' about their illness, it is little wonder that many women turn to the complementary, fringe or holistic health care, which appear to offer women a measure of control and power over their lives.
>
> (Wilkinson and Kitzinger 1994: 129)

The feminist critique of the medical encounter was noted earlier and as Wilkinson and Kitzinger (1994) suggest a logical response is for women to look to non-orthodox practitioners. Although based on rather uncertain data, the increase in the use of non-orthodox practitioners and the increase in the range of non-orthodox practice has been identified as a particular feature of contemporary society (Giddens 1991; Sharma 1992; Saks 1995). There is a wide range of approaches to health and treatments available within non-orthodox medicine. These include, homoeopathy, aromatherapy, osteopathy, reflexology, naturopathy, spiritual healing, bioenergetics and many more. Such approaches challenge medical dominance in two ways. Firstly, they remain in direct competition for clients despite the Medical Registration Act. One of the functions of the Act was to define orthodox medicine and hence accord a less privileged status to all the competing therapeutic approaches. The very terminology such as 'non-orthodox', 'alternative' and 'complementary' is indicative of the power of medicine. Conventionally, non-orthodox therapies are seen to range from those which can complement orthodox practice such as homoeopathy and aromatherapy to those which contain profoundly different concepts of health to medicine and act as alternatives (Sharma 1992; Saks 1995). The early exclusionary strategies of the medical profession have been well documented and were related to a number of campaigns against 'quackery' as well as reference in medical journals to the 'so-called science of healing' (*Lancet* 1889, cited in Saks 1995: 232). Nearly a hundred years later, the BMA (1986) report on alternative therapy reflected a similar view in arguing that non-orthodox practices had to provide scientific evidence for the validity of their treatments before they could be taken seriously. In the report, medicine is closely associated with the public interest which it protects by warning of the 'risks of great harm' presented by some therapies. This again is an interesting echo of nineteenth-century concerns about quackery and shows just how consistent exclusionary strategies can be. The whole report was hostile to non-orthodox therapies and the largest section of it was devoted to showing how rigorous and scientific medical science was. Continued interest in non-orthodox therapies and the growing consumer demand for them contributed to a further BMA report in 1993. The title *Complementary Medicine: New Approaches to Good Practice* indicates a more conciliatory attitude. Effectively, the report made the case for the professionalization of the more complementary approaches with professional bodies and recognized training, in what can be seen as a demarcationary professional strategy.

The GMC permits GPs to refer patients to non-orthodox practitioners but they retain responsibility for the patient and the NHS is unlikely to pay for the treatment. Payment for non-orthodox therapies is an important characteristic which forces clients to make choices and demand 'value for money'. To some extent, the practitioner–client (rather than 'patient') relationship is transformed because the client's knowledge is recognized and is often central to treatment and clients have to make active choices.

In a public health care system the patient does not pay directly for the therapy and has not sought the particular practitioner out as part of an active quest for healing, often arriving at the consulting room through a process of bureaucratic referral. Under such circumstances, might not the treatment be less satisfactory, the motivation of both patient and therapist being different?

(Sharma 1992: 211)

There is an interesting reflection here of the nature of the medical encounter. The emphasis shifts from the biological to the social, with the client as experiencing subject being at the heart of the therapy. Balint's (1957) conceptualization of the encounter as therapy in itself remains true in non-orthodox encounters.

Secondly, the threat from non-orthodox approaches may ironically develop due to the expansion of medical expertise and knowledge. Illich (1976) argued that one facet of medicalization was the 'deskilling' of lay people who lost faith in their knowledge about health. Giddens (1991) suggests that expanding expertise is a feature of late modernity that can lead to a 'reskilling' of people who become 'empowered' to pursue their own interests. He highlights the proliferation of self-help groups and uses a medical problem to illustrate his argument. Herzlich and Pierret (1987) also claim that self-help groups are a recent development and form part of a wider protest movement evident in modern societies. The groups that sprang up around AIDS illustrate the point as they formed powerful venues for collective action that influence decisions about biomedical research and practice. At a more individual level, they offer emotional support and can, through the expertise of members, provide an alternative or at least a critique of medical practice. Similarly, feminist self-help groups have formed around breast cancer and supported alternative treatments to radical surgical interventions (Wilkinson and Kitzinger 1994). As Giddens (1991) points out, the widespread availability of health-related material in popular culture and literature aimed at consumers makes it possible for people to develop their expertise in the areas of health that concern them. This in itself constitutes a threat to the exclusive nature of medical knowledge which is facilitated by evolving medicine diversity (Bury and Gabe 1994). The rapidly increasing use of the Internet as more people put their computers 'on-line' and the creation of what has been called the 'network society' (Castells 1996) has enabled them, not only to have immediate access to international health resources, but also to have direct access to knowledge that was previously inaccessible to the lay public. Both general medical journals such as the *British Medical Journal* and specialized electronic journals are freely available either partly or as complete electronic copies. Furthermore, through email, lay people can get in touch with self-help and pressure groups as well as other individuals, both lay and expert. Taken together, these developments disperse medical knowledge and go some way to undermine its claims on the exclusivity of medical expertise (Hardey 1999). 'Reskilled' lay people can make informed choices and challenge medical decisions. Clearly, non-orthodox therapies represent one of the choices open to them. However, more pessimistic expectations about the social impact of information technologies point to the divide between the information 'rich' and 'poor'. From this perspective, those – the poor – who do not have the same access to the Internet as the better off, will be further marginalized. Furthermore, the diversity and uncontrolled nature of Internet material means that the information available to people may be inadequate, wrong or misleading (Impicciatore 1997).

Conclusion

The establishment of the NHS placed medicine at the centre of the health-care system and confirmed its domination over other professions. Despite various reorganizations of the NHS (see Chapter 3), it is widely held that they had a limited effect on the dominant position of the medical profession (see Harrison *et al.* 1990). In Britain, the NHS provided an organizational structure which helped to retain the historical divisions between and within professional groups. Gender has had an important influence on the healthcare professions and it is a matter of speculation whether the greater number of women students in medical schools will change the culture of the profession. On past experience, there are few grounds to predict any great changes especially while nursing remains a firmly female profession. The challenges that are more likely to change medicine and more widely the biomedically dominated healthcare system come from outside the professions and the NHS. Reflecting wider social changes associated with the move from modernity to postmodernity, the basis upon which the professions have been based for the past hundred years or more are being questioned.

Social divisions and health

CHAPTER 5

Introduction

There are few areas of public or scientific debate that have attracted so much controversy than that about 'social divisions and health' also described as 'inequalities in health' or 'variations in health'. The terminology and data used in the debate are often problematic and this reflects the involvement of a range of scientific disciplines, ideologies and political position that are engaged in understanding differences in health. This is both a strength, in providing a rich, diverse set of data and explanations, and a weakness, in obscuring trends in health and the production of clear interventions to decrease observed variations in health. The purpose of this chapter is to explore the relationship between the social and economic structure and health experiences. This entails not only considering the impact of social class position, ethnic origin and gender on health but also involves examining the implications of unemployment, poverty and poor housing conditions for the health and well-being of adults and children.

In 1977, the Labour Government commissioned 'The Working Group on Inequalities in Health' which was chaired by Sir Douglas Black and included a number of academics who had played a role in the 'rediscovery of poverty'. This had challenged the idea that the welfare state had effectively ended poverty and that other measures were creating a more equitable society. Part of the remit of the Working Group was to collect information about social class and health and to explain why there were disparities in health related to social class. The group presented what is now universally known as the Black Report in April 1980, after Margaret Thatcher had won an election victory for the Conservative Party. Only 260 copies of the original report were published as the Government attempted to minimize the impact of the report. This hostile reception reflected the end of the post-war consensus over the social and economic role of the state and the desire of the new government to develop a non-interventionist welfare policy based on an individualistic philosophy. It also marked the beginning of a series of conflicts between the state and academics over the production and publication of information about poverty, health and unemployment. In 1987, the Health Education Council published an update of the Black Report called 'The Health Divide' which was later revised (Whitehead 1992). Again there was an attempt to lessen the impact of press coverage on the report's publication (Townsend and Davidson 1982; Townsend *et al.* 1992). The issues of health and inequality remain contentious. Significantly inequality is not mentioned in *The Health of the Nation* (DoH 1992) and 'variations' in health is commonly found in official publications. The Black Report has had an enduring impact on the debate about the links between social divisions and health (Morris 1979; Davey Smith *et al.* 1990) and was compared to the Bible in the *British Medical Journal* as 'much quoted, occasionally read and largely ignored when it comes to action' (*British Medical Journal* 1986: 91).

Health statistics

Within sociology in general, there is a degree of scepticism about quantitative methods, statistics and in particular official statistics. Abercrombie (1994) in the *Penguin Dictionary of Sociology* represents this scepticism: 'the categorisation of data reflects the interest of government and may not be meaningful to sociologists'. This view is reinforced by the Government Statisticians' Collective who noted that: 'the methods and concepts developed and used for official statistics are shaped by the sorts of policies powerful people in the state wish to consider and by the concerns which preoccupy them' (*Government Statisticians' Collective* 1993: 153). Bulmer (1980) provides a more considered account of why sociologists tend to neglect official statistics and draws attention to the benefits that can be gained from such material. Irvine *et al.* (1979) also argue that statistics should be recognized as the outcome of complex historical, political, economic and cultural processes that give rise to particular categorizations and data. Texts that are concerned with quantitative methods and the use of statistics draw attention to the need to understand the production of statistics (e.g. Dale *et al.* 1988; Slattery 1986; Reid 1987; Stewart and Kamins 1993). Texts about health provide critical accounts of statistical data which is dominated by the Black Report approach. Statistical material must therefore be seen as a social product and cannot be considered to be scientific, value neutral and have the status of 'social facts'.

The census has provided important data for, and analysis of, health since the last century but there is also a range of large-scale surveys that have been used to examine the health of the population. The number of surveys has grown in the past decade. This is partly a result of the government's

Table 5.1 Selected major national surveys in Britain

Survey title	Size	Collected	Main topics
Census of population	20 million households	Decennially	Household composition, occupation, etc.
Family Expenditure Survey	12,000 households	Annually	Household composition income/expenditure, etc.
General Household Survey	20,000 individuals in 10,000 households	Annually	Employment, education, fertility, health, etc.
Labour Force Survey	60,000 households	Quarterly from 1992	Employment, economic activity, housing, etc.
British Social Attitudes Survey	3000 individuals	Annually	Family, health, politics, welfare, etc.
Health Survey in England	16,000 individuals	Annually from 1991	Cardiovascular disease, risk factors, etc.
Family Resources Survey	26,000 households	Annually from 1993	Household income, benefits, etc.

desire to collect statistics to support planning and policy (e.g. National Health Service Central Register was central to the reorganization of the NHS) and partly as a consequence of improved technological resources that make the analysis and storage of such data easier and cheaper. During the 1980s the HIV/AIDS crisis highlighted the need for new levels of health data. It also promoted a public debate about the role of the state in the collection of data on the population. The *National Survey of Sexual Attitudes and Lifestyles* was deprived of government funding on the basis that the state should not attempt to elicit information about sexual practices. The survey was later supported by the Wellcome Trust (Wellings 1994). The *British Social Attitudes Survey* became a significant source of social data during the 1980s and reflects an increased concern with public opinion. Table 5.1 shows some of the more important surveys. A number of these surveys are longitudinal in that data are collected repeatedly from the same sample cohort over relatively brief intervals (for example, the *Labour Force Survey* has collected data on a quarterly basis since 1992).

The growth in the number of national surveys is reflected in a rising tide of smaller scale local surveys and commercially produced data. In the face of this expanding activity and the increasing potential for the state to collect data on the population, a review of the Government Statistical Service was undertaken in the 1980s. Significantly, it recommended that 'information should not be collected primarily for publication [but] primarily because government needs it for its own business' (Privy Council Office 1981: 182). This highlights the need to examine the creation of statistics and some of the often 'taken-for-granted' assumptions and categories that are used. All major surveys use social class which was one of the earliest and most influential statistical categories upon which mountains of analytical work and rhetoric have been erected over the years.

Determining social class

The desire to know about the health of the population in Britain was the motivating force behind the development of the first major social class classification scheme. At the end of the nineteenth century, one of the more significant debates was that between hereditarian eugenicists and environmentalists. The former argued that intelligence was primarily inherited and thus it was essential that the 'more intelligent' sections of the population should reproduce themselves. The increasing ability of middle-class women to take responsibility for their fertility and early feminist calls for more adequate birth control contributed to the momentum of the eugenics debate. T.H.C. Stevenson was a keen advocate of the environmentalist side of the debate and he was also a medical statistician in the General Register Office. The office was responsible for recording births, marriages and deaths. Stevenson was also an advocate of public health measures that would improve the infant mortality rate (Rose 1995). Stevenson's detractors argued that such interventions would prompt a further rise in the 'less intelligent' working-class population and therefore undermine the Darwinist project of social selection. Stevenson was instrumental in devising the first major attempt by government to utilize occupational groupings in the analysis of the census (Leete and Fox 1977). He hoped that data on infant mortality broken down by social class would provide evidence to support the environmentalist cause and consequent health policy. The Registrar General's classification of occupations which Stevenson developed was established in 1911 and built on earlier schemes that began in the 1850s. Groups of occupations were hierarchically ranked according to the degree the status and the 'general standing' of the occupation. These groupings reflected the hierarchical model of society in which the basic distinction was between the upper, middle and working classes. Stevenson's scheme involved a more detailed eightfold classification with three industrial groups for those engaged in mining, textiles and agriculture. However, it should be noted that from its inception, this scheme did not distinguish between ownership of resources and waged income, thus making it difficult to identify capital ownership that is central to a Marxist analysis.

The relative importance and standing of the industries identified in 1911 and the nature of work has been transformed in the following decades. There have therefore been a number of significant revisions to the scheme which are often ignored. The first major revision took place in 1921 when the established three industrial groups were re-allocated into a new five-class scheme. A stronger emphasis was given to 'skill' and Rose (1995: 1) claims that there is evidence that this 'revision was constructed in the light of knowledge of mortality rates. Thereby it produced the mortality gradients

Table 5.2 Current Standard Occupational Classification

Social class	Classification	Example of occupations
I	Professional occupations	Lawyer, doctor.
II	Intermediate occupations	Teacher, nurse
III (non-manual)	Skilled non-manual occupations	Clerical worker, shop assistant
III (manual)	Skilled manual occupations	Bricklayer, bus driver
IV	Semi-skilled manual occupations	Porter, farm worker
V	Unskilled manual occupations	Labourer, cleaner
Other	Armed forces, economically inactive	

so long cherished by those who use RGSC for this purpose'. Such claims may not invalidate the resulting data but highlight the interplay between the development of apparently 'value neutral scientific tools' and the social and cultural context in which such tools were developed and used. Contemporary variations on this classification of occupations are still used on birth and death certificates, decennial censuses and in a range of health research. It should be noted that the reliability of data recorded on death certificates can be questioned (Carr-Hill 1990). The 1921 revision produced the basic and now familiar fivefold scheme.

Since 1921, changes have been made to the allocation of particular occupations to social classes on a routine basis. For example, in the 1931 census male clerks were moved from class II to class III and in the 1961 census postmen and telephone operators were moved from class II to class IV. Such changes represented attempts to keep pace with economic and technical changes that have an impact on occupations and the nature of employment. They also affect the range of occupations and number of people allocated to particular social classes. This process of economic, social and technical change had by the end of the 1960s produced considerable growth in occupations falling into social class III. In 1970, this grouping was divided into class III (Non-Manual) and III (Manual). This classification remains in use and is shown in Table 5.2 with some illustrative occupations.

The 'level of occupational skill' (OPCS 1980) rather than 'the general standing in the community' (OPCS 1970) became the defining criterion for the classification of occupation in 1980. In practice, the need to retain comparability of data over time and the association of 'skill' with prestige and income led to relatively few changes in the ranking of occupations. This had led to the claim that, despite the changes in 1970 and 1980, there are no important differences in the relationship between the groupings and 'a wide variety of social, educational and health variables (Brewer 1986: 131). The balance between the number of people allocated to different classes is dynamic. For example, the size of social class I and social class V were about equal in 1991 but fifty years previously social class V was seven times larger than social class I (Carr-Hill 1990). As Illsley (1986: 152) notes, 'valid comparisons involve the comparisons of like with like' which becomes difficult when there are underlying changes in the extent and dispersal of social class groupings.

The Registrar General's classification is a status-based approach to social class that implies a major division between people involved in manual and non-manual work. In practice, it is the 'household' rather than individuals which is measured. Since most people live in households for the major part of their lives, and marriage or more recently cohabitation, represent significant routes to social mobility, this reflects social reality. The Registrar General's classification is also embedded in a 'male breadwinner' model of employment that bases classification where possible on the male 'head of household'. Therefore, social class defined only on the occupation of the male head of household may not adequately reflect the circumstances and experiences of other members of the household. Indeed, there is evidence to suggest that the distribution of resources within the household may be such that the health experiences and risks may not always be represented by the apparent class position of the male head of household (Burghes *et al.* 1997). The Black Report argued that the occupational status of both husband and wife needs to be examined when analysing the relationship between social factors and health. Women are thus relegated to a secondary status and the role of housewife has never be accorded the status of an occupation. Only unmarried employed women living alone are classified according to their own occupation. It was as late as 1986 that birth registrars were required to record the occupation of a baby's mother as well as its father (unless the birth was registered outside marriage and without an acknowledged father). There have been calls for housewifery to be classified (e.g. Walby 1986) and some have argued for a combination of household and individual classifications that encompass a wider definition both of occupation and living arrangements (e.g. McRea 1986). As Macfarlane (1990: 24) notes 'one of the biggest gaps in the information about women in official statistics is about the association between their paid employment and their health'. A purely occupation-based scheme also fails to capture adequately the experiences of other groups such as men and unmarried women who are unemployed or retired who are classified according to their last occupation. For those experiencing long-term unemployment, such a classification may not provide a satisfactory indicator of social and economic circumstances. Furthermore, there is evidence to suggest that in some instances there is a significantly poor response rate from certain sections of the population such as young men in the 20–30 age range. In the 1991 Census, this poor response may be partly due to the heritage of the Community Charge that may have promoted the 'missing million' to disappear from official records (Heady 1994).

As an 'occupational class' scheme the Registrar General's classification is skewed in that it reflects a gendered occupational structure. Ideas about femininity and masculinity that are associated with gender have a significant impact on what is considered to be men's and women's occupations. Therefore, relatively large numbers of men are found, for example, in manual occupations while women dominate in non-manual office work. In particular, work involving caring such as nursing is subject to a high degree of gender segregation. It should be noted that women who are informal or unpaid carers are not accorded an occupational classification in their own right. Within occupations, women tend to be concentrated in lower status jobs. In the medical professions women are underrepresented in consultants' posts and in the high status areas such as surgery and forensic psychiatry (Oakley 1983). This gendering of work produces an occupational structure in which men occupy the top and the bottom positions and women are grouped in the middle (Marshall *et al*. 1988).

Following Whitehead (1990 revised 1992: 312), the problems with the male-centred approach to the social categorization of women can be summarized as follows:

◆ The majority of married women are engaged in either full-time or part-time employment. By classifying them according to their husband's occupation, potentially significant information concerning the health risks associated with their own occupation is lost.
◆ Employed wives make a vital contribution to family finances and in some cases they may be the main income earner. In such circumstances, the husband's occupation may not reflect the household economic or social situation.
◆ It is not possible to compare the health of employed women with those in other categories such as housewives, informal carers and the unemployed.

The Registrar General's classification of social class provided a dependent variable that can be used to show how the different sections of the population experience marked differences in levels of morbidity and mortality. It has become the main measure of social class and remains widely utilized in social, health and medical research. The major virtues of the classification are: its longevity which make it possible to make comparisons over time; its simplicity in that large amounts of data can be easily ranked; and its high level of utilization which makes it feasible to compare across individual pieces of research. As Brewer (1986: 139) suggests, the Registrar General's classification is 'an arbitrary and crude, but well used, measure of social inequality'. It has also been described as 'commonsensical' (Crompton 1994) and as 'intuitive' (Rose 1995). In referring to the theoretical debate about social class Edgell (1993: 54) notes that 'bias is built into the language of class'. In lay understandings of social differentiation, notions of status, economic success and culture are bound up with the language and imagery of class. The way in which the social class fits common-sense notions is both a strength and a weakness. Every ten years occupational descriptions and rankings are reviewed by a closed group of officials and experts (Marshall *et al.* 1988). The thinking behind their decisions is not known and so it is not possible to judge how 'commonsensical' or 'intuitive' the process is. It has been suggested that this exercise is shaped by a wish to retain existing health gradients across the classes (Leete and Fox 1977; Bloor *et al.* 1987). The validity of the social class classification has not been examined in any depth (Wilkinson 1986) and so it is hard to establish the veracity of such claims. Should there be any substance to them the persistent health gradients that have been identified would be questionable at a fundamental level. The allocation of occupations to a hierarchy of occupational skills should reflect a 'common-sense' consensus over the 'standing' and material rewards of different occupations. The existence of such a consensus has been challenged (e.g. Edgell 1993) and furthermore linked to the 'obsolete and discredited' notion of society 'as a hierarchy of inherited natural abilities' (Marshall *et al.* 1988: 19).

Part of the 'crudeness' of the Registrar General's classification is that it is essentially pragmatic and not overtly grounded in a theoretically framework. The debate about the role and nature of social class has a long theoretical and pragmatic heritage. The substantial literature that arose out of the tensions between Marxist and Weberian approaches to social class were joined in the early 1970s by feminist challenges to assumptions about the labour market made in class analysis (Marshall *et al.* 1995). A significant feature of the debate is that it is grounded in theory and thus general concerns about how to conceptualize social change and human action. The actual debate itself is beyond the scope of this book (see Lee and Turner 1996). It may be more appropriate to use the term 'occupational class' rather than 'social class' in relation to a scheme that is purely based on occupation alone. In the introduction to *Inequalities in Health* it is noted that '. . . occupation is basically a pragmatic guide to that person's social position and his or her likely command over resources, and as such has its limitations. It is only an approximate indicator of family living standards or social position' (Townsend *et al.* 1992: 14).

Ethnicity, social class and identification

The ethnic mix of the British population is complex. Established immigrant populations that largely originated from Ireland and Europe were joined by large scale post-war migration from British colonies in South Asia and the Caribbean. This formed the basis of the current diversity of the ethnic population which has been defined variously in terms of skin colour, religion, nationality and so on. Language is a problem and words such as 'black' in common with other labels such as 'queer' and 'lesbian' have been reclaimed through political movements to take on a new meaning (Hall 1991).

Table 5.3 shows the proportion of the population in Britain identified in the 1991 Census as belonging to a ninefold classification of ethnicity. The

Table 5.3 Ethnic Classification, 1991 Census

Ethnic group	Proportion of population in Great Britain (per cent)
White	94.5
Black, Caribbean	0.9
Black, African	0.4
Black, other	0.3
Indian	1.5
Pakistani	0.9
Bangladeshi	0.3
Chinese	0.3
Other groups	0.9

Source: OPCS 1992.

nature of this material remains highly contested and the production of the data in Table 5.3 was the outcome of a sometimes acrimonious debate. For a long time, country-of-birth data was the main source of information about race. In the 1950s and 1960s, such data may have identified immigration from the 'New Commonwealth and Pakistan' with the associated implication of skin colour but it could contribute little to understanding the experiences of people who were identified with various ethnic minorities. Furthermore, information based on country of birth becomes increasingly unreliable as the number of heads of households from ethnic minority groups born in Britain increases. By the early 1970s, the country-of-birth classification was used in statistics relating to migration and unemployment as well as various local surveys of local house tenure. Such material reflects the concerns of the time. Moser wrote in 1972 that the focus on the New Commonwealth and Pakistan population in official statistics

> reflects public interest focused upon the potential and actual social issues arising from the increase in immigrants of ethnic origins previously represented in the country to only a small extent. These issues relate, among other things, to language difficulties, the concentration of some immigrants within urban areas of decayed housing and the differences in general social and cultural traditions.
>
> (Moser 1972: 20)

This suggests that the production of data stemmed from the perception that the presence of ethnic minorities created particular problems. The quantification of these problems may have eventually contributed to policies to address the needs of ethnic minorities but it also helped to legitimate racist arguments.

In the 1960s, the incidents of tuberculosis among recent immigrants (mainly black) gave rise to concerns that it would spread across the population (mainly white) (*British Medical Journal* 1962). Despite evidence that the rate of tuberculosis related to public health resources, housing and nutrition (McKeown 1976), it became seen as an 'immigrant disease' imported from 'dangerous and exotic' countries. In the 1970s, an editorial in the *Lancet* called for compulsory X-ray screening of all immigrants and providing medical legitimization of racist immigration policies (Ahmad 1993). In 1969, the Hospital In-Patient Enquiry (now the Hospital Episode System) and a year later the Mental Health Enquiry for England began to collect data on the place of birth of patients. The 1971 Census included a question on the place of birth and on parents' place of birth. The *Labour Force Survey* and the *General Household Survey* also attempted to identify ethnicity during the 1970s. By the end of the 1970s, a number of tests had been undertaken by the Office of Population Censuses and Surveys (OPCS) in order to include a categorization of ethnic identity in the 1981 Census (see Sillitoe 1978: 81). There was a General Election in 1979, and much debate about the Nationality Act 1981 which increased the opposition to ethnic categorization to such a degree that it was dropped from the 1981 Census. Many members of ethnic minority communities were concerned about the use to which such information would be put. The risk that non cooperation with the census would invalidate the whole exercise was high (White 1990). However, following further tests and refinements a ninefold categorization that combines notions of race, ethnic identity and nationality was included in the 1991 Census (see Table 5.3).

The census classification of ethnic identity conflates a number of characteristics which it is assumed are a fixed. Other surveys such as the *General Household Survey* which use interviews to collect data include an interviewer's assessment of colour in the data. However, ethnic identities (like sexual identities) are dynamic and subject to change. Furthermore, ethnic taxonomies inevitably allocate people into single categories which hide significant variations (for example 'Asian' identifies a highly diverse social group). According to Banton (1977), racialization is 'the way in which scientific theories of racial typology were used to categorise populations'. Racialization therefore suggests that 'race' is a natural, scientific and primary categorization of the population which implies that distinctive social characteristic and behaviours are determined by race. Ahmad (1993: 19) make the point that: 'A major issue in the racialization of health research is that it is assumed that the populations can only be meaningfully divided into "ethnic" or "racial" groups, taking these as primary categories and using these categories for explanatory purposes.' The danger is that other explanations or analytical models are made marginal or not even considered, so that 'race' becomes an independent variable in health research. As noted in Chapter 1, biomedical research has a history of racialized research. The higher incidents of rickets among Asian children is a well-known example of racialization which resulted in the 1970s of the emergence of the new category of 'Asian rickets'. This was causally linked to 'pathological' practices in Asian culture (Ahmad 1993). However, rickets had been a disease of poverty that was instrumental in the introduction of free school milk and the fortifying of margarine with vitamin D.

Miles (1989: 9) argues that from a Marxist perspective 'the influence of racism and exclusionary practices is always a component of a wider structure of class disadvantage and exclusion'. The interplay between social class and ethnic group is complex and it is all too easy to ignore the dimensions of racial discrimination and harassment in occupational class. Equally, it must be remembered that not all people from ethnic groups experience the same levels of discrimination and disadvantage or believe that they are subject to these processes. Social, epidemiological and biomedical research using ethnic taxonomies must be treated with caution. This does not mean that such research should not be undertaken or discounted, but its results will remain contested.

The Economic and Social Science Research Council (ESRC) is undertaking a review on behalf of the OPCS of the measurement of social circumstances in order to provide an improved measure for the Census of 2001. The issues of gender and race form a central part of this review. Part of this exercise will be to attempt to make British measures more compatible with those used in other European countries. This potentially will make it easier to make reliable statements about the health experiences of different social groups across the European Community. A further dimension is the problem of how to classify people who are retired and may have last been economically active many decades ago. This reflects both the rise in early retirement and increased longevity.

Alternative measures of social position

Although the Registrar General's scheme has a dominant position in researching health, there have been many attempts to develop alternative schemes that overcome some of the difficulties encountered in this approach. These schemes go beyond the classification of occupations to provide composite measures that may include home and car ownership, education and factors related to locality such as environmental deprivation. For example, the Jarman 'underprivileged areas score' index was used to measure deprivation in relation to the provision of general practitioners (Jarman 1983, 1984). Like other systems, it attempted to include information about the locality in which people live as well as household-based data. This recognizes that locality may have a determining effect on the opportunities and constraints individuals face in making choices whether it is about employment or a healthy diet. Such a quantification of deprivation attempts to combine an assessment of deprivation such as poor housing and overcrowding with measures of the number of people at 'risk' of deprivation, such as single-parent households and elderly people living alone enable the identification of clusters of morbidity or mortality that are related to particular areas. The Department of the Environment produced an attempt to operationalize

Table 5.4   Department of the Environment Index of Deprivation (1983)

Per cent of economically active persons who are unemployed
Per cent of households defined as overcrowded
Per cent of households with single parent family
Per cent of households lacking exclusive use of two basic amenities
Per cent of pensioners living alone
Per cent of population change
Standardized mortality rate
Per cent of households in which the head was born in the New Commonwealth or Pakistan

deprivation with its indicators of urban deprivation shown in Table 5.4. In practice, such scales can produce results that are to a greater or lesser extent an artefact of the weightings given to the various dimensions of the scales. Both of the scales outlined have produced results that suggest that London has the majority of 'most-deprived' areas (Townsend 1987; Whitehead 1992). This is caused by the relatively large number of single-parent and ethnic minority households in London, skewing the analysis. The more dimensions that are included in a scale, the more open it becomes to the problem of skewing. This suggests that a basic scale of four indicators:

♦ unemployment
♦ overcrowding
♦ lack of resources
♦ home tenure

may be more reliable (Townsend 1987). However, despite the potential problems, such basic scales do not produce the detail possible in more complex schemes such as those designed to measure multiple deprivation. In assessing all these scales, it is important to separate the measurement of deprivation from the households and people who experience deprivation. As Townsend states:

> Otherwise there is a danger of treating age, ethnicity and single parent-hood as causes of the phenomenon under study. It is wrong in principle to treat being black or old and alone or a single parent as part of the definition of deprivation. Even if many such people are deprived it is their deprivation and not their status which has to be measured. And many people having that status are demonstrably not deprived.
>
> (Townsend 1987: 89)

It should also be remembered that 'deprivation' itself is a contested concept. It is based on the economic and social experience of conditions which are markedly different from those experienced by the majority of the population. In particular, deprivation implies a lack of material and/ or social resources that are taken for granted by the general population. It can be distinguished from poverty which may be defined in terms of resources (e.g. income) that are directly available to individuals or households. Deprivation is therefore a broader concept and can be linked to debates about citizenship, the 'underclass' and social exclusion. As Berthoud (1976: 180) notes, it should also be distinguished from inequality: 'If inequality can be seen as a hill, deprivation is a ravine into which people should not be allowed to fall.'

Life, death and the Black Report

Mortality was the main focus of the Black Report because it provided a crude but crucial indicator of the life chances of different groups of people. It also has a resonance with common-sense ideas about life expectancy which in Britain perceives deaths that occur below the retirement age as untimely. Furthermore, there is a considerable amount of data available about mortality that makes it possible to identify changes related to time and place. Infant mortality (deaths that occur in the first year of life) in particular has proved to be a sensitive indicator of the health of women and wider social conditions. During the second half of the twentieth century the infant mortality rate has followed a broad downward trend. In 1950, there were 31 infant deaths for every 1000 live births; this figure had fallen to 12 by 1980 and 8 by 1990 (Central Statistical Office 1992). During the period from 1971 to 1991, the infant mortality rate in England and Wales fell by 58 per cent (Botting 1995). This is the largest fall in any age group and much of the decline can be accounted for by a reduction in the neonatal mortality rate (deaths during the first 28 days of life). In this period, deaths are closely linked to medical care which diminishes social class differences. The post-neonatal rate (deaths over 28 days and under a year) remained fairly stable over the same period. However, there was a marked increase in sudden infant death syndrome (SIDS) throughout the 1980s which became the main cause of post-neonatal deaths. Deaths in this category which in the past may have been classified as caused by other factors tended to be assigned to SIDS, so that the apparent change in the cause of death is due to changes in the identification of medical conditions on the death certificate. Death attributed to SIDS declined gradually after 1988 due to parents' awareness of SIDS and changes in the sleeping arrangements of their infants (Dunnell 1995). The perinatal mortality (stillbirths or death in the first week of life) rate also declined with the stillbirth rate falling from 10.3 per total births in 1975 to 4.7 in 1989. This general improvement in infant mortality hides important differences related to social class.

> For the death of every one male infant of professional parents, we can expect almost two among children of skilled manual workers and three among children of unskilled manual workers. Among females the ratios are even greater.
>
> (Townsend and Davidson 1982, 1992: 44)

Table 5.5   Perinatal and infant mortality rates per 1000 total births 1978–9 and 1992 compared by social class (for marriage births only)

Social class	Perinatal		Infant	
	1978–9	*1992*	*1978–9*	*1992*
I	11.9	6.3	9.8	5.0
II	12.3	6.1	10.1	4.6
III (non-manual)	13.9	6.8	11.1	5.5
III (manual)	15.1	7.0	12.4	5.6
IV	16.7	7.4	13.6	5.8
V	20.3	8.9	17.2	7.9
Other	20.4	10.2	23.3	10.5
Ratio of social class V : I	1.71	1.7	1.8	1.6

Source: Poverty, Oppenheim and Harker, 1996, table 4.2: 79.

Table 5.5 shows the rates of perinatal and infant mortality by social class for births within marriage. The table shows that 9 out of every 1000 babies born to parents in social class V in 1992 were stillborn or died during the first week of life compared to 6 out of every 1000 babies born to parents in social class I. A similar gap between the social classes can be seen in the infant mortality rate of 8 per 1000 for babies born into social class V compared to 5 per 1000 for babies born into social class I.

The risk of death during the first 12 months of life is related to the age of the mother, marital status at the time of the child's birth, birthweight and the number of previous births. Perinatal and infant mortality rates are highest for mothers under 16 years of age and next highest for those over the age of 35 years. The lowest rates are experienced by mothers between the ages of 25 and 35 years (Macfarlane *et al.* 1995), however, inequalities related to social class remain. The majority of infant deaths occur to low-birthweight babies, that is, babies weighing under 2500 grams at birth. Women in households in which the main wage earner is in social class V are more likely to give birth to low-weight babies than mothers from other households. It is women who are living on the social and economic margins who are most at risk of having a low birthweight baby. Such social disadvantages and associated health behaviours such as smoking mean that lone mothers are more likely to give birth to a low birthweight baby than married mothers. Mothers who were born in the New Commonwealth also have a higher risk of having a low birthweight baby than British-born mothers. Social class also has an impact on the survival rate of low-weight babies with low birthweight babies born to mothers in social class V more likely to die than babies born to mothers in social class I (Macfarlane *et al.* 1995).

Table 5.5 does not include the growing number of births outside marriage (Burghes *et al.* 1997). Stillbirth and post-neonatal mortality rates are higher for babies born outside marriage than for children born to married couples in social class V. Marital status is also associated with social class with births to married couples being more common in social classes I and II. As Whitehead has remarked:

> The inescapable conclusion is that occupational class differences are real sources of difference in the risk of infant mortality.
>
> (Whitehead 1992: 266)

The risk of death among children between the ages of 1 and 14 years is twice as high for boys and girls born to fathers in social class IV and V than among those in social class I (OPCS 1991). The Black Report shows that the differences in mortality between classes I and V are due mainly to accidents and respiratory diseases. Accidents account for the largest single cause of death in childhood with a higher incidence in the lower classes. They are also higher among boys. Accidents relate directly to social circumstances such as living in inner-city urban areas in an environment that makes it hard for parents to supervise children. Furthermore, it is difficult for poor parents who may be living in low-quality housing to afford to buy safety equipment such as fireguards or stair gates. This is reflected in the marked social class differences in home accidents that involve children. There is also a marked class gradient in childhood deaths from traffic accidents, with boys and girls from social classes IV and V at greatest risk. As Holman (1991: 7) concludes 'children whose parents cannot afford a car are knocked over by those that can'.

Inequalities between the social classes in mortality extend throughout the lifecourse. The Black Report identified a persistent inverse relationship between social class and mortality. *The Health Divide* (Whitehead 1990) showed that between the 1950s and the 1980s, the mortality rates for social classes IV and V had remained the same or had marginally increased for people over 35 years of age. In contrast, there had been a marked improvement in the mortality rates for those in social classes I and II. Standardized mortality ratios (SMRs) are used to make allowances for changes in the age structure of the population. First calculated in 1931, a base year such as 1980 is taken from which shifts in the SMR can be detected. The average for the population is 100 so that a SMR below 100 indicates a lower than average chance of death whereas a figure above 100 suggests a higher than average chance. Table 5.6 provides SMRs for adult males for 1970–2, 1979–80 and 1991–3 and illustrates not only the existence of a distinct gradient from class I to class V but indicates that class inequalities increased over the period in question. For the period 1970–2, the SMR for class V was 1.8 times that of class I; in 1981–3, it was 2.1 times as high.

A number of significant diseases that often lead to an early death have a distinct social class distribution that can be identified by collapsing the six social classes into non-manual and manual groups. This reveals that, for example, for men in the 20–64-year age group, the SMRs for lung cancer

Table 5.6 Standardized mortality ratios for adult males, England and Wales

Class		1970–2	1979–80	1991–3
I	Professional	77	66	66
II	Intermediate	81	74	72
III	Skilled, non-manual	99	93	100
III	Skilled, manual	106	103	117
IV	Semi-skilled	114	114	116
V	Unskilled	137	159	189

Source: *Population Trends* (1996).

for non-manual and manual workers were 65 and 129, respectively, in the early 1980s (Marmot and McDowall 1986). In the same age group, the manual classes also showed an above average SMR for coronary heart disease. Further studies have confirmed that for men, mortality is consistently lowest among those in professional and managerial jobs and highest among men in labouring and other manual occupations (Bethune *et al.* 1995). As Whitehead (1992) suggests, diseases which have in the past been associated with affluence or 'executive stress', such as coronary heart disease, appear to be more common in the manual classes. The significance of the influence of wider social factors and economic circumstances on mortality rates is indicated when she states: 'Clearly in this country nowadays "diseases of affluence" have all but disappeared and what is left is a general health disadvantage of the poor' (Whitehead 1992: 232). This picture of class-based differences in mortality is reflected in studies of people within one occupation such as the longitudinal study of civil servants in Whitehall (Marmot *et al.* 1991). In general, it can be shown that lower-grade civil servants have a higher death rate than those in higher grades.

There is a clear and persistent social gradient in mortality rates at all ages. The rates for stillbirths, infant mortality, deaths in childhood and adult mortality are higher in the lower social classes than in the higher social classes. For men there is an 'increasing mortality disadvantage, each social class shows higher mortality than the social class above' (Harding 1995: 34). Of the 66 major causes of death, 62 are more prevalent in social classes VI and V than in other social classes. Rather than diminishing, it appears that such differences are increasing (DoH 1995).

Social class and morbidity

While mortality was the main focus of the Black Report, it is important to see whether there are social class differences in the rates of illness experienced by people while they are living. As Blaxter (1990: 7) suggests, 'inequalities in health may not be the same as inequalities in death'. However, it is evident that disparities in morbidity can be identified and that health surveys have consistently recorded higher rates of self-reported illness among manual classes than among non-manual groups (Blaxter 1990). A number of surveys of self-perceptions of health have shown that men and women in social classes I and II are far more likely than men in social classes IV and V to state that they are in very good health (White *et al.* 1993). It is also evident that people in social classes IV and V say that they experience four times as much bad health than men and women from social class I and II report. Other surveys show similar patterns; for example, one national survey of self-perceived health found 12 per cent of men in class I believed their health was fair or poor compared to 36 per cent of men from social class V (Cox *et al.* 1987). The study used a number of different measures of health and Blaxter concludes that 'at all ages, and for each dimension of health, there was a tendency for experience to be poorer as social class declined' (Blaxter 1990: 63).

As was noted earlier, low birthweight is a significant determinant of perinatal mortality and it can also have implications for the future health of the child (Barker 1991). In the 1990s, about 66 per cent of babies born to mothers on benefits had a below average birthweight and consequent higher risk of ill health (OPCS 1996). White *et al.* (1993) noted that people from manual social class households were nearly twice as likely than those from non-manual households to experience breathlessness.

As we saw earlier, measures of social class based purely on the occupation of the husband do not necessarily accurately reflect the circumstances and experiences of other members of the household. Such limitations need to be borne in mind when considering morbidity statistics and social divisions. It has been suggested that occupation-based measures constitute a 'summary measure' which 'can best be regarded simply as a starting point for the investigation of social circumstances and health' (Blaxter 1990: 61).

Explanations of social divisions in health

The key to the controversy that developed in the wake of the Black Report can be found in the question it posed: 'Why does social class continue to exercise so significant an influence on health?' (Townsend and Davidson (1982, 1992: 112). It is the explanations offered in the report that have dominated the debate and arguments about health inequalities. The report offered four central theoretical explanations which it referred to as:

- ◆ artefact explanations
- ◆ theories of natural or social selection
- ◆ materialist or structuralist explanations
- ◆ cultural/behavioural explanations.

Before the main characteristics of these explanations are considered, it is worthwhile noting the point made by some critics that the report offers no review or discussion to explain why or how these explanatory categories had been generated (Vågerö and Illsley 1995).

The artefact explanations

One artefact argument suggests that the link between material resources and physical well-being reflect changes which have taken place in the occupational structure rather than a 'real' association. This involves highlighting the decline in the number of people employed in manual occupations and the increase in the numbers engaged in non-manual work over the past few decades. It is further claimed that changes in the size and composition of the Registrar General's occupational class categories make comparisons between mortality rates for the different groups over time difficult. Furthermore, the contraction of social class V, which contains a disproportionate number of older workers who have a higher risk and incidence of chronic sickness, may distort the data on mortality and morbidity. This suggests that underlying changes in the social structure and distribution of social class may mean that any data based on social classes should be questioned. The logic of this argument is that observed class-based inequalities in health are not real but artificial and constructed out of the measurement process. However, health research using a diversity of methodologies has universally found an association between social position and health. Problems associated with measurement and the definition of categories can contribute to the extent and distribution of observed inequalities. However, the opposite is also true in that 'the measurement process may be concealing as well as generating inequalities of health' (Bloor *et al.* 1987).

Theories of natural or social selection

There is a tension in the Black Report between what may be regarded as genetic and social mobility explanations of social selection. There are resonances of Darwinism in the genetic social selection thesis which we examined in exploring the development of social class measures earlier in this chapter. The Black Report notes 'that men and women who by virtue of innate physical characteristics are destined to live the shortest lives also reap the most meagre rewards (Townsend and Davidson 1982, 1992: 113). The use of 'innate' points to some notion of genetic rather than social factors driving individuals' health prospects (Vågerö and Illsley 1995). This has echoes of sociobiological explanations of societies which focus on what is seen as the primary role of genes (e.g. Wilson 1975). The major objection to a genetic explanation is what is called the 'genetic fallacy'. This points out that it is impossible to reach any conclusions about the role of genetic fitness in the face of an absence of information about the distribution of genes among the social classes (Vågerö 1991).

Social selection explanations accept the existence of inequalities in health. It is argued that the concentration of poor health in the lower classes is a reflection of 'health discrimination' on social mobility (West 1991). Using data from the 1946 National Survey of Health and Development, Wadsworth (1986) shows how unhealthy people are more likely to experience downward social mobility. He describes how those men who had been seriously ill during childhood appeared to be more likely than others to have experienced downward mobility by the time they reached their mid-twenties. Social class differences in health are interpreted as a result of the healthy becoming upwardly mobile and the unhealthy becoming downwardly mobile (Stern 1983). Thus social class position is more or less a consequence of health status rather than vice versa. Poor health is not only a predictor of what is sometimes referred to as 'downward occupational drift' but can also be seen as a factor that prevents or restricts upward mobility. The overall result is a tendency for high social class groups to shed their unhealthy members and gain healthy individuals who have risen from the lower social classes. It is therefore claimed that the result of this mobility process in the groups is a clustering of high mortality and morbidity rates in social classes IV and V. It is important to distinguish between social selection explanations and genetically based explanations. Failure to do this means that social factors may be neglected in an overall rejection of the social selection approach due to its association with a genetic explanation of human diversity (Vågerö and Illsley 1995). Evidence from a number of studies has suggested ways in which foetal and infant development can be affected by material and structural factors so that there is a high risk of ill health and early death in adult life (e.g. Barker 1991). Barker agues that there is a 'biological programming' that for example may link low birthweight with cardiovascular disease. This suggests that there is a process of social selection that may be 'programmed' before birth that effectively makes those born into the social and economic margins more at risk to chronic conditions. Thus the concentration of morbidity and mortality in social classes IV and V may in part be explained by this process.

Materialist and structuralist explanations

The Black Report from its examination of the relationship between social class and health gave more weight to materialist and structuralist explanations than the others it offered. More recently, an article in the *Lancet* that reconsidered the Black Report ten years after its publication noted that 'poverty and deprivation were the principal cause of premature death and lesser life expectancy of the lowest classes' (Morris 1990: 304). In a similar review of trends over the decade, the *British Medical Journal* anticipated the confirmation of a widening health gap following the analysis of the 1991

Census (Davey Smith *et al.* 1990). In the same issue, the editorial stated that 'as the gap between rich and poor in Britain has widened half our children live in poverty' (Smith 1990: 349). A comparison of male mortality in the early 1970s with the early 1990s revealed a relative widening of the gap between social class V and social classes I and II (Drever *et al.* 1996). In terms of specific causes of mortality, a fivefold difference in death due to lung cancer and a fourfold difference in suicide between social class V and social class I was noted.

It is important at this stage to examine what might be indicated by 'poverty'. Seebohm Rowntree (1901), in a classic study of the poor in York, defined poverty as having an income which was not enough to buy 'the minimum necessities of merely physical' existence. He went to considerable efforts to develop a list that would fulfil the needs of 'subsistence living'. Such a definition is based on basic biological needs and represents what is known as 'absolute poverty'. This definition of poverty can be seen as universal and 'scientific' in that it was originally drawn up with the help of the new science of nutrition. Poor nutrition, low birthweight, retarded physical and mental development and impaired resistance to disease are all associated with living at or below absolute poverty. Such poverty is common in many developing countries and helps to account for the falling level of health in some parts of Eastern Europe. Starkly, absolute poverty can be defined in terms of whether an individual has just enough to eat. However, such assessments ignore the judgemental dimension of 'subsistence' which is bound within a social and cultural context (for example, Rowntree held that tea was essential). Changing living standards have an impact on what is considered to be the minimum necessities. Furthermore, it ignores any psychological, cultural or social needs.

Townsend (1979: 125–6) in his study of *Poverty in the UK* states that individuals 'can be said to be in poverty when they lack the resources to obtain the types of diet, participate in the activities and have living conditions and amenities which are customary, or at least widely encouraged or approved, in societies to which they belong'. This suggests that poverty is not just subsistence or physical needs but that it is also related to exclusions from what are considered normal aspects of social life. However, as Blaxter notes (1990), when 'poor' people are interviewed about their health, they do not often talk about their material circumstances or structural constraints. One common approach to defining poverty (that was used in the Black Report) is to regard people who have an income that is between 100 and 140 per cent of the supplementary benefit level, as living in or on the margins of poverty. Although this benefit has been recently replaced, the intention to ensure that people have a minimum income remains the same. Another approach is to focus on concepts of 'customary' and 'encouraged or approved' and undertake public opinion surveys to identify what is regarded as a minimum standard of living. A further approach is the index of deprivation considered earlier which provides a set of fixed measures.

Clearly, relative poverty does not have the health risks that are starkly attached to absolute poverty especially as found among the poor in many developing countries. It also has no universal form and so, for example, the *British Medical Journal* editorial noted above used indicators relating to half the average income. The uncertainty over the identification of relative poverty has led some to argue that there is a danger that it overlooks 'an irreducible absolutist core' (Sen 1994) which can be quantified.

Materialist and structuralist explanations of health inequalities concentrate on how people located in the lower social classes tend to have limited educational and employment opportunities with poorer access to financial and material resources than those located in other social classes. By examining material deprivation and social disadvantage, these explanations explore the part played by structural factors in determining life circumstances and influencing the life chances of people. It should be recognized that there are blurred boundaries between the materialist and structuralist and the cultural and behavioural explanation. For example, there is an interaction between poverty, poor housing and smoking behaviours (Graham 1993b). In exploring aspects of deprivation and disadvantage, emphasis will be placed on income, housing and unemployment.

Differences in income

> The poorer you are, the more likely you are to die young. The child of a manual labourer can expect to die eight years younger than the child of a lawyer. Early death, and greater illness during life, are firmly linked to money.
>
> (*Which* 1989: 26)

The quotation above claims that income differences are an important cause of social class differences in health. Income, poverty and social class are sometimes seen as nearly equivalent (e.g. Blackburn 1991). However, relative differences between social classes (e.g. between social class II and social class III non-manual) may have different implications for health. The Black Report orientates its discussion of income inequalities to its general concern with the material and structural explanation of inequalities. While a number of studies have highlighted the problems of living on a low income, there is no simple correlation between what may be defined as a low income and health. Furthermore, it can be hard to discern what might be identified as the outcome of health behaviour, for example choosing a high-fat and high-salt diet, and as an outcome of low income, for example living in temporary accommodation without cooking facilities and local shops. There are complex measurement problems associated with linking income to health. For example, to take earnings from employment as the sole measure of income is to ignore other important sources such as 'fringe benefits' (e.g. private healthcare) and releasable capital gains (e.g. shares). There may also be significant income differences within one social class. For example, the non-manual social class III includes many low-grade salaried clerical and administrative staff who are relatively low paid while the manual group includes more highly paid skilled workers who can increase their basic pay by working overtime. Furthermore, it is often the income available to a household and its distribution within the home rather than an individual income that shapes the health, lifestyle and consumption patterns of family members. At a basic level, it can be difficult for researchers to obtain accurate figures on individual incomes and hard to take account of factors such as unearned income and material resources such as home ownership. Such difficulties are reflected in the greater degree of research on those dependent of benefits or low incomes that are supplemented by benefits.

In a study of the relationship between income and mortality, it was shown that those occupational categories which have experienced the fastest rise in income also recorded the fastest fall in death rates, whereas those occupational groups displaying the slowest rise in income also experienced the slowest fall in mortality rates (Wilkinson 1986, 1992). This suggests that the lower occupational groups that have been subject to the restructuring of the labour market, loss of trade union power and relatively declining real incomes are more likely to experience lack of self-esteem, stress and a sense of being unable to fully participate in society. Since the publication of the Black Report, the gap between the low waged and others in employment has increased. There has been a deregulation of employment law that has made many low-skilled jobs less secure. Furthermore, disadvantage in the labour market through, for example, racial discrimination will be reflected in health disadvantage (Nazroo 1997). In Black Report terms, the introduction of minimum wage legislation may increase the lifestyle choices open to those on a low income and potentially lower their risk of poor health.

Division in housing
An association between poor housing and poor health has been described since early studies of social conditions in the nineteenth century. Chadwick's 1842 report on the unsanitary conditions found in urban working-class areas noted that overcrowding, poor ventilation and damp houses help to spread infectious diseases and thereby increase mortality rates (Conway 1994). Florence Nightingale's comment that 'the connection between health and the dwellings of the population is one of the most important that exists' (quoted in Lowry 1991: 149) is still true today. This is reflected in the prominence given to housing in the deprivation indexes noted earlier. While improvements in general living conditions and the quality of houses, have helped to reduce the incidence of infectious diseases common in the last century, evidence of links between housing and health remains (Conway 1995). ('Housing' here is taken to cover all forms of accommodation (e.g. flats, bedsits, etc.) and tenure unless stated otherwise.)

A disproportionate number of infant deaths occur in households in which basic amenities are lacking, people are living in overcrowded conditions or where facilities are shared with other families (Fox and Goldblatt 1982). A study of low-income households in London, Edinburgh and Glasgow used surveys and interviews to establish a link between reported incidence of ill health and inadequate and damp housing (Hunt 1990). It was found that a range of symptoms including coughs, nausea and high blood pressure increased as the quality of the housing decreased. A similar pattern in children's health has been identified (Platt *et al.* 1989). Adults and children living in damp housing reported more respiratory symptoms than those living in dry surroundings. Furthermore, it was found that these differences persisted even when factors such as income, overcrowding and the incidence of smoking were taken into account. Poor housing conditions are not only associated with increased ill health and mortality. Brown and Harris' research into depression among women concluded that housing problems were 'highly associated with chronic psychiatric conditions' and had a clear aetiological role in depression' (1978: 199, 276).

The form of, as well as the quality of, housing can have an impact on health. The inability of residents to control the entrance to their homes together with structural defects, poor maintenance and vandalism may create a social malaise and contribute to mental health problems (Hunt 1990). The location of housing is also important. Some large housing estates and deck access housing schemes lack recreational facilities and safe play areas for children. Often located on the outskirts of towns and cities they have poor access to shops and healthcare service, reinforcing a sense of physical and social isolation. More broadly, mortality and morbidity patterns are associated with geographical location with, for example, people living in prosperous rural areas experiencing better health and those living in inner urban areas (Charlton and White 1995). Significant differences in accident rates, health status and psychological distress have been found between people who live in an estate which is seen as having poor environmental conditions and housing compared to those who occupy similar housing in an estate with better conditions (Blackman *et al.* 1989). Housing that incorporates materials that are now recognized as dangerous to health, such as asbestos and lead pipes, can cause cancers and reduced child development (Lowry 1991).

From the inception of the welfare state until the 1970s there was a twin-track housing policy which embraced owner-occupation and council-rented housing. The latter provided the majority of social housing for those on low incomes and did much to end the squalid housing described by Chadwick and others. Support for council housing gradually diminished and housing associations have been encouraged to provide housing for those who cannot compete in the private sector (Ginsberg 1992). Because of the links between tenure, income and social class it is not unexpected that there should be tenure-based health differences. For example, men and women living in local authority housing have been found to have a higher SMR than owner-occupiers for malignant neoplasms, respiratory and circulatory diseases (Fox and Goldblatt 1982). In the 1980s, the Conservative Government granted new rights to council tenants, enabling them to purchase their homes from the council. Restrictions were also placed on local authorities preventing them from using the proceeds from council house sales to finance the building of more houses. By the 1990s, two-thirds of homes were owner-occupied (OPCS 1991). At the same time, demographic changes such as the increase in divorce and lone parenthood since the 1970s was contributing to what has been called the 'feminization of poverty'. Tenure is one of the main divisions between lone parents and other families with children. Lone parents are more likely to be housed in 'hard to let' accommodation and have a higher risk of homelessness than other families (Hardey and Crow 1991). There is also evidence that Black families are more likely to be offered inferior housing (Ginsberg 1992).

It is difficult to measure the total number of homeless persons in Britain partly because there is a gap between the number of people who apply to local authorities to be classified as homeless and the number accepted as such. The Housing (Homeless Persons) Act 1985 imposes a duty on local authorities to provide accommodation for homeless people deemed to be in 'priority need' as defined by the Act. The categories of 'priority need' are: families with young children; pregnant women; and those who are considered vulnerable on account of age, physical disability, mental handicap or illness. Thus single persons, childless couples and those considered to have made themselves intentionally homeless are largely excluded from the figures. Local authorities do extend help to these groups but they are under no statutory obligation so to do. Pressure groups like Shelter and Roof claim that official figures seriously underestimate the nature and extent of the homeless problem. They refer to the existence of the 'hidden or concealed homeless' that is, those people whom the system fails to provide for and those living in substandard, overcrowded housing. It is also likely that people in marginal housing will not be included in the major surveys and the census.

In order to meet their statutory requirements under the Housing Act, local authorities have had to place families in temporary accommodation in private lodging houses, hostels and hotels. In 1995, there were 46,160 households in such short-term accommodation (Oppenheim and Harker 1996). However, 'temporary' can translate to over a year for some families. The living conditions experienced by individuals and families living in temporary accommodation can be a direct cause of health problems. In particular, children have a higher risk of accidents and mental health problems.

Divisions in unemployment
Since the publication of the Black Report, the recessions of the 1980s and early 1990s have led to considerable debate about the nature and extent

of unemployment. The first and most obvious effect of unemployment is a marked drop in income as earnings are replaced by state benefits. It has been suggested that 'with the possible exception of the down-and-out homeless, direct measures of hardship show there is no poorer group of people than unemployed couples with children' (Berthoud 1986: 2). Therefore, unemployment has a close association with poverty and material deprivation which is likely to become worse the longer people remain unemployed. It can also be difficult to determine the degree to which poor health leads to unemployment or whether unemployment causes a deterioration in health. A longitudinal study of the mortality records and employment histories of men over a ten-year period from 1971 to 1981 found that those men who were unemployed and actively seeking work in 1971 had higher mortality rates than those men who were in continuous employment throughout the period (Moser et al. 1984). As the study excluded men who were unemployed as a result of chronic sickness, the findings can be seen to support the view that raised mortality was a consequence of unemployment rather than the result of pre-existing poor health. The wives of unemployed men were also found to have relatively high mortality rates. This suggests that unemployment has an impact on the unemployed themselves and other family members (Moser et al. 1984). Less is known about the problems of unemployed women than men, despite the considerable increase in the full- and part-time employment of women. As we saw earlier, the official statistics neglect the links between employment and women's health (Macfarlane 1990). It can also be difficult to measure the social class of unemployed women who have been relatively inactive in the formal labour market. Arber (1989) suggests that *General Household Survey* data indicate that the general female mortality gradient is as steep as the male.

There are physical and psychological health problems associated with the unemployed and their families. An in-depth case study of 22 families (Fagin and Little 1984) indicates the nature of these problems. A distinction was made between those families in which health problems were present prior to unemployment and those in which health problems occurred following unemployment. Unemployment was identified as a cause of stress in all the families and it was this stress which was seen as a possible mechanism by which job loss leads to illness. The authors point out the difficulties of disentangling the effect of unemployment from other stress-producing life events which may be experienced at the same time, such as the death of a member of the family or marital separation. The study found that following unemployment spouses with a record of poor health had a tendency to suffer a recurrence of their previous illnesses. In a number of cases, the unemployed reported an increase in some physical symptoms, such as headaches and backache, which may be triggered by psychological mechanisms. Job loss is viewed as setting in motion certain psychological changes, which for some produce feelings of hopelessness, loss of self-esteem and violent

High	Low
Opportunities --- Constraints	
Stress on individual responsibility	Stress on social structure

Figure 5.1   Continuum of health explanations

outbursts of temper. In a few cases, health improved during unemployment. This may be related to work-related stress or poor working conditions during employment. The effects of unemployment can be felt by all members of the family. Children in families where the father had been out of work for a long time experienced more health and behavioural problems. Furthermore, there is some evidence that children in households where both parents are unemployed are more likely to be unemployed themselves and to suffer early heart disease (Vågerö and Leon 1994).

A number of studies have identified a relationship between suicide or parasuicide (non-fatal deliberate self harm, i.e. attempted suicide) and unemployment. Data from the OPCS longitudinal study indicate a two- to threefold increase in suicide among the unemployed in England and Wales (Moser *et al.* 1988). An investigation into hospital admissions for parasuicide in Edinburgh between 1968 and 1982 established strong links with unemployment. Only in one year during the study period did the relative risk of attempted suicide for the unemployed fall below a level of tenfold that of the employed. The risk of parasuicide was also higher for men with long terms of unemployment (Platt and Kreitman 1984). Not only does suicide or parasuicide increase with unemployment, it also follows the geographical pattern of unemployment, with higher rates in areas that experience high rates of long-term unemployment.

Cultural and behavioural explanations

The Black Report stresses individual behaviour when cultural and behavioural explanations are considered. It argues that 'such explanations, when applied to, often focus on the individual as a unit of analysis, emphasising unthinking, reckless or irresponsible behaviour or incautious lifestyle' as the main determiner of poor health (Townsend and Davidson 1982, 1992: 110). The interaction between material and structural factors and cultural and behavioural factors is complex and in the Black Report there is a clear emphasis on the former. Cultural and behavioural explanations can be situated along a continuum Figure 5.1. At one end of the continuum, individualistic explanations of health suggest that unhealthy behaviours and their associated outcome such as smoking, high-fat diets and low levels of exercise are a matter of personal choice. In other words, individuals are able to choose a healthy or unhealthy lifestyle so that consequent poor health is the responsibility of individuals. At the other end of the continuum, individual health behaviours are shaped by their social and material circumstances. In other words, people may have little choice in the lifestyle and health behaviours they adopt and they should not be held responsible for consequent poor health. As we saw earlier (Chapter 2), unhealthy choices such as smoking do not have a simple relationship with cost that would suggest price increases would be followed by a lower consumption (i.e. a healthy choice) by those with few material resources. Explanations situated at the initial left side of the continuum were favoured by the state at the time the Black Report was published. The introduction to *Inequalities in Health* (1992) quotes the then Health Minister who identifies government policy with the left side of the continuum:

> I honestly don't think the problem has anything to do with poverty. My family grew up in Liverpool and they didn't have two beans, but as a result of good food, good family and good rest, they grew up fit and well. The problem very often is, I think, just ignorance.
> (Quoted in Townsend and Davidson 1982, 1992: 12)

The interpretation of cultural and behavioural explanations of health behaviour contained in the Black Report should therefore be seen in the context of the hostile reception the report and later revisions received from official bodies that wanted to reject or minimize the role of materialist and structural explanations of health (Bury 1997; Vågerö and Illsley 1995). The cultural and behavioural aspects of health behaviour were considered in Chapter 2.

Social divisions

'Race' and inequalities in health

There are relatively few substantial empirical studies that examine the health status of ethnic minority populations as opposed to social classes (Coleman and Salt 1996; Modood *et al.* 1997). For example, reports from the *Health and Lifestyle Survey* which was based on a study of 9000 adults provided an analysis based on 'race' (Blaxter 1990). Many empirical studies restrict their analysis to 'racial' groups born abroad in order to deal with the problems of definition noted earlier (Balarajan and Bulusu 1990). Others have used self-classification (e.g. the census) or used a classification arrived at by an interviewer. Less is known about patterns of morbidity than mortality, although some studies suggest that incidents of self-reported health are worse for South Asian and Caribbean populations (Balarajan *et al.* 1991). However, such data may hide significant differences within such broad categories as 'South Asian' (Modood *et al.* 1997). Thorogood's (1990) research into the health beliefs and practices of the Caribbean community in Britain suggested that women adopt a multifaceted approach to health that incorporates Western and non-Western medicine (Nettleton 1993). As we saw earlier (see Chapter 2), this makes the quantification of self-reports difficult and may help to account for difference between populations.

The perinatal mortality rates in England and Wales are higher among births to immigrant mothers than among babies of UK born mothers (Balarajan and Botting 1989). Although there has been a decline in infant mortality rates in all ethnic groups since such data was collected, differentials remain. For example, the infant mortality rate for those of Pakistan and Caribbean origin are nearly twice that of the UK as a whole. Between 1982 and 1985, the average post-neonatal mortality rate for mothers born in the UK was 4.1 deaths per 1000 live births. The rate for babies of mothers who were born in Pakistan was the highest at 6.4, but babies born to mothers from India and Bangladesh experienced below average risks at 3.9 and 2.8. This points to a wide variation of health and mortality within the 'black' population with some groups such as Bangladeshis tending to experience worse general health than others (Andrews and Jewson 1993).

The *Immigrant Mortality* study provides a picture of mortality rates of immigrants over twenty years of age, occurring between 1970 and 1978 (Marmot *et al.* 1984). This showed that general mortality rates were higher in comparison with the UK average. However, lower mortality rates were noted for some conditions such as obstructive lung disease and liver cancer. Between 1970–2 and 1979–83, mortality from ischaemic heart disease declined by 5 per cent in men and 1 per cent in women in England and Wales. Over the same period, mortality increased for those born on the Indian subcontinent by 6 per cent in men and 13 per cent in women (Balarajan and Raleigh 1993). People born in the Caribbean have lower rates of coronary heart disease than the general population (Nazroo 1997). The social class gradient in adult mortality, from low mortality in high social class groups to high mortality in the lower social classes, was replicated in the case of immigrants from Ireland. While there was a downward gradient from class I to class III among Indians, this trend did not follow through to the manual working-class categories. For immigrants from the Caribbean, the highest mortality rate was recorded in social class I. Figure 5.2 shows the association between reported health and social class in the recent Policy Studies Institute survey (Modood *et al.* 1997). It indicates a clear relationship with poor health and social class with a more marked difference between manual and non-manual households for ethnic minority respondents (Nazroo 1997).

The links between health status and wider social, economic and environmental factors are indicated by the comparatively higher rate of mortality due to violence and accidents experienced by immigrants. This highlights the problem of differentiating 'racial' differences that may shape health and

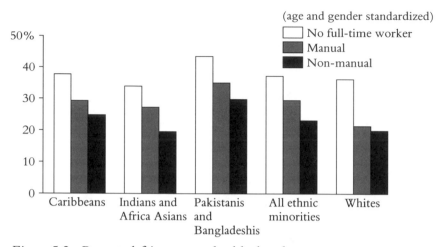

Figure 5.2 Reported fair or poor health, by class
Source: Policy Studies Institute Survey (Modood *et al.* 1997)

other factors such as housing, environment and education. For example, Polednak (1990) reports that age-specific mortality rates are high for men from ethnic minorities compared to white men but when account is taken of educational level the age specific mortality rate for men from ethnic minorities was lower. Therefore, there are complex interactions and relationships between 'racial' status and health (Modood *et al.* 1997). Data about the relationships between 'race' and health have 'a remarkable pattern of diversity and change' and represent 'a challenge to many orthodox explanations for inequalities' (Andrews and Jewson 1993: 142).

Differences in health based on 'race' did not form a significant part of the Black Report although Whitehead's (1992) review pays more attention to 'race'. This reflects the problems with large-scale data on 'race' and health as well as the general emphasis on materialist and structural dimensions of inequalities. As we have seen, there is a problem in relating 'race' with social class. More generally, it may be that observed health differences arise through the experience of deprivation. Blackburn (1991: 37) makes this point when she notes that 'Black people share the disadvantages of white working-class people and more'. Evidence for the 'and more' can be found, for example, in the twice as high unemployment rate experienced by ethnic minorities in 1994 (Sly 1995). Furthermore, people from the ethnic minorities are more likely than whites to be employed in low paid and insecure jobs (Oppenheim and Harker 1997; Modood 1997). In the Black Report, divisions in health related to 'race' therefore tended to be marginalized into the wider concern for material and structural explanations. In recognition of the lack of knowledge about 'race' and health, Ahmad (1993: 31) has called for research that concentrates on 'black people's perceptions and perspectives on health'.

Table 5.7   Life expectancy (years) in Great Britain at birth, by gender

Gender	1901	1931	1961	1991	1996	2001
Men	45.5	57.7	67.8	73.2	74.4	75.4
Women	49.0	61.6	73.6	78.7	79.7	80.6

Source: Adapted from *Social Trends 26*, 1996, table 7.3: 130.

Gender inequalities in health

The Black Report and other research on social divisions in health when referring to 'gender and health' tend to mean 'women'. Their perceptions and experiences of illness are defined as a problem compared to the 'good' health of men. This is significant because women are seen to suffer 'poor' health in relation to the 'good' health of men. Men's poor health, in general, remains relatively neglected and the debate about gender differences remains largely embedded in biological assumptions about sexual difference and related social and psychological differences.

The average life expectancy of a woman born in 1996 has been estimated at 80 years compared to 75 for men. From Table 5.7 it can be seen that there has been a significant increase in life expectancy for men and women but that women have a consistently higher life expectancy than men. This gender gap in life expectancy is common to all Western industrial countries. A small amount of this gap is accounted for by sex-based physiological differences. Women may be protected to some degree from ischaemic heart disease through female sex hormones while men are at risk from conditions directly related to the X-linked recessive mutations. However, the differences in mortality are generally attributed to differences in health behaviours and lifestyles (e.g. Townsend and Davidson 1982, 1992; Blaxter 1990).

In aggregate, while women live longer than men they experience more acute and chronic sickness. Women, for example have a higher rate of rheumatoid arthritis and mental illness than men. An analysis of the *Health and Illness Survey* data and the *West of Scotland-07 Survey* data found that for specific chronic conditions women reported a greater incidence of illness in six out of seventeen conditions identified in the surveys (Macintyre *et al.* 1996). Women had a greater incidence of high blood pressure, varicose veins, depression or nerves, migraine, piles or haemorrhoids. However, the picture becomes difficult to evaluate as age increases due to the lower numbers represented in the data, the earlier mortality among men and the representation of symptoms from survivors of earlier interventions to address conditions such as heart disease. Later life for a significant number of women may be characterized by poverty, disease and depression. In other words, longer life may not mean better quality of life and should be seen in the context of the higher risk of poverty experienced by women (Glendinning and Millar 1992).

It has been suggested that, although women report more symptoms and make greater use of the health services, they may not actually suffer more ill health than men. Information about morbidity produced from self-reported symptoms in health surveys and records of GP consultations and hospital visits may reflect the difference between how men and women perceive and respond to symptoms. It is argued that men are more likely than women to ignore symptoms or be less likely to seek medical advice (Blaxter 1990). In addition, it is argued that men may be more reluctant to disclose details of any illnesses in a health survey interview. Consequently, there may be underreporting and underrecording of illness in the male population that makes it appear that men experience better health. However, a review of research has argued that there is only limited evidence for a significant gender difference in the interpretation of symptoms (Verbrugge 1989a). Women consult their GPs more often than men do, but as Graham (1993a) notes, this can be partly accounted for by the fact that it is usually mothers who take their sick children to the doctor. Menstruation, contraception, pregnancy, childbirth and the menopause are subject to increasing medical interventions which demand that women engage with the healthcare system. Such factors do not fully account for the excess of women's minor health problems (Popay *et al.* 1993) and point to the importance of social factors in shaping the perceptions and behaviours of both women and men.

Post-war psychological theories advocated by Bowlby (1953) and Winnicott (1957) stressed the significance of secure attachments for children and argued that inadequate parent–child bonding could lead to delinquency. It was assumed that mothers would 'naturally' gain fulfilment through mothering and that women who failed to meet the expectations of the role or rejected it were pathological. This view of gender roles was deconstructed by feminist research in the 1970s which revealed the negative aspects of the 'natural' home-centred role of wife and mother. For example, Oakley (1974) and Bernard (1972) argued that the role of housewife had low status, involved monotonous work, served to socially isolate women and can have adverse consequences for their physical health and mental well-being. This may account for the higher levels of chronic sickness and poorer health in general that women who are full-time housewives experience compared to women who work in some capacity outside the home. Brown and Harris (1978) in a study of clinical depression in women identified the lack of employment outside the home as one of four factors responsible for the greater susceptibility to depression of working-class women compared with middle-class women. Research in the United States suggests that employment does have a positive effect on the health status of women (Nathanson 1975).

The *General Household Survey* has been used to circumvent the problems that arise in measuring the social class of women (e.g. Arber 1990; Arber and Ginn 1993). This analysis found that full-time employment had a detrimental effect on health for women who were under 40 years of age, had children and were engaged in lower non-manual and manual occupations. Little adverse effect was noted among women, over 40 years of age, without children and in similar types of employment. Fulfilling the multiple roles of housewife, mother and employee can place a physical and mental strain on women and increase the risk of ill health. However, for some women, role accumulation has its advantages. For example, women employed in professional and managerial occupations not only obtain the social and psychological rewards associated with these jobs, but also have the financial resources which enable them to spread the burden of childcare and housework. In other words,

> . . . the adverse consequences of occupying the roles of mother, housewife, and full-time worker are less for women in more 'privileged' structural positions. Indeed there may be positive benefits of role accumulation for these women. For other women freedom to work may be a dubious freedom if it means that they have little time to do anything except paid work, unpaid domestic tasks, and routine childcare.
>
> (Arber 1990: 91)

Women's employment patterns have changed considerably since the publication of the Black Report. In the 1990s, in the majority of families with children, both parents are employed although in two-thirds of married couples only the father works full time (Burghes et al. 1997). Paid work is therefore likely to have an increasing impact on patterns of female morbidity although because of the gendered nature of employment divisions, Arber (1990) argues that one of the problems with many of the studies dealing with the impact of role accumulation on women's health is that they have failed to give sufficient consideration to the material circumstances within which the roles are located. Not all work outside the home provides women with an escape route from the dull routine and monotony of housework. This is particularly the case for women who are already in a disadvantageous structural position. Economic necessity may force them into accepting work which is unskilled, tedious and offers no opportunity for personal development. The major difference between this kind of employment and housework is that it constitutes paid, as opposed to unpaid, labour. However, the level of pay is unlikely to be sufficient to enable them to buy the support services necessary to help them to fulfil their domestic roles. The same roles can have different consequences depending on the social and economic circumstances of women's lives. For example, fulfilling parental, marital and employment roles will not be the same experience for a mother working part time, with an unemployed husband and living in shared accommodation, as it is for a part-time professional worker with children, married to a business executive and living in a large house in a residential suburban district. Therefore, occupational class alone is of limited explanatory value in understanding differences in women's health. In order to understand women's health status it is necessary to appreciate the combined influence of occupational class, parental roles, marital roles and employment status.

Conclusion

This chapter has examined some of the main dimensions of the unequal and systematic distribution of 'good' and 'bad' health. This distribution is related to variables that include social class, 'race' and gender. People respond to their structural, material and cultural circumstances in subtle and complex ways that produce patterns of mortality and morbidity that have to be interpreted with care. In particular, the tension between material explanations of mortality and morbidity patterns and explanations based on individual behaviours or lifestyles remains an important focus for debate. However, the weight of evidence points to a significant link between such stark indicators as mortality patterns and material deprivation (e.g. Phillimore *et al.* 1994). The concentration of deprivation in particular localities not only restricts the opportunities of those who live there but places considerable strain on local health services (Johnson *et al.* 1997). The creating of 'health action zones' reflects government recognition of the manifest problems of inner urban areas. The fallout from the Black Report hangs over the ongoing debate about the nature and extent of health inequalities as well as the policy debate about the role of the state in shaping such inequalities.

Gender and health

Introduction

The US psychoanalyst Robert Stroller made a distinction between sex and gender in his book *Sex and Gender* (1968). This duality was popularized in Britain by Ann Oakley in her book *Sex, Gender and Society* (1985, first published 1972) and it has been widely accepted within social science since. Introductory sociology texts such as Giddens' *Sociology* (1997), O'Donnell's *A New Introduction to Sociology* (1992), Lee and Newby's *The Problem of Sociology* (1992) and Haralanbos and Holborn's *Sociology: Themes and Perspectives* (1991) all make use of the distinction. It is based on a theory of natural difference that is rooted in biological differences between men and women. Oakley (1985) states:

> 'Sex' is a word that refers to the biological differences between male and female: the visible difference in genitalia, the related difference in procreative function. 'Gender', however is a matter of culture: it refers to the social classification into 'masculine' and 'feminine'.
>
> (Oakley 1985: 16)

This conceptualization of gender provides the space to examine gender as a dynamic cultural product. Oakley (1985) used this to explore the social roles of women and how they were socialized into them. Subject to socialization, 'gender' can be deconstructed and reformed around new cultural, political or social ideals. However, adherence to this distinction gives 'sex' up to the scientific and medical world where it apparently remains fixed unproblematically in the biology of the body. The links between femininity or masculinity and the female or male body are less certain than traditional biological distinctions claim. Connell (1987) makes the interesting assertion that the enormous effort that is made to sustain gender differences indicates the fragility of the biological basis of sex difference. He points to the way gender is reproduced through the provision of different colour baby clothes for girls and boys and expectations that male babies will be 'strong' and girls 'weak'. This initial gender differentiation is entirely social, as the babies involved have no conception of gender difference and their performance of activities that range from feeding to urination can be dealt with identically. This analysis draws attention to the unequal social categories of men and women which are generated from social expectations about biological difference. Generalities such as 'all men are stronger than women' hide the diversity of physical forms which mean that some women are stronger than some men. Research on homosexual and transsexual identities show the way the biology of the body interacts with identity so that the boundaries between gender and sex are broken down (Plummer 1995). As Turner (1996: 60) argues, '"gender" is a social construct which mediates another social construct of "biology"'.

The growing interest in the 'body' since the mid-1980s reflects increasing consumerism and the emphasis on individual responsibility for health. Turner (1992) suggests that contemporary society is what he calls a 'somatic society' in which the body is a central focus of individual, cultural and political concern. Feminist critiques of medical practice and professions as well as new social movements that have developed around fertility, contraception, AIDS and other issues, are seen as indicators of the centrality of the body. Individuals express and shape their sense of identity through their bodies. It has replaced the traditional existential certainties of religion as the key factor in the negotiation of self-identity (Shilling 1991; Turner 1992).

Health expressed through the body can be conceptualized as a 'positional good' (Leiss 1983). Positional goods help to establish and maintain an individual's position in the social hierarchy and thus can be seen as part of the 'habitus' of particular social groups (Bourdieu 1984; Elias 1978, 1939). 'Habitus' broadly refers to embodied dispositions that shape how people, or more generally generations and cultures, perceive and understand the world around them. Habitus may be precognitive but it is expressed by 'techniques of the body' which include walking, accent, handshakes, kissing and so on (Mauss 1979). Turner (1992) illustrates this process with Elias's (1991) example of how babies have an innate ability to smile and how adults tend to respond to a smile. While growing up, people learn the complexities of smiling and become able to distinguish between, for example, a leer and a smile. Bourdieu (1984), developing the ideas of Elias (1978, 1939), argues that the body is the 'most indisputable materialization of class taste' which is manifest in people's attachment to particular types of food, exercise, work, sport, art and so on. As Shilling (1991, 1993) and Mellor and Shilling (1997) have shown, bodies can take the form of physical capital. Based on the work of Bourdieu and Elias, Shilling argues that people who occupy different social positions perceive and use this physical capital differently. The functional orientation to health that is prominent in working-class accounts of health (see Chapter 2) treats the body as a 'means to an end' such as domestic labour or paid employment. They may also try and convert their physical capital into other forms of capital by using their bodies in, for example, sports. This reflects the tradition of working-class boys becoming boxers, footballers or more recently bodybuilders in the hope of acquiring economic and social capital. The use of steroids by male bodybuilders in order to create a massive, muscled body which may not only undermine the sexual capacity of the body but present a serious threat to health (Klein 1995), indicates the potential hazards of such 'body projects' (Shilling 1993). The experience of a fictional bodybuilder in Fussell's (1991) novel *Muscle* graphically illustrates the tension between appearance and the functioning of the male body that has been reconstructed through considerable effort:

> Thanks to the drugs and my diet, I couldn't run 20 yards without pulling up gasping for air. My ass cheeks ached from innumerable steroid injections, my stomach whined for sustenance, my whole body throbbed from gym activities and enforced weight loss. Thanks to my competitive tan, my skin was breaking out everywhere. Vinnie and Nimrod explained that all this was perfectly normal . . . 'Big Man, this is about *looking* good, not feeling good'.
>
> (Fussell 1991: 193; original emphasis)

Body projects represent one of the few areas of control people have in an uncertain and diverse society. 'If one feels unable to exert control over an increasingly complex society, at least one can have some effect on the size, shape and appearance of one's body' (Shilling 1993: 7). The more complex explanations of health offered by the middle class include a perception of the body as 'an end in itself'. As Shilling argues, they know that the body's 'appearance, size, shape and even its contents, are potentially open to reconstruction in line with the designs of its owner' (p. 5). Middle-class participation in sport is primarily for the enjoyment and sensation they derive from it. They may also be using their bodies to send out messages about their self-identity and aspirations by, for example, both the activities they engage in (e.g. golf, squash, etc.) and the 'designer' equipment they utilize. There is therefore a direct association between bodies and the consumer culture.

Modern medicine has provided an increasing number of techniques that can be used in body projects. These range from surgical interventions to reshape the body (e.g. breast enlargement or penal 'enhancements') and infertility treatments (e.g. IVF and GIFT) to pharmaceutical interventions (e.g. steroids, psychotropic drugs). There is clearly a direct link between the body and consumer culture. For example, a study of middle-class consumption patterns found that higher income groups were the largest consumers of health and body care products (Savage *et al.* 1992). The diversity of consumer culture with its ephemeral fashions, emphasis on style, leisure centres with multiscreen cinemas and night clubs, out-of-town shopping and consumer programmes have been seen as a reflection of postmodern society (Turner 1992). The cultivation of the thin and 'beautiful' body has become a significant body project which may impose considerable degrees of surveillance and discipline on the body. This 'consumer body' represents a massive market for 'health food' (e.g. 'low fat' margarine, skimmed milk, etc.) and diets of various kinds. At one extreme, this can lead to mental ill-health problems and death through eating disorders.

The family and health

It is often forgotten that the majority of health work is undertaken in the private sphere of home and family. This is because it is unpaid and largely undertaken by women as part of their 'natural' role (Stacey 1988). Graham (1985) notes that the caring role of women in the family places them at the 'interface between the family and the state' and frequently makes them the 'go-between linking the informal health care system with the formal'. This has been central to the rationale adopted by many researchers for focusing on women as the subjects of their research and partly accounts for the relative lack of similar research on men (Calnan and Johnson 1985; Mullen 1993). For both men and women, health is often experienced, negotiated and expressed through their roles as members of a family (Brannen *et al.* 1994). Although there are now more 'single-person households' than ever before, most single people will have parents, relatives and sometimes non-resident partners and children.

'Fatherhood' is as O'Brien (1991) argues, 'abstract and involuntary' and is given meaning by its social context. Indeed, some men can be unknowing biological fathers so that they are never aware of their fatherhood. In her feminist analysis, O'Brien argues that childbirth and reproduction give women a knowledge of the natural world that men cannot appreciate. As Hearn (1987) suggests, men have access only to the abstract idea of being a parent before the birth of their child. In a sense they are alienated from their children and the experience of birth. The attempt to overcome this alienation, O'Brien argues, is manifest in the dominant position traditionally given to fatherhood within marriage. In the private sphere of the home and in the public sphere, men seek to exert control over women and children. By confining women to the private sphere and dominating the public sphere men attempted to recapture something which they felt they had been denied by biology. Writing in the 1920s, Bertrand Russell (1929) asserted that the 'non-existence' of fathers 'might be a positive advantage to children'. The powerful but absent family patriarch depicted by Russell is an enduring image of fathers that many influential nineteenth and early twentieth century men sought to perpetuate. As O'Brien (1991) suggests, fathers' relationship with their children was characterized by oppression and the desire to control. Father–son relationships were a particular source of anxiety and conflict, while daughters were assumed to be the proper business of mothers. Ironically, by the early twentieth century the most popular ideas about father–son relationships were articulated by men who never married or married very late. Baden-Powell summed up this approach when he explained that 'manliness can only be taught by men, and not by those half men, half old women' (cited in Tosh 1991). However, such images of fatherhood are biased towards those who have left work relating to their experiences in diaries or other accessible forms. Trudy King's book *Feeding and Infant Care* was first published in 1913 and remained influential for several decades. Its emphasis on the need for regularity in mothering tasks was reinforced in the 1920s by popularizing the work of scientific behaviourists which restated the need for the routine management of children. These theories held that emotional parenting was detrimental to children's development so that proper mothering should be mechanical and task-led. In contrast, the New Psychology movement that gathered momentum in the wake of dealing with the traumas caused by the First World War emphasized the importance of emotions and reciprocity in mother–child relationships. This prepared the ground for the popular success of Bowlby's *Child Care and the Growth of Love* which was first published in 1953. Most of the childcare manuals and professional literature of this period were concerned with young children and took for granted the distant patriarch model of fatherhood. By the 1950s, the combined influence of the behaviourist and the popular psychologists had produced an almost complete consensus about the mother's duty as the main if not sole provider of care for children.

The influence of Parsonian sex-role theory and Bowlby (1953) and Winnicott (1957, 1971) as advocates of Freud's notion of pre-Oedipal relations is evident. For Parsons, the father had an unambiguous role in transmitting the gendered division of labour that underpinned the stability of the modern state. Bowlby's work stressed the significance of secure attachments for children and argued that inadequate parent–child bonding could lead to delinquency. It was assumed that mothers would 'naturally' gain fulfilment through mothering and that women who failed to meet the expectations of the role or rejected it were pathological. There is an irony here in that unmarried and, in particular, young unmarried mothers were encouraged to give up their babies to adoption. Biology in such cases was not a determinant of motherhood and stigmatized natural mothers displayed their 'pathological' tendencies by deviating from norms about the proper context for motherhood. Medical and social work professions reinforced the norms of good mothering to the extent that some single mothers were categorized as insane (Spensky 1992). This emphasis on pathology stems from the research on 'unwanted' infants and deviant children that formed the basis for the theories of such influential figures as Trudy King, Watson and Bowlby. The emphasis on the first few years of life as formative to later development reinforced the focus on mothers rather than fathers. Consistent with the previous expectations about fathering, it was accepted that a father would treat boys and girls differently by 'encouraging instrumental behaviour in his son and expressive behaviour in his daughter' (Biller 1971). Thus, part of becoming a 'man' was learning to become detached from pain and bodily sensation (Morgan 1992). The father–son relationship remained central to the development of male (heterosexual) identity and healthy adults. Articulated through the 'maternal deprivation' thesis, fathers were present as breadwinners and providers of moral support to mothers in caring for children. The cultural norm that gradually weakened over the decades was that 'a child whose father performs the mothering functions both tangibly and emotionally while the mother is preoccupied with her career can easily gain a distorted image of masculinity and femininity' (Bell and Vogel 1968: 586).

Smart (1997: 54) has identified the 1970s as a 'discursive high point in the history of motherhood' and a time when 'motherhood stood on the threshold of independence [from the governance of men and marriage] and in sight of a proper means of economic support'. Caring for children was thus no longer presented as a woman's inevitable moral duty or sacrifice. Women could – and do – choose various options in caring for children as was evident by the growth in single mothers. More recently, the rise in the number of never-married mothers has led to further claims that a 'new type' of mother has emerged, who does regard the partnership of a man as unnecessary (Beck and Beck-Gernsheim 1995). Significantly, there were a number of attempts by men to reassert their power as fathers. The debate surrounding illegitimacy in the late 1970s reflects this in that the Law Commission initially called for an extension of the rights of unmarried fathers that would give biological fathers automatic parental rights. Thus interest in fatherhood increased in response to feminism, social change and as part of the redefinition of masculinity (Morgan 1985; Brittan 1989). Over the decade about 10 per cent of all lone parents have been men. It is tempting but erroneous to assume that lone fathers are men who 'mother' (Hipgrove 1982). Lone fathers have significantly different demographic characteristics from lone mothers and their social and economic position is defined primarily by their gender. The majority care for school-age children and unlike lone mothers, most are employed full time. This highlights the significance of the labour market which works to the advantage of fathers as workers but largely to their disadvantage as parents (see Hardey and Crow 1991). It also points to the way employment and economic circumstances are related to men's opportunities to act as parents. The increase in step-parenthood has drawn attention to the problems associated with forming and maintaining relationships with stepchildren. While stepfathers' legal position has been clarified as families become more complex throughout the rise in cohabitation and remarriage, the boundaries around fatherhood have become more complex. Pragmatic reasons such as distance and new relationships are often seen as factors that lead to non-resident fathers losing contact with children. However, more non-resident fathers claim they remain in contact with their children than is apparent in the degree of contact reported by lone mothers (Burghes *et al.* 1997). This points to the emotional problems that confront non-resident fathers and the value they place on the appearance of contact with their children.

In Britain, Mount (1982), Scruton (1986) and others attempted to ensure the place of 'the family' (in traditional form) at the centre of state policy by asserting that it was the fundamental source of social stability. It was argued that increases in youth crime and 'lax' moral values were linked to the decline of a natural and universal form of family (Mount 1982). This is clearly not new in that it effectively reasserts Bowlby's thesis but the focus is on the father rather than the mother. It follows that fathers have a vital social role and a duty to be involved in the raising of children, thus rejecting the distant patriarchal model of fatherhood. Furthermore, fatherhood conducted from within the family was seen as 'an indispensable civilising force' (Murray 1984) for young men who were failing to act as breadwinners or responsible citizens. In the United States, the growth in lone-mother households and the apparent displacement of men from these families was seen as producing a threatening and crime-ridden underclass. Originally associated with urban black populations, the underclass model is widely influential and has been used to highlight the dangers of 'families without fatherhood' (Dennis and Erdos 1992) or of a 'fatherless society' (Blankenhorn 1995). Translated into popular culture, the label 'deadbeat dads' or in practice settings 'errant fathers' indicates a general shift from a focus on fathers' rights to their responsibilities. Economic and social changes that involve the loss of many traditionally male-dominated industries and the increased participation of women in the workforce lies behind this approach to fathers as a social problem. In particular, it was the widening gap between the poor families and the increased affluence of the majority that lent weight to ideas such as the underclass thesis. Finch (1989) argues that British social policy has been shaped by assumptions based on a 'gendered, modified extended family' model in which mothers and fathers 'normally' take on appropriate responsibilities towards their children.

In the majority of families with children, both parents are employed, although in two-thirds of married couples only the father works full time (Central Statistical Office 1995). Furthermore, as working and 'unsocial' hours increase, the opportunities for fathers in particular to participate in domestic work and interact with children become limited (Burghes *et al.* 1997).The *British Social Attitudes Survey* indicates that women still inevitably take responsibility for the mundane tasks such as washing and cooking (*Social Trends* 1996, table 12.1: 216). Such domestic tasks have a significance beyond the actual labour involved because the 'very ideas of "the housewife" and "the husband" are fusions of emotional relations, power and the divisions of labour' (Connell 1987: 125). It has been suggested that while more engaged in parenting than previously recognized, fathers' involvement is biased towards the less routine and pleasant tasks such as playing with children (Lewis 1986; Burghes *et al.* 1997). This gives some credence to Jackson's (1990) conclusion about the emotional engagement fathers have with children and the value they place on children in terms of defining their own sense of self (McKee and O'Brien 1982). It may also help account for the way that mothers generally take responsibility to seek medical help for children's symptoms. What is less clear is the degree to which fathers are involved in the lay referral system. However, the distribution of household tasks and resources is a highly complex and dynamic process that is strongly shaped by employment patterns and social class (Pahl 1990). Oakley's (1974) study of housework, for example, associated it with isolation and stress and it would be a mistake to assume that domesticity is any less open to such stresses for men. Furthermore, the increasing recognition of physical and sexual abuse represents the dark side of masculinity (*Feminist Review* 1988). A number of tragic and well-publicized cases of child abuse resulted in something of a panic over father–child relationships. Changes in public policy, especially in areas of employment that involve children, have reinforced the idea that men who work, for example in nurseries or primary schools, are breaking normative gender divisions and have questionable constructions of masculinity. All fathers are now aware that sexual interpretations can be placed on their interactions with children and many fathers remain concerned that public expressions of affection will be misinterpreted.

In the United States and later in Britain, work on masculinity and identity sought to explore men's experience of fatherhood and relate it to their experience and identity as 'men' (Brittan 1989; Connell 1987; Connell 1996). This work conceived of fatherhood as a part of male identity that can embrace a caring enjoyable and emotional involvement with children and women. A number of autobiographical accounts of becoming fathers have explored this emotional experience of fatherhood and laid claim to the 'new nurturing' father (e.g. Jackson 1990). Giddens (1992) argues that in post-industrial or 'high modern' societies, personal and domestic relationships are characterized by emotions rather than considerations of material gains such as property or the potential social contacts gained by a GP in the ninteenth century by a 'good marriage' (see Chapter 5). This 'transformation of intimacy' (ibid.) means that people expect to gain personal satisfaction, self-knowledge and self-realization through the intimate relationships they engage in. However, the traditional emphasis on employment and increasing working hours constrains the space men have for developing successful relationships. A father, in Brannen *et al.* (1994) articulates, this dilemma in his relationship with his son who he said had 'everything':

> . . . possibly he hasn't had my love over the years . . . because I was never here to give it to him . . . you get what I mean . . . I don't think

we have ever been on holiday together . . . so basically he never got
nothing from me . . . which when you look back, you think . . . you
should have made some sort of effort to do it.

(Brannen *et al.* 1994: 48)

Fatherhood has been reconceptualized so that it symbolizes the 'successful' emotionally committed relationship. This goes some way to
account for men's desire in new relationships to have biological children
even when both they and their partners may already have children from
previous relationships (Corea 1985). The recognition of fatherhood can
be seen in the presence of fathers in the delivery room (Tew 1995). This
represents a reinterpretation of the bonding thesis that had emerged in
the midwifery and psychological literature. This suggested that fathers
would be more likely to form a close relationship with a child if they had
witnessed the birth. Associated with changes in midwifery practice, the
presence of fathers was instigated by mothers rather than called for by
fathers.

Women, men and marriage

In one of the few references to direct health in the 'founders' of sociology
as a discipline Durkheim (1951, 1897) in his study of suicide argued that
marriage improved the well-being of men. The trend towards cohabitation
makes it harder to evaluate the impact of marriage. Data on cohabitation
have only recently been available in Britain (Burghes *et al.* 1997) but analysis
suggests that, in cohabitation, the experience of health corresponds more
closely with that of married rather and single people (Foster *et al.* 1995;
Murphy *et al.* 1997). In most Western societies, mortality data indicate that
for almost all causes of death, married people are better off than single
people, who in turn experience better mortality rates than the divorced
(Macintyre 1992). Morbidity is difficult to assess; however, a general picture
emerges which suggests that married people experience better mental and
physical health and that this better health persists into old age (Umberson
1992; Wyke and Ford 1992). Factors which include social class, age at
marriage and health behaviours have been controlled for in various studies
which still report a health advantage for the married. The use of clinical
indicators such as blood pressure also produces a significantly lower report
for the married compared to the single (Macintyre 1992). Marriage also
appears to provide men with a greater improvement in health than their
partners (Zick and Smith 1991; Macintyre 1992). This is in accord with the
feminist literature which draws attention to marriage as an unequal relationship under which men gain more than women (e.g. Gove 1984; Morgan

1980). The explanations for these differences in health can be formed into three groups, namely, social selection, social protection and the negative consequences of being single.

Social selection explanations argue that unhealthy people are less likely to get married or stay married than the healthy. Chronic illness may affect the individual's opportunities to meet potential partners. Factors such as the stigma that may attach to some conditions and the poverty that accompanies persistent ill health may act as a barrier to the formation of relationships (Kiernan 1988). The increasing use of genetic tests may detect hidden problems that may also hinder the formation of relationships where a partner expects to have children. Such factors also have an impact on remarriage. Social protection explanations emphasize the social aspects of marriage. It is suggested that marriage provides an important level of emotional support and access to wide kin network (Macintyre 1992; Wyke and Ford 1992). Such networks can be important in maintaining health and help people to recover faster from episodes of illness (Bloom 1990). This echoes Durkheim's (1951, 1897) point about the way marriage integrates people into the social structure. Reflecting the expectation that women mediate families' health, there is some evidence that wives discourage unhealthy behaviours and lifestyles. In particular, the diet of the household is likely to be shaped by women and this has made them the primary target for health promotion (Bunton and Macdonald 1992). Graham (1984, 1996) has described how women ensure that children and partners get enough to eat sometimes at the cost of their own diet. Women with children may discourage partners from smoking (Marsh and Matheson 1983; Graham 1984). However, the dynamics of family life may also reinforce unhealthy behaviours (Mullen 1993). Furthermore, for men, in particular, their partners are likely to be their first recourse of lay referral and care (see Chapter 2). The increasing importance of women's employment suggests that the material aspect of marriage is significant. Two incomes in one household can not only increase housing opportunities but also reduce stress through the provision of holidays and paid childcare in households with children (Marsh and Matheson 1983; Zick and Smith 1991). Marriage also provides the partners with a well-defined and accepted social role. For women, it provides a venue to have children and men, as we have seen, are able to become fathers. In both cases, this confirms their identity and provides a sense of belonging in a 'world of couples' (Hardey and Crow 1991). Single people face a degree of social exclusion that increases with age and the acquisition of deviant statuses such as becoming a lone parent. Single people may also find it harder to abandon unhealthy behaviours such as smoking (Graham 1984) or adopt healthy dietary habits (Burgoyne and Clarke 1983). Single working-class men, for example, are more likely to adopt 'risky lifestyles' than married or middle-class men (Morgan 1980; Wyke and Ford 1992; Mullen 1993). The perception that marriage changes men's health behaviour is captured by one of Mullen's (1993) informants:

being married has altered my whole approach. I am not saying that if I had not got married I would have been an alcoholic kind of thing. I could have been an extremely unhealthy person.

(Mullen 1993, R682: 141)

An important and long-established negative consequence of being single relates to divorce and bereavement. Divorce has long been associated with psychological problems and ill health. The stress associated with the transition through divorce or bereavement has a negative effect on health which is compounded by the loss of support networks (Murphy *et al.* 1997). Factors related to 'loss' (Gerhardt 1989) may generally increase individual vulnerability to ill health. It is those who already have relatively fewer material resources (expressed in social class) and emotional resources (e.g. social networks) that are most susceptible to problems linked to loss. The gender advantage of marriage to men can be seen in the relatively higher mortality rate experienced by widowers compared to widows (Murphy *et al.* 1997) and men's greater vulnerability to depression following widowhood (Umberson *et al.* 1992).

The evidence suggests that men 'do better' than women in terms of health from marriage, regardless of differences in social class or 'race'. This suggests that marriage is 'bad' for women and it is the inequalities in emotional and physical domestic labour that is cited as a major cause (see Oakley 1974; Graham 1985). The emphasis on the mother's as opposed to the father's nutritive role and the increasing expectations of employment point to the multiple roles that confront women. Hochschild's (1989) observational study of married couples with children found that when both adults were working full time, only the wives do most of the domestic work. A number of these mothers believed that their partners should do more to help but were afraid of potential conflict if they pressed their case. The multiple roles women undertake within families can be a major source of stress, especially when they are coupled with a sense of relative powerlessness in the household. These gender inequalities may transcend social class because, even in more affluent households, women are generally responsible for home-making and caring. They can, however, 'buy their way out' of some of the dilemmas by, for example, employing domestic help that is frequently provided by women from low-income households. It is in these households where the stress and strains of marriage are most exposed and divorce is more likely (Burghes *et al.* 1997). Care has to be taken in any study of family dynamics that an overdeterministic analysis is not provided in the search for causal relationships. Furthermore, while cohabitation is now being taken into account, other 'married-like' relationships such as those in gay and lesbian households are underrepresented in the health literature. Connell (1987) indicates how complex family life is:

Far from being the basis of society, the family is one of its most complex products. There is nothing simple about it. The interior of the family is a scene of multi-layered relationships folded over on each other like geological strata. In no other institution are relationships so extended in time, so intensive in contact, so dense in their interweaving of economics, emotion, power and resistance.

(Connell 1987: 121)

This complexity, with its potential social and health implications, can be seen in the examination of eating disorders.

Concern about anorexia nervosa has increased over the past thirty years both in popular culture and the medical literature. It was not until the 1970s that diagnostic criteria for anorexia came into general use. The degree to which this represents a 'real' increase in the incidence of eating disorders is less clear (van't Hof and Nicolson 1996) but they have been regarded as 'paradigmatic illnesses' (Shilling 1993) that reflect post-industrial culture. A study of 16-year-olds' perception of different male and female body shapes revealed that a far narrower range of female body shapes than male shapes were regarded as attractive (Furnham and Radley 1989). This difference in sensitivity to body shape has been noted in a number of studies of post-industrial societies and is reflected in Turner's (1996) notion of the 'somatic society'. Associated with thinness and beauty, eating disorders mainly affect women and appear to peak between the ages of 14 and 18 years (Heavan 1996). Bulimics and anorectics perceive their bodies as being larger than they actually are and consequently attempt to lose weight. This is achieved by occasional unrestrained eating followed by purging (bulimia) or severely restricting the intake of food (anorexia). A number of feminists have shifted attention from the link to body image to the relative lack of power of women (e.g. Orbach 1988: Banks 1992). They argue that women's bodies are the only area over which they have full control, therefore deliberate starvation is a form of protest and call for freedom. This draws attention to tensions within the family as a significant element in eating disorders and some treatments involve family members as well as the patient (Heavan 1996). Food may be the focus for struggles over power in families and reflect wider social forces. A Muslim father of Middle East origin living in Britain illustrated this process when he spoke to a researcher about his daughter who did not believe in God and desired to follow a non-Muslim lifestyle.

I try to eat the evening meal with the household. My daughter doesn't comply. It's part of her attitude to food, her attitude to freedom. Generally she likes to please herself, eat what she likes. I've tried to persuade her eating isn't just eating, it's a social situation . . . Nasreen doesn't comply . . . In the weekend I apply a little pressure.

(Brannen et al. 1996: 152)

The 'new' problem of infertility

It is in the area of reproduction that some of the starker differences in gender are experienced. Until recently, parenthood has either been natural through fertilization and birth, or social through step parenthood or adoption. Surrogacy must now be added to the potential forms of motherhood (Stacey 1988). Interventions into fertility can be divided into four groups (Stanworth 1987). Firstly, there are fertility controls such as the condom, the contraceptive pill, intrauterine devices, the diaphragm and RU486 (the 'aftersex pill'). Despite clinical trials of the male contraceptive pill and the increased use of condoms since the health campaigns that developed out of AIDS, most of these interventions are targeted on women. The contraceptive pill gave rise to a 'contraceptive revolution' in the 1960s. Pharmaceutical companies made considerable profits from marketing 'the pill' and its use rapidly spread across the globe. Reliable contraception contributed much to the involvement of women in the public sphere, but as Doyal (1996) notes, it has still failed to reach many women in the developing world. Furthermore, the testing of new contraceptive technologies such as the injection-based Depo Provera in developing countries has been controversial (Newman 1985). Orally taken drugs such as RU486, which can prevent pregnancy after sex has taken place, have been attacked by some groups as amounting to a form of abortion. Secondly, there are those controls that manage labour such as episiotomies, caesarean sections and forceps (see Chapter 4). Thirdly, there are those techniques that involve screening such as ultrasound and amniocentesis (see Chapter 4). Fourthly, there are the increasing range of techniques that attempt to overcome infertility. In vitro fertilization (IVF) and gamete intrafallopian tube transfer (GIFT) have become available under the NHS as well as providing a growing business for the private sector. Although the site for these interventions is largely women's bodies, a number of studies have suggested that the low fertility of male partners can often be the main problem. Alternatives such as adoption may be acceptable to the woman but it is often the desire on the part of the man for his biological child that prompts recourse to the new treatments (Lasker and Borg 1989). This is significant in that the higher rates of divorce, remarriage and cohabitation create new families relatively late in life. In such instances, one or both partners may have children from previous relationships but the men in particular may want to confirm the relationship by 'their' biological child (Corea 1985).

While IVF techniques are the most recent and often the most dramatic intervention into fertility, self-insemination or artificial insemination by donor (AID) have been long established (Pfeffer 1987). These 'low-technology' methods do not require any medical intervention and may be undertaken at home without the involvement of the state. A number of self-help and feminist groups provided advice and promoted a political and ethical debate in the 1980s. The Warnock Report (1985) was the result of a wide-ranging enquiry that restated the centrality of the two-parent conventional family as the preferable situation for children to be raised. This reflected the concern that low-technology methods could be used by such 'deviant' families as single people, gays and lesbians. In practice, it proved impossible to bring such informal methods under the direct control of the medical profession or the state except in terms of the law. A number of legal cases that arose out of conflicts between people who had made fertility arrangements established male sperm donor's right to access to resulting children. This applies only where private arrangements have been made, not to the medically supervised donation of sperm through anonymous sperm banks. During the 1990s, the case of a woman who demanded access to sperm taken from her dead husband provoked further ethical and legal debate.

Both low and high technologies can marginalize the role of the father to that of supplier of genetic material. High technologies may reduce biological mothers to the status of 'mother machines' (Corea 1985). A survey of popular and medical texts found terms like 'egg mother', 'biomother' 'nurturant mother' and many others were used to describe the previously simple category of 'mother' (Treichler 1990). Oakley (1986) has drawn attention to the birth by caesarean section to brain dead women, how it has reduced the mother to the status of a biological environment. A discourse about 'test-tube babies', 'artificial wombs', gestation carriers' and 'ripe eggs' not only hides the wider impact of treatment on women but also depicts women's bodies as a set of parts that are available for medical surveillance and intervention (Steinberg 1990). The prospect of Aldous Huxley's 'brave new world' where babies are grown in bottles in a scientifically led society, can be glimpsed in academic and popular writing on the subject. The 'flight from nature' suggested by high technologies is misleading, as the experience of pregnancy and birth that results from high-technology interventions is the same as those resulting from 'natural' fertilization (Stanworth 1987). The eugenic potential of such interventions is evident in both the screening for 'defects' and the selection of people as donors of genetic material and subjects for treatment. In Britain, there is a tension between the principles of free blood donation and the more onerous procedure of egg donations (Stacey 1988; Foster 1995). The Royal College of Obstetricians and Gynaecologists (1983) suggested that women could be rejected for treatment on social grounds and that single women should not be treated. This sort of policy shows how interventions reinforce existing class, racial (as a disproportionate number of the ethnic minority population is located in the lower social classes) and gender inequalities (Wood 1997).

The NHS has given a low priority to infertility treatment which has led to strict criteria being developed for inclusion in the programmes. Foster (1995) cites one NHS programme which expected applicants to fulfil the same social criteria as couples who hope to adopt. This is likely to exclude single women and people in 'unconventional' relationships that are disadvantaged in current adoption procedures. There has been a significant growth in private sector treatment to fill the gap left by the lack of NHS provisions (Abel-Smith 1994). The high costs and uncertainty of infertility treatment (which is excluded from health insurance schemes) means that it is relatively inaccessible to the less well off (Pfeffer 1992). This commercialization of IVF and GIFT effectively provides a mechanism of social selection whereby only those able to pay are able to receive the treatment. The well-rehearsed debate about whether pregnancy should be conceptualized as an 'illness' (see Chapter 2) is relevant here in that it is argued that the NHS should not use resources to 'cure' women of infertility who are not 'ill'. Technological developments have not only extended the areas of medical intervention but defined 'infertility' as pathological:

> The way in which 'childlessness' is seen as physiological 'dysfunction' locates it firmly (and only) within the domain of medical science. It posits not only the state of 'childlessness' but those individuals who are childless (defined as 'infertile') as appropriately, even necessarily, medical territory.
>
> (Beagan 1989: 91)

The impact of a process of social selection can be seen in recent demographic figures. The number of twin, triplet and higher births increased during the 1980s as IVF treatment became available. Between 1975 and 1995, there was over 60 per cent increase in the number of multiple births to couples in the non-manual social classes, with a tenfold increase in the rate for women aged between 35 to 29 years (Wood 1997: tables 3 and 4). Such multiple births are also more common among couples from non-manual social classes living in the south-east of England where there are more private medical resources than in other parts of the country.

At a time when the age at birth of the first child is increasing and a significant number of women are having their first child in their late thirties (Wood 1997), the potential of 'curing' infertility appears to create new choices. However, as we have seen, these new choices are relatively constrained for many women. This in part accounts for the diversity of feminist responses to the new technologies, ranging from those who argue that they epitomise men's desire to control women's bodies (O'Brien 1991; Corea 1985) while others accept the techniques but are critical of the social processes whereby they are applied (e.g. Stanworth 1987; Doyal 1987).

Families and informal care

The family has always had a central place in social and health policy. This is nowhere more evident than in policies related to informal care, which as Finch and Groves (1983) have pointed out, are dependent on the unpaid care of women. They go on to conclude that 'in practice community care equals care by the family, and in practice care by families equals care by women' (p. 494). In the 1980s, policy shifted from 'care in the community' to 'care by the community' (see Chapter 5). At one level, the utilization of unpaid female labour appears economically effective from the perspective of the state. However, this does not take account of the opportunity costs of the potential earning power of women who become full-time carers. There is a tension here between recognizing the desirability of offering people the opportunity to be cared for by their relatives and the problem that this may lock a female relative into being a carer. The review *Community Care: Agenda for Action* (Department of Health 1988) recommended a shift to the individual and away from statutory provision, with an enhanced role for private and voluntary care. It also suggested that the state should adopt an 'enabling' role through the social services to take responsibility for this. Most of the recommendations were implemented under the Community Care Act 1990. Case management was introduced and gave those in need of care the right to individual care assessments. These could be undertaken by a combination of health and social workers. A market model of provision similar to the NHS was proposed with social services becoming purchasers rather than direct providers of care. However, the financial and organizational problems involved meant that the transition to the market model did not begin until 1993. While community care policies may assume the availability and willingness of largely female relatives to provide care, in practice there is considerable diversity in the extent of informal care (Finch and Mason 1993).

In households where a chronically sick person is cared for, the distribution of caring labour is unequal. Ungerson (1987) has suggested that 'unequal sharing' took place in the households in her study in that husbands tended to contribute little to caring tasks even when the elderly person is his parent. This supported the earlier findings of Nissel and Bonnerjea (1982) who concluded that 'not one woman said her husband or children helped with feeding, washing or washing clothes for the dependent relative'. Husbands' contributions tend to take the form of 'treats' or transport rather than the labour of personal care. Although most informal carers are women, husbands of chronically sick spouses make up a significant number of carers (Arber and Ginn 1991). However, there is evidence that the men become carers when they are the only possible providers of care (Thompson 1993). Furthermore, men who undertake caring work often get more help from friends and family than women do (Allen 1994) and are more likely than female carers to gain help from support agencies (Harding 1996). While the provision of respite care and other support services through voluntary agencies have improved since the 1980s, it remains difficult to identify and define need (Harding 1996). Indeed, it is possible that the 'state withdraws once family resources have been mobilised or are seen to be on hand' (Parker 1981: 23). Unlike services for children, the recognition and detection of incidents of abuse or the neglect of elderly people remains underdeveloped. The association of poverty with chronic illness and disability exacerbates the experience of social and economic deprivation. The inequalities in health experienced earlier in life are carried forward into old age. An analysis of *General Household Survey* data on women in their late sixties found that the incidence of moderate or greater disability was about two-thirds as high among women classified as unskilled than those from higher occupational groups (Arber and Ginn 1991).

Gender and mental health

It is in mental health that biomedicine recognizes the fragility of its relationship to science and the uncertainty of diagnosis and treatment. Since the nineteenth century, there has been an increasing rise in the number of women diagnosed as mentally ill, but this may reflect the generation of new categories of mental illness rather than any absolute rise in poor mental health in the population (Busfield 1989; Pilgrim and Rogers 1993). The new categories of ill health that can cause mental health problems include postnatal depression, anorexia and premenstrual tension. These and many other conditions have replaced the previous broad category of 'hysteria' (Ussher 1991). 'Hysteria', premenstrual tension, menopausal depression and other conditions 'have "real" symptoms, but at the same time are ideological constructions which signify the social, rather than the biological vulnerability of women' (Turner 1996: 193). The higher incidence of mental health problems reported for women is a reliable and clear indication of a gender gap in health (Macintyre *et al.* 1996). Women are overrepresented among those diagnosed as suffering from neurosis, affective psychoses and vague mental disorders (Verbrugge 1984). Examinations of psychiatric texts have detected a gender bias that makes it more likely that women will be diagnosed as suffering from psychological problems (Busfield 1982). As Foster (1995) points out in her exploration of textbooks, the boundaries around psychiatric diagnostic categories are often blurred and uncertain. The gender bias at the theoretical and training level is a more plausible explanation of bias in diagnosis than the argument that it can be accounted for by the male domination of the psychiatric and medical profession. Feminist writers have argued that the identification of mental health problems relates directly to the stark operation of patriarchy that pathologizes women's lives (e.g. Chesler 1972). However, where such patriarchal practices are evident they are likely to be operating in a complex manner so that they are mediated through female practitioners who now outnumber men practitioners in psychiatry (Miles 1991; Parkhouse 1991). Given the powerful impact of medical socialization and the nature of medical knowledge, it is not surprising that women doctors do not differ greatly in their diagnostic practices from their male colleagues (Riska and Wegar 1995). Lay advice reflects the prevailing medical culture that regards psychiatric drugs as a useful way of addressing a variety of symptoms. Female networks are particularly important in normalizing the use of psychiatric drugs for 'sleeplessness' and 'stress' (Miles 1988; Ettorre and Riska 1995). When men are diagnosed as suffering from mental health problems they are to be identified as having schizophrenia, alcoholism, personality disorders or a range of psychosomatic disorders (Verbrugge 1984).

Valium, Ativan, Librium, Mogadon and many other tranquillizers and sleeping pills have become so well known that they have entered popular culture and are traded illicitly. Their use became widespread by the 1970s with women being twice as likely as men to receive prescriptions (Ettorre 1992). In 1965, less than five million benzodiazepine prescriptions were issued compared to 30.7 million by 1979 (Gabe 1991). The new psychotropic drugs can be broken down into four main groups:

- Antidepressants for the relief of depression
- Neuroleptics for the relief of psychotic problems such as schizophrenia
- Tranquillizers for the relief of anxiety
- Hypnotics–sedatives for the relief of insomnia

They, therefore, offer the potential to address a wide range of human behaviours. As Ray (1991) has pointed out, they also represent the most profitable and extensive section of the pharmaceutical industry. Analysis of the advertising aimed at doctors in the 1970s show how strongly the pharmaceutical industry associated the use of its new products with women (Mant and Darroch 1975). An examination of advertisements for tranquillizers in the *British Medical Journal* found that 91 of the 115 advertisements directly referred to women patients (Melville 1984). Depictions of women as depressed housewives were common and serve to reinforce gender stereotypes. While drug treatment can relieve anxiety, stress and depression it cannot address many of the causes. Brown and Harris's (1978) influential study of depression in London identified a number of factors that made it significantly more prevalent among working-class women. These included, three children under 14 years old and living at home, the lack of an 'intimate' relationship and unemployment. Not surprisingly, lone mothers experience twice the rate of long-term illness including mental health problems than mothers with partners (McKay and Marsh 1994). This once again reflects the association between social class and illness. However, this is not a simple relationship that points to the use of psychotropic drugs as a palliative for material deprivation. In a study of black and white working-class women in London, Gabe and Thorogood (1986) found that white women were more likely to be long-term users of psychotropic drugs. They argued that this was related to both how 'stress' and 'depression' was perceived as well as the relative isolation from social networks of the white women. This suggests that it is the combination of material deprivation and social exclusion that makes people more likely to display symptoms that lead to the prescription of psychotropic drugs. Support for this can be found in the *Health and Lifestyle Survey* (Blaxter 1990) which reported that women married to men at the lower end of the social class hierarchy reported more incidence of anxiety, depression and stress than any other group. Critics of the use of psychotropic drugs have argued that they have been used in a way that amounts to social control (e.g. Chesler 1972). It is argued that the anger and frustration that arise from deprivation are diverted away from potential political action by the use of drugs which address the individual problems of 'anxiety' or 'stress' as opposed to the collective problems of poverty.

Concern about the addictive and other effects of psychotropic drugs came to prominence in the 1980s and coincided with a growing concern within the NHS for the cost of the drugs (Miles 1988). Despite a reduction in the prescribing of psychotropic drugs, a new range of antidepressants were introduced in the late 1980s. Prozac and other antidepressants were seen by the pharmaceutical industry as an answer to an increasing amount of criticism about the addictive nature of psychotropic drugs. The use of such drugs in the United States has been called 'cosmetic psychophar-macology' (Kramer 1993) because of the way they can change individual behaviours to fit the prevailing cultural norms.

we value the assertive woman and shake our heads over the long-suffering self-sacrifice. Perhaps medication now risks playing the role that psychotherapy was accused of playing in the past: it allows a person to achieve happiness through conformity to contemporary norms.
(Kramer 1993: 43)

For many feminist critics, this points to the potential for the unequal prescribing of drugs to reinforce masculine values and behaviours.

Conclusion

Women in post-industrial societies are increasingly taking on obligations in the public sphere while largely retaining their established responsibilities in the private sphere. As mothers, paid workers, unpaid carers, frequently women occupy more social roles than most men. A study of survey data in the United States suggested that rather than contributing to an increase in women's ill health, employment increased their sense of well-being (Nathanson 1980). The study found that women with no paid employment experienced greater incidence of ill health and that the largest gap between the employed and unemployed was observed among lower-class groups. It also reported that the women with young children and full-time employment were most likely to seek early medical advice about any symptoms noticed in themselves or their children. Employed mothers with children appear likely to experience the best health (Verbrugge 1976). Health inequalities between men are broadly associated with unemployment and social class. Between women unemployment or lack of paid work, social class, marital status and the absence of dependent children help account for health differences (Arber *et al.* 1985: Arber 1989). Employment is therefore pivotal in the health of both men and women, but for women it is less strongly linked to material factors. It is suggested that satisfactions gained through work activities and the social aspects of employment in themselves end social exclusion.

Gender differences in health have become one of the standard categories in the literature on divisions in health. It has been observed empirically both in survey and qualitative data and has been reported in most Western countries. However, this orthodoxy may be hiding some 'paradoxes' (Verbrugge 1989a) as well as failing to take account of the changes that have taken place over the past decades that have witnessed the emergence of post-industrial or high modern society. Macintyre *et al.* (1996) in an analysis of the *Health and Illness Survey* data and the *West of Scotland-07 Survey* data found that a simple comparison revealed that more women across all ages reported a greater degree of symptoms than men. When the symptoms were divided up into 'malaise' (e.g. nerves, difficulty concentrating, tiredness, etc.) and 'physical' (back trouble, headaches, palpitations, constipation, etc.) women reported more malaise symptoms at all ages but there was no significant physical difference until after the age of 40. For specific symptoms, there were interesting different patterns of symptoms. For example, men reported more symptoms related to 'stiff or painful joints' at younger ages while the position was reversed for ages over 40. A greater incidence of women reporting 'sickness, nausea or stomach trouble' was observed only in the Scottish study from women aged 18 years (table 5, p. 620). The authors conclude that:

> The research which has accumulated over the last decade or so seems increasingly to support the view that gender differences in health are rooted in social roles, against a backdrop of some male biological disadvantages.
>
> (Macintyre *et al.* 1996: 623)

It is therefore important to recognize the complexities of gender differences rather than accept the 'reality' of reported incidence of various inequalities. In particular, the increasingly rapid changes in post-industrial societies need to be taken into account when examining such data. Furthermore, it is important that the focus on gender-based differences does not obscure differences related to factors such as 'race' and sexuality.

Opportunities and constraints in health

Health and lifestyle

In contemporary society, health can be invested in, produced, purchased, used and displayed in a diversity of ways. The lack of health can also be identified, defined, resisted, diagnosed, treated and managed by recourse to a diversity of theoretical approaches and therapies. Pluralism has diminished the overarching authority of biomedicine (Bury 1997) but yet not loosened its grip on the boundaries of legitimate healthcare which are maintained through control of the research agenda, professional status (Saks 1995) and public policy. People therefore have the insecurity and uncertainty of choices that are partly shaped by their position within the social and economic hierarchy. These opportunities and constraints are often manifest in the rather ill-defined term 'lifestyle' (Blaxter 1990). This reflects Sobel's (1981: 1) suggestion. 'If the 1970s are an indication of things to come, the word lifestyle, will soon include everything and mean nothing, all at the same time'. It has been used by Giddens (1991) to show how a self-identity is manifest through the choices individuals negotiate. A lifestyle according to Giddens is

> . . . a more or less integrated set of practices which an individual embraces, not only because such practices fulfil utilitarian needs, but because they give material form to a particular narrative of self-identity. [The choices that lifestyles consist of constitute] decisions not only about how to act but who to be. The more post-traditional the settings in which an individual moves, the more lifestyle concerns the very core of self-identity, its making and remaking.
>
> (Giddens 1991: 81)

Furthermore, the self-identity is 'the self as reflexively understood by the individual in terms of his or her biography' (p. 244). Biographies are also reflexive (Beck 1992) as people have greater opportunity to shape, choose and manage them. The established certainties of, for example, social class and identity are reduced as society becomes more dynamic and fractured. Pervasive reflexivity and the dynamic construction of identities which are focused on the body characterize high-modernity society (Shilling 1993). Consumption is a central factor in forming and displaying identity and lifestyle in post-industrial societies. Health is a major component of this conceptualization of lifestyle (Bourdieu 1984). Body maintenance, which in previous times was associated with rigorous denial and exercise for spiritual ends, is focused on more hedonistic pursuits and expressions of identity (Nettleton 1995; Featherstone 1991; Mellor and Shilling 1997).

Commodification through the market and manifest in advertising encourages individualism: '. . . the project of the self becomes translated into one of possession of desired goods and the pursuit of artificially framed styles of life' (Shilling 1993: 198). This may contribute to anxiety about making the 'wrong' choices but as Bauman (1988: 65) points out 'lifestyle advertising' and 'style' television programmes and magazines help to reassure people that 'choices are right and rational'. In response to pressure from anti-smoking groups and state legislature the tobacco industry has developed ever more abstract advertising campaigns that have sought to associate life*style* (with an emphasis on 'style') with cigarettes. Bunton and Burrows (1995) show that there is a strong link between social class, gender and particular brands of cigarettes. The marketing of the brand 'Death Cigarettes' with a skull and crossbones on a black packet is a good example of the inversion of the health promotion message as part of a style product indicative of rebellion, independence and danger. The 'self-surveillance of bodily health' (Featherstone 1991: 184) forms a part of both commercial and state attempts to encourage 'health bodies and healthy lives'. This embraces a general sense of risk and threat (see Chapter 1) which is expressed in terms of the consumption of 'healthy' foods and habits. This consumption includes the perceived reduction of health risks through, for example, not smoking or avoiding 'fatty foods'. Health promotion has for some time given voice to the link between the consumption of saturated fats and an increase in the risk of cardiovascular disease. Consumers, whatever their degree of expertise in matters such as diet, may find it difficult to make objective choices of foods because packaging does not carry sufficient or comprehensive information. At a more general level, a whole industry devoted to risk assessment has grown up and public policy is increasingly concerned with 'safety legislation'; for example, seat belt legislation was an early attempt to reduce the risk of injury in car accidents. The irony of the risk/safety boundary is illustrated by car design which, while making cars safer for drivers, may also make them feel less exposed to accidents and so more likely to take risks. Choices are informed by perceptions of style and risk. Both are dynamic and different expectations of risks help to 'lubricate' the market with a 'constant supply of new well publicised dangers' (Bauman

1993: 204). Children, in particular, become a site for parents' concern about apparent risks to them. Their apparent vulnerability to risks that range from concerns about the nutritional value of school meals to fears about paedophiles enhances dependence and is expressed in the protective behaviour of parents. The transportation of children at all ages to local schools by parents, which ironically increases the risk to children of car accidents and indirectly pollution, is one of the clear examples of this behaviour. Risk therefore restrains the opportunities of children and young people and is a factor in making less clear and extending the transition to adulthood (Furlong and Cartmel 1997).

Concerns about salt in foods or genetically modified soya or tomatoes creates the space for more products under a 'with' and 'without' dualism. Ironically 'low fat' foods are a good example of the dictum 'more is less' in that such products and 'natural' food cost more than those which include additives or fats of various kinds.

As Giddens (1992) notes.

> With the increased efficiency of global markets, not only is food abundant, but a diversity of foodstuffs is available for the consumer all year round. In these circumstances, what one eats is a life-style choice influenced by and constructed through, vast numbers of cookbooks, popular medical tracts, nutritional guides and so forth.
>
> (Giddens 1992: 32)

The concept of risk is central to various conceptualizations of lifestyle and this points to the related concept of choice. Choice is partly constrained by people's inability to afford for example, good housing or a 'healthy' diet. Social divisions and material differences are therefore a significant dimension of lifestyles. A theme running through this and many other books about health is the association of ill health with material deprivation and social exclusion. Beck (1992: 35) acknowledges risks are increased with deprivation: 'Like wealth, risks adhere to the class pattern, only inversely: wealth accumulates at the top, risks at the bottom . . . Poverty attracts an unfortunate abundance of risks.' During the 1980s, the number of people living in relative poverty (below half the average income) grew. Such deprivation is reflected in mortality rates which between 1982 and 1992 show that there was no improvements in mortality rates among young men (aged 20–40) and only small improvements among younger women (Phillimore 1994; Tickle 1996). Deaths from suicide, AIDS, violence and cirrhosis increased among young men. Rising social and material inequality has an impact on such stark health indicators as the mortality rate. It is the persistence of a significant minority population living in relative poverty that helps to account for such sharp differences in mortality (Wilkinson 1996).

Blaxter highlights an important element of the relationship between social position and health behaviours when she writes: 'Unhealthy behaviour does not reinforce disadvantage to the same extent as healthy behaviour increases advantage' (1990: 233). Smoking provides something of a classic example for the complex relationships between choices and health behaviours. A general decline in smoking in Britain can be traced back to the 1960s (Lader and Matheson 1992). However, smoking among young people has gone against this general trend since the 1980s. The study of 800 16-year-olds by Brannen *et al.* (1994) found that 30 per cent of women and 17 per cent of men described themselves as smokers. There were also significant ethnic differences with, for example, 10 per cent of Asian young people compared to 28 per cent of white young people being smokers. The family also had an effect on smoking behaviour with those least likely to smoke living in households with both parents and those most likely to smoke coming from a small group living in single father households. The lifestyle of parents in terms of their smoking behaviour has been explained by Graham (1987a: 55) in her study of lone mothers: 'in a lifestyle stripped of new clothes, make-up, hairdressing, travel by bus and evenings out, smoking can become an important symbol of one's participation in an adult centred world'. Echoing the old theme of teenage rebellion it has also been suggested that some young people may become antismoking from living in a household where a parent smokes (Oakley *et al.* 1992). Overall, there is a widening social class gap between the middle and working classes with a inverse relationship between income and smoking becoming increasingly evident. As Burrows and Nettleton (1995) note most research on health behaviours has concentrated on the relatively disadvantaged. Their study of middle-class smokers identified a minority made up of more men than women who had a lifestyle which involved the overconsumption or indulgence in food, drink and smoking. Associated with a 'London lifestyle', such risky health behaviours appear to express a particular set of male values which are displayed by visible consumption. Smoking at a young age as Plant and Plant (1992: 22) report has a significant impact on later mortality as 'among every 1000 young adult males in England and Wales who smoke cigarettes on average about 1 will be murdered, 6 will be killed on the road and 250 will be killed before their time by tobacco'. Changes in women's smoking habits in France and Italy have already had an impact on the sharp rise in female lung cancer (Graham 1996). Even without taking account of passive smoking, this highlights why cigarettes have become a major site for health promotion activity with increasing restrictions on advertising.

Like tobacco, alcohol is associated with the transition to adulthood and the latter has become attractive as smoking has become increasingly stigmatized and marginal in many public venues. 'Soft' alcoholic drinks have been introduced supported by vivid advertising and images intended to associate them with youth culture and lifestyles. The production of 'sweet' and fruit-based drinks are particularly aimed at women who traditionally drink less than men and prefer wine over the traditional 'male' beers and lagers. By 16 years of age, most young people will have experienced alcoholic drinks (Heaven 1996) and most drink at home (Oakley *et al.* 1992). Heavy drinking only occurs among a minority with one study reporting about 1 in 10 young men and half as many women aged 14–16 years drinking more than eleven units of alcohol on the last occasion they drank (Fossy *et al.* 1996). However reflecting wider social attitudes, alcohol is the preferred drug for most young people (Rice 1992), with a lowering of the age when it is first experienced. Indeed it may be accepted by parents as part of household practices and a less harmful alternative to other drugs. The consumption of alcohol by young people attracts considerable public attention with images of 'lager louts' and public drinking resulting in legislative attempts to prevent drinking in public spaces such as parks. However, it is the activities such as vandalism, petty crime and violence associated with drinking, especially among young men, that form the basis for this concern. This is reflected in figures that state that 60 per cent of all indictable crimes are being committed by the 14–25 age group (Home Office 1993). The boundaries around health, lifestyle, deviance, crime and social policy and so forth become blurred. 'Problem' drinking is defined and addressed through medicine and health promotion.

Social differences, health and control

The Black Report (Townsend and Davidson 1982, 1992) highlighted the role of housing in shaping health and later studies have reiterated its significance (e.g. Blackburn 1991). The 'health problems' of poor housing and homelessness have been addressed by policies ranging from wholesale redevelopment to targeted programmes to rehouse disadvantaged groups. The exchange of short term or inadequate housing with permanent individual housing could be expected to improve health. This reflects the early public health model which did so much to provide clean water and better housing in the past. However, the provision of a better physical environment may not in itself improve people's actual or perceived health. A study of Bangladeshi and Somali families in London indicates the importance of social factors and health. These families who were classified as homeless and living in temporary accommodation in Tower Hamlets were resettled in Stepney and the Isle of Dogs (Collard 1996: 25). During an interview after resettlement, they were asked about health and 'a surprising number mentioned racial harassment as a key factor affecting health and well-being'. Despite their satisfaction with their new home, as one respondent said, '. . . we feel like prisoners in our own homes, children are kept in the house like in cells' (p. 24). Such restrictive lifestyles can have a significant effect on children's health and more general social behaviour (Lundberg 1991). More than a year after resettlement, most families achieved a higher score on a health profile survey that indicated poor health than they did on the same profile before the move. Over one-third reported a marked deterioration in health. In spite of improvements in living conditions, the social exclusion manifest in racial harassment in the new neighbourhoods was more significant in people's health. Poverty as a form of social exclusion experienced for example as racial discrimination, has a direct and clinically measurable effect on ill health (Bhopal 1997).

Environmental deprivation is a long-established factor in the health of populations. The 'black triangle' which includes neighbouring parts of the Czech Republic, Poland and former East Germany is the most polluted area of Europe. The sulphurous smog is obviously related to heavy industrial plant and reinforced through domestic fuel burning and traffic. There are echoes here of the industrial past in Britain. However, the relationship between pollutants, ill health and mortality remains contested (*Lancet* 1992), especially in the face of other factors such as poverty and deteriorating healthcare systems. In this context, the degree of control local communities have over their health is marginal because individuals and families cannot escape the consequences of living in their polluted environment. The boundaries around lay perceptions and biomedical science are significant here. The 'Love Canal' in New York State was polluted with wastes legally discharged by a large electrical manufacturer (Phillimore and Moffatt 1994). Polluted water contaminated homes and playgrounds and gave rise to increasing local concern over the impact on residents' health. However, lay perceptions of risk and 'proof' differed from the more cautious scientific approach, which effectively delayed dealing with the waste. The words of a woman who lived near to a coking works indicates how lay knowledge of environmental factors is grounded in biography and observation.

> I have always believed that the cokeworks were to blame for all my sinus problems as I never had any symptoms before I exchanged houses to my present address. I lived at my previous home for seven years without any sinus problems.
>
> (Phillimore and Moffatt 1994: 147)

Such individual observations do not constitute 'scientific' evidence, and combined with a political immobility or inability to address the root causes of pollution, produce little action. The localized nature of environmental problems means that there are a diversity of beliefs and forms of action that lack the coherence and power of scientific research and state policy (Ingelehart 1990). There is a similarity here with lay understandings of health and the medical establishment. The lack of a clear link (Phillimore and Moffatt 1994) between the public and the realm of science is significant. However, the growth of access to the Internet may provide a new mediating structure which is characterized by a lack of overall ownership or control. The rhetoric of the consumerism and citizenship that became a central plank of Conservative Administrations (1979–97) contributed to the importance of social movements. The role of social movements such as AIDS activists and various disability groups in health will become increasingly significant as national and local political structures seek consumers' views and representation. An account of AIDS activism in the United States has traced its development from an initial demand to 'get drugs into bodies' to current demands for basic research (S. Epstein 1995). This led to the 'expertification' of activists which allows activists to achieve 'advisory jurisdiction' in funded research projects. Similar trends can be seen in Britain, with research councils promoting 'user involvement' in research applications. The debate about Gulf War syndrome in Britain, where activists are campaigning to achieve recognition of the role of chemicals used in the conflict with various health problems, highlights the ability of such campaigners to keep their concerns on the political agenda. The discourse about 'responsibility' and 'community' that developed in the 1980s at the political level contributed to New Age campaigns against major developments, the Poll Tax protests of the 1980s and other social movements. The election of the new Labour Government in 1997 and the response to the death of Diana Princess of Wales reflect the general sense of the possibility of social action largely absent in the 1980s and early 1990s. However, despite the incorporation of some lay people into decision-making bodies, the boundaries around 'expert' and lay knowledge and power remain. The degree to which the new Labour Government and notions of 'stakeholding' will make it easier for the lay voice in health to be taken seriously remains to be seen.

When asked in the abstract, 'What makes people unhealthy?' Blaxter (1993: 125) in an examination of HALS data, found that the 'most popular form of answer: "My life is unhealthy because I can't control my weight, because I smoke; it is healthy because I take exercise, because I watch my diet"'. However, while at one level there is little difference across the social classes, Blaxter argues that the more deprived respondents who have relatively constrained lifestyle choices are unwilling to acknowledge their lack of control. In a sense they are seen to articulate a false consciousness of responsibility and choice. This moral stoicism is well expressed by a resident of an estate in the Rhondda which had few services, a high turnover of residents and high unemployment:

> It's a cradle to grave care as promised by the Welfare State . . . it is also about people being active in their own care . . . many people around here need to be prodded into taking care of themselves especially women who are especially reluctant to bother doctors who appear to be unsympathetic and impatient with them.
>
> (Peckham *et al.* forthcoming)

This neatly captures the values of self-reliance and alienation from the middle-class world of medicine (see Chapter 2). Graham (1987b) has highlighted the significance of control over 'small' domestic aspects of life that were symbolized by smoking for lone mothers. Williams (1993), in an enthographic account of chronic illness suggested that 'dirt' symbolized 'disorder and loss of control'. His representation of Mrs Field, a 62-year-old widow with rheumatoid arthritis, shows how she attempts 'to enact a story about herself as she wishes to be understood, regardless of whether the enactment is the optimum way for her to proceed in the given circumstances' (p. 103). This suggests that it is not so much false consciousness that is being expressed by people in deprived circumstances, but a desire to situate their health experiences within a biographical context that focuses on their success at being able to make choices and develop a lifestyle. The formation and discourse of ideas about the 'right' values and orientations to health are shaped by such factors as an individual's position in the social structure, cultural capital, biography and so forth.

Preventative screening programmes are designed to detect diseases early so that treatment can be less radical and more successful. They are targeted on the 'healthy' but scientifically defined 'at-risk' populations. Risk is identified and assessed by biomedical and epidemiological processes that can, for example, establish an association between blood pressure and stroke. However, the relatively low number of specific cases identified in such programmes (Abramson 1997) prompts the debate between the 'efficiency' of putting resources into prevention as opposed to the illness services of the NHS (see Chapter 5). The *Health of the Nation* (DoH 1992) identified targets for preventative programmes and general practitioners are expected to undertake routine screening of patients. Women are a particular target of screening with established programmes for breast and cervical cancer. The elderly population are also seen as at risk, and general practitioners are expected to monitor their health on an annual basis following the 1986 White Paper *Promoting Better Health* (DHSS 1986). There are grounds to see this as an extension of the medical gaze to healthy populations (Armstrong 1995) and the way it reshapes the boundaries around those 'at risk'. Screening programmes in the guise of a health 'check up' have been promoted by private medicine and sometimes offered free as an inducement to join a health insurance scheme. Those who are 'too risky' are unlikely to be pressed into membership.

What Armstrong (1995) has called 'surveillance medicine' reflects not only the blurring of the boundaries around categories such as illness and health but also the centrality of health to individual lifestyles. He argues that Ackerhnecht's (1967) conceptualization of 'hospital medicine' was the precursor to surveillance medicine that characterizes contemporary medical practice. 'The techniques of Surveillance Medicine – screening, surveys and public health campaigns' . . . attempt . . . 'to transform the future by changing the health attitudes and health behaviours of the present' (ibid.: 402). These techniques and resulting data are increasingly shared by the realm of health and social care. Health visitors have a long-established ambiguous position of being a 'family' (or more precisely the mother's) friend and at the same time being engaged in health and social surveillance of parenting.

Surveillance is not applied uniformly across the population, but is targeted on those who are perceived to be more at 'risk' – in other words, people who live on the social and economic margins. This reinforces the association of deprivation with 'inappropriate' social and health behaviours. However, this problematization of the poor can give a false picture. Child sexual abuse has been linked with deprivation and household dissolution but a comprehensive Department of Health study has found that social position or household form is not directly linked to it (Sharland *et al.* 1996). The rise of surveillance medicine is not necessarily accompanied by a rise in traditional medical power. Ideas about risk and a prevailing sense of insecurity extended to a decline in awe towards medical knowledge and practice. Patients in the passive and compliant role cast by Parsons' notion of the sick role are transformed in postmodern societies into active consumers of health who have increasing access to a diversity of information about health and treatments. The old family health book with its explanation of signs and symptoms that once had a place in every home is being supplanted by a computer with access to a global network of information that offers a diversity of explanations. The resulting challenges to medical power are often expressed in the general practitioner's surgery as one doctor put it:

> The number of women that come along and demand, as of right, HRT [hormone replacement therapy] now because Dr Kindness in *Women's Own* has said . . . 'go along and see your male chauvinist pig of a doctor and tell him it's your right to have HRT'.
> (Weiss and Fitzpatrick 1997: 319)

At the same time, doctors are facing restrictions on their 'autonomy' by the introduction of health management and the implementation of such policies as the 'Limited List' of prescription drugs. This gives some ground for Haug's (1973) identification of a 'deprofessionalisation' of medicine (Weiss and Fitzpatrick 1997) particularly at a time when non-orthodox therapies are increasingly popular. However the consumption of NHS resources is constrained to a 'supermarket model' (Winkler 1987) under which the consumer has little say in the range of products on offer, or in the case of general practitioners little choice in choosing to change to a different 'supermarket'. The blurring of boundaries around health and social care as well as the incorporation of some non-orthodox techniques in orthodox medicine further undermines established medical boundaries. Changes to professional groups such as nurses who are beginning to act in roles previously the province of doctors also point to a redefining of the professional boundaries. It would be wrong to assume that everyone has become this new 'critical and informed' health consumer. Faith in medicine remains taken for granted by many people who seek to understand or come to terms with their health problems. However, state policy is unlikely to undo the principles expressed in the *Health of the Nation* (DoH 1992).

Conclusion

Medicine remains a powerful presence in both public and personal life. Its success was assured in the nineteenth century when orthodox medical practice was defined and a place at the centre of government was established. The transformation of industrial societies in the late twentieth century, a general increase in the standard of living and education and the decline of organized religion has created new spaces for the use of medical knowledge. At the same time, traditional boundaries around biomedicine and the social world fracture when the generation of such knowledge is revealed as a social process. The dilemmas and uncertainty of post-industrial life not only presents individuals with opportunities but also new sets of constraints that are partly defined and shaped by notions of risk and style. Dilemmas about lifestyle and identity can be resolved and constructed by recourse to ideas about health. 'Healthy' bodies and lifestyles are promoted in the media and popular culture as essential in establishing successful relationships and employment opportunities. Those who reject or are unwilling or unable to participate in such a dynamic and individualized society may be excluded and defined as a 'problem' to be addressed through social or health interventions.

References

Abercrombie, N. (ed.) (1994) *Dictionary of Sociology* (3rd edn). London: Penguin.

Abel-Smith, B. (1960) *A History of the Nursing Profession*. London: Heinemann.

Abel-Smith, B. (1994) *An Introduction to Health: Policy, Planning and Financing*. London: Longman.

Abramson, J.H. (1997) Epidemiology – to be taken with care. In M. Sidell *et al. Debates and Dilemma in Health Promotion: A Reader*. London: Macmillan.

Ackerhnecht, E. (1967) *Medicine at the Paris Hospital 1774–1848*. Baltimore, MD: Johns Hopkins.

Aglietta, M. (1987) *A Theory of Capitalist Regulation*. London: Verso.

Ahmad, W.I.U. (ed.) (1993) *'Race' and Health in Contemporary Britain*. Buckingham: Open University Press.

Ahmad, W.I.U. (1993) Making black people sick: race, ideology and health research. In W.I.U. Ahmad (ed.) *'Race' and Health in Contemporary Britain*. Buckingham: Open University Press.

Allen, S.M. (1994) Gender differences in spousal caregiving and unmet need. *Journal of Gerontology*, 49(4): 187–95.

Andrews, A. and Jewson, N. (1993) Ethnicity and infant deaths: the implications of recent statistical evidence for materialist explanations. *Sociology of Health and Illness*, 15(2): 137–56.

Arber, S. (1989) Gender and social class inequalities in health: understanding the differentials. In J. Fox (ed.) *Health Inequalities in European Countries*. Aldershot: Gower.

Arber, S. (1990) Opening the black box: understanding inequalities in women's health. In P. Abbott and G. Payne (eds) *New Directions in the Sociology of Health*. Brighton: Falmer Press.

Arber, S. (1991) Class, paid employment and family roles: making sense of structural disadvantage, gender and health status. *Social Science and Medicine*, 32: 375–436.

Arber, S. and Ginn, J. (1991) *Gender and Later Life: A Sociological Analysis of Resources and Constraints*. London: Sage.

Arber, S. and Ginn, J. (1993) Gender and inequalities in health in later life. *Social Science and Medicine*, 36(1): 33–46.

Arber, S., Gilbert, N. and Dale, A. (1989) Paid employment and women's health: a benefit or source of role strain? *Sociology of Health and Illness*, 7(3): 375–400.

Armstrong, D. (1983) *Political Anatomy of the Body: Medical Knowledge in Britain in the Twentieth Century*. Cambridge: Cambridge University Press.

Armstrong, D. (1993a) From clinical gaze to a regime of total health. In A. Beattie *et al.* (eds) *Health and Wellbeing: a Reader*. London: Macmillan.

Armstrong, D. (1993b) Public health spaces and the fabrication of identity. *Sociology*, 27(3): 393–410.

Armstrong, D. (1995) The rise of surveillance medicine. *Sociology of Health and Illness*, 17: 393–404.

Ashmore, M., Mulkay, M. and Pinch, T. (1989) (eds) *Health and Efficiency: A Sociology of Health Economics*. Milton Keynes: Open University Press.

Ashton, J. and Seymour, H. (1988) *The New Public Health*. Milton Keynes: Open University Press.

Audit Commission (1993) What Seems to be the Matter: Communication between Hospital and Patients. London: HMSO.

Baggott, R. (1994) *Health and Health Care in Britain*. London: Macmillan.

Baker, D. (1991) The foetal and infant origins of inequalities in health. *British Journal of Public Health Medicine*, 13: 64–8.

Bakx, K. (1991) The 'eclipse' of folk medicine in Western society. *Sociology of Health and Illness*, 13: 20–38.

Balarajan, R. and Bulusu, L. (1990) Mortality among immigrants in England and Wales 1979–83. In M. Britton (ed.) *Mortality and Geography: A Review in the Mid 1980s*. London: OPCS.

Balarajan, R. and Raleigh, V.S. (1993) The ethnic population of England and Wales: the 1991 Census. *Health Trends*, 29: 113–16.

Balarajan, R., Raleigh, V. and Yuen, P. (1991) Hospital care amongst ethnic minorities in Britain. *Health Trends*, 23(3): 390–3.

Balint, M. (1957) *The Doctor, His Patient and Illness*. London: Pitman.

Baly, M.E. (1995) *Nursing and Social Change* (3rd edn). London: Routledge.

Banks, C.G. (1992) 'Culture' in culture-bound syndromes: the case of anorexia nervosa. *Social Science and Medicine*, 34(8): 95–8.

Banton, M. (1977) *The Idea of Race*. London: Tavistock.

Barker, D. (1991) The foetal and infant origins of inequalities in health. *British Journal of Public Health*, 13: 64–8.

Barrett, J.F., Jarvis, G.J., MacDonald, H.N. *et al.* (1990) Inconsistencies in clinical decisions in obstetrics. *Lancet*, 366: 549–51.

Bauman, Z. (1988) *Freedom*. Milton Keynes: Open University Press.

Bauman, Z. (1993) *Postmodern Ethics*. Oxford: Blackwell.

Beagan, B.L. (1989) Jargon, myth and fetishes: Language use and the new reproductive technologies resources for women. *Feminist Research*, 18(4): 4–9.

Beardshaw, V. and Robinson, R. (1990) *New for Old? Prospects for Nursing in the 1990s*. London: King's Fund.

Beck, U. (1992) *The Risk Society: Towards a New Modernity*. London: Sage.

Beck, U. and Beck-Gernsheim, E. (1995) *The Normal Chaos of Love*. Cambridge: Polity Press.

Bell, N. and Vogel, E. (eds) (1968) *A Modern Introduction to the Family* (revised edition). New York: Free Press.

Bennett, P. and Murphy, S. (1997) *Psychology and Health Promotion*. Buckingham: Open University Press.

Berger, P.L. and Luckman, T. (1971) *The Social Construction of Reality*. Harmondsworth: Penguin.

Berliner, H. and Salmon, J. (1980) The holistic alternative to scientific medicine: history and analysis. *International Journal of Health Services*, 10: 133–45.

Bernard, J. (1972) *The Future of Marriage*. New York: World Publishing.

Berthoud, R. (1976) The disadvantages of inequality: A study of social deprivation. *PEP Report*. London: MacDonald and Janes.

Berthoud, R. (1986) *Selective Social Security*. London: PSI.

Bethune, A., Harding, S., Scott, A. and Filaki, H. (1995) Mortality of longitudinal study 1971 and 1981 census cohorts. In F. Drever (ed.) *Occupational Health: Decennial Supplement*. London: HMSO.

Bhopal, R.S. (1986) The inter-relationship of folk, traditional and western medicine within an Asian community in Britain. *Social Science and Medicine*, 22: 99–105.

Bhopal, R. (1997) Is research into ethnicity and health racist, unsound, or important science? *British Medical Journal*, 7096: 1710–15.

Biller, H. (1971) *Father, Child and Sex Role*. Lexington, MA: Heath.

Blackburn, C. (1991) *Poverty and Health: Working with Families*. Milton Keynes: Open University Press.

Blackman, T., Evason, E., Melaugh, M. and Woods, R. (1989) Housing and health: a case study of two areas in West Belfast. *Journal of Social Policy*, 4: 56–62.

Blankenhorn, D. (1995) *Fatherless America*. New York: Basic Books.

Blaxter, M. (1983) The cause of disease: women talking. *Social Science and Medicine*, 17: 56–69.

Blaxter, M. (1990) *Health and Lifestyle*. London: Heinemann.

Blaxter, M. (1993) Why do the victims blame themselves? In A. Radley (ed.) *Worlds of Illness*. London: Routledge.

Blaxter, M. and Patterson, E. (1982) *Mothers and Daughters: A Three Generational Study of Health, Attitudes and Behaviour*. London: Heinemann Educational Books.

Bloom, J.R. (1990) The relationship of social support and health. *Social Science and Medicine*, 30(5): 635–7.

Bloor, M., Samphier, M. and Prior, L. (1987) Artefact explanations of inequalities in health: an assessment of the evidence. *Sociology of Health and Illness*, 9(1): 231–64.

Botting, B. (1995) A review of the health of our children, decennial supplement. *Population Trends*, 82: 27–32.

Bourdieu, P. (1984) *Distinction: A Social Critique of the Judgement of Taste*. London: Routledge.

Bowlby, J. (1953) *Child Care and the Growth of Love*. Harmondsworth: Penguin.

Brannen, J., Dodd, K., Oakley, A. and Storey, P. (1994) *Young People. Health and Family Life*. Buckingham: Open University Press.

Braverman, H. (1974) *Labour Monopoly and Capitalism*. New York: Monthly Review Press.

Brewer, R. (1986) A note on the changing status of the Register General's classification of occupations. *British Journal of Sociology*, 37: 131–40.

British Medical Association (1986) *Report of the Board of Science and Education on Alternative Medicine*. London: BMA.

British Medical Association (1993) *Complementary Medicine: New Approaches to Good Practice*. Oxford: Oxford University Press.

British Medical Journal (1962) Tuberculosis in immigrants [Editorial] *British Medical Journal*, i: 1397–8.

British Medical Journal (1986) Whatever happened to the Black report? *British Medical Journal*, 293: 91–2.

Brittan, A. (1989) *Masculinity and Power*. Oxford: Blackwell.

Brown, G. and Harris, T. (1978) *The Social Orgins of Depression*. London: Tavistock.

Brown, G.W. (1973) The mental hospital as an institution. *Social Science and Medicine*, 7: 407–24.

Bulmer, M. (1980) Why don't sociologists make more use of official statistics? *Sociology*, 14: 505–23.

Bunton, R. and Burrows, R. (1995) Consumption and health in late modern medicine. In R. Bunton, S. Nettleton and R. Burrows (eds) *The Sociology of Health Promotion: Critical Analysis of Consumption Lifestyle and Risk*. London: Routledge.

Bunton, R. and Macdonald, G. (1992) *Health Promotion: Disciplines and Diversity*. London: Routledge.

Bunton, R., Nettleton, S. and Burrows, R. (1995) (eds) *The Sociology of Health Promotion: Critical Analysis of Consumption Lifestyle and Risk*. London: Routledge.

Burghes, L., Clarke, L. and Cronin, N. (1997) *Fathers and Fatherhood in Britain*. London: Family Policy Studies Centre.

Burgoyne, J. and Clarke, D. (1983) You are what you eat: food and family reconstruction. In A. Murcott (ed.) *The Sociology of Food and Eating*. Aldershot: Gower.

Burrows, R. and Nettleton, S. (1995) Going against the grain: an analysis of smoking and 'heavy' drinking amongst the British Middle Classes. *Sociology of Health and Illness*, 17(5): 668–80.

Bury, M. (1982) Chronic illness as biographical disruption. *Sociology of Health and Illness*, 4(2): 167–82.

Bury, M. (1988) Meanings at risk: the experience of arthritis. In R. Anderson and M. Bury (eds) *Living With Chronic Illness: The Experience of Patients and their Families*. London: Unwin Hyman.

Bury, M. (1991) The sociology of chronic illness: a review of research and prospects prospect. *Sociology of Health and Illness*, 13(2): 451–68.

Bury, M. (1997) *Health and Illness in a Changing Society*. London: Routledge.

Bury, M. and Gabe, J. (1994) Television and medicine: medical dominance or trial by media. In J. Gabe, D. Kelleher and G. Williams (eds) *Challenging Medicine*. London: Routledge.

Busfield, J. (1982) Gender and mental illness. *International Journal of Mental Health*, 11: 46–66.

Busfield, J. (1989) *Managing Madness: Changing Ideas and Practice*. London: Unwin Hyman.

Busfield, J. (1996) *Men, Women and Madness: Understanding Gender and Mental Disorder*. Basingstoke: Macmillan.

Calnan, M. (1987) *Health and Illness: The Lay Perspective*. London: Tavistock.

Calnan, M. and Johnson, B. (1985) Health, health risks and inequalities: an exploratory study of women's perception. *Sociology of Health and Illness*, 7(1): 55–75.

Camus, A. (1971) *The Plague*. Harmondsworth: Penguin.

Carr-Hill, R. (1990) The measurements of inequalities in health: lessons from the British experience. *Social Science and Medicine*, 31(3): 393–404.

Carr-Sauders, A.M. and Wilson, P. (1933) *The Professions*. Oxford: Clarendon Press.

Carricaburu, D. and Pierret, J. (1995) From biographical disruption to biographical reinforcement; the case of HIV-positive men. *Sociology of Health and Illness*, 17(1): 65–88.

Cartwright, S.A. (1851) Report on the diseases and physical peculiarities of the Negro race. Reprinted in A.L. Caplan, H.L. Engelhart and J.J. McCartney (eds) (1981) *Concepts of Health and Disease: Interdisciplinary Perspectives*. Reading, MA: Addison-Wesley.

Cassell, E.J. (1991) *The Nature of Suffering and the Goals of Medicine*. Oxford: Oxford University Press.

Castells, M. (1996) *The Rise of the Network Society: Volume One*. London: Blackwell.

Central Statistical Office (1992) *Social Trends 22*. London: HMSO.

Central Statistical Office (1995) *Social Focus on Women*. London: HMSO.

Charlton, B.G. and White, M. (1995) Living on the margins: a salutogenic model for socio-economic differentials in health. *Public Health*, 109: 235–43.

Chesler, P. (1972) *Women and Madness*. New York: Doubleday.

Christman, N.J. (1977) The health seeking process: an approach to the natural history of illness. *Culture, Medicine and Psychiatry*, 1: 351–77.

Clark, D. (1993) *The Sociology of Death*. Oxford: Basil Blackwell.

Clegg, S. (1989) *Frameworks of Power*. London: Sage.

Cockburn, C. (1990) *Brothers: Male Dominance and Technological Change*. London: Pluto Press.

Coleman, D. and Salt, J. (eds) (1996) *Ethnicity in the 1991 Census. Volume One*. London: HMSO.

Collard, A. (1996) *Homing In: Providing for the Health and Resettlement Needs of Rehoused Homeless Families*. Oxford: THHSG.

Connell, R.W. (1987) *Gender and Power*. Cambridge: Polity Press.

Connell, R.W. (1996) *Masculinities*. Cambridge: Polity Press.

Conway, J. (1995) Housing as an instrument of health care. *Health and Social Care in the Community*, 3: 141–50.

Cooter, R. (ed.) (1988) *Studies in the History of Alternative Medicine*. London: Macmillan Press.

Corbin, J. and Strauss, A. (1988) *Unending Work and Care: Managing Chronic Illness at Home*. San Francisco, CA: Jossey-Bass.

Corbin, J. and Strauss, A. (1991) Comeback: the process of overcoming disability. In G.L. Albecht and J.A. Levy (eds) *Advances in Medical Sociology*, vol. 2. Greenwich, Conn: JAI Press.

Corea, G. (1985) *The Mother Machine*. New York: Harper Row.

Cornwell, J. (1984) *Hard-Earned Lives: Accounts of Health and Illness from East London*. London: Tavistock.

Cowie, B. (1976) The cardiac patient's perception of his heart attack. *Social Science and Medicine*, 10(2): 87–96.

Coward, R. (1989) *The Whole Truth: The Myth of Alternative Health*. London: Faber and Faber.

Cox, B., Blaxter, M., Buckle, A.L.J. *et al.* (1987) *The Health and Lifestyle Survey*. Cambridge: Health Promotion Trust.

Cox, D. (1991) Health service management – a sociological view: Griffiths and the non-negotiated order of the hospital. In J. Gabe, M. Calnan and M. Bury (eds) *The Sociology of the Health Service*. London: Routledge.

Crawford, R. (1977) You are dangerous to your health: ideology and politics of victim blaming. *International Journal of Health Services*, 21(3): 423–39.

Crawford, R. (1980) Healthism and the medicalization of everyday life. *International Journal of Health Services*, 19: 365–88.

Crompton, R. (1994) *Class and Stratification*. Cambridge: Polity Press.

Culyer, A.J. (1976) *Need and the National Health Service*. Oxford: Martin Robinson.

Currer, C. (1986) Concepts of mental well- and ill-being: The case of Pathan mothers in Britain. In C. Currer and M. Stacey (eds) *Concepts of Health, Illness and Disease: A Comparative Perspective*. Leamington Spa: Berg.

Dale, A., Arber, S. and Proctor, M. (1988) *Doing Secondary Analysis*. London: Unwin Hyman.

Davey Smith, G., Barlety, M. and Blane, D. (1990) The Black Report on socio-economic inequalities in health 10 years on. *British Medical Journal*, 301: 373–7.

Davidoff, L. and Hall, C. (1987) *Family Fortunes: Men and Women of the English Middle Class 1780–1850*. London: Hutchinson.

Davies, C. (ed.) (1980) Rewriting Nursing History. London: Croom Helm.

Davies, C. (1992) Gender, history and management style in nursing: towards a theoretical synthesis. In M. Savage and A. Witz (eds) *Gender and Bureaucracy* (Sociological Review Monographs). London: Blackwell.

Davison, C., Davy Smith, G. and Frankel, S. (1991) Lay epidemiology and the prevention paradox: the implications of coronary candidacy for health promotion. *Social Science and Medicine*, 13(1): 1–19.

Davison, C., Davy Smith, G. and Frankel, S. (1992) The limits of popular lifestyle: re-assessing 'fatalism' in the popular culture of illness prevention. *Social Science and Medicine*, 34(6): 675–85.

De la Cuesta, C. (1983) The nursing process: from development to implementation. *Journal of Advanced Nursing*, 8: 365–71.

Delaport, F. (1986) *Disease and Civilisation*. Cambridge, MA: MIT Press.

Dennis, N. and Erdos, G. (1992) *Families Without Fatherhood (Choice in Welfare No. 12)*. London: IEA Health and Welfare Unit.

Department of the Environment (1983) Urban deprivation. *Information Note No. 2*. Inner Cities Directorate. London: Department of the Environment.

Department of Health (1988) *Community Care: Agenda for Action*. London: HMSO.

Department of Health (1989a) *Working for Patients*. Cmnd 555. London: HMSO.

Department of Health (1989b) *General Practice in the National Health Service: The 1990 Contract*. London: HMSO.

Department of Health (1991) *The Patient's Charter*. London: HMSO.

Department of Health (1992) *The Health of the Nation*. London: HMSO.

Department of Health (1993) *Changing Childbirth: Part 1. Report of the Expert Maternity Group*. London: HMSO.

Department of Health (1995) *The Health of the Nation, Variations in Health: What can the Department of Health and the NHS do?* London: HMSO.

Department of Health and Social Security (1968) *Seebohm Committee on Local Authority and Allied Personal Services*. Report. Cmnd 2703. London: HMSO.

Department of Health and Social Security (1976) *Prevention and Health: Everybody's Business*. London: HMSO.

Department of Health and Social Security (1983) *NHS Management Inquiry* (Griffiths Report). London: HMSO.

Department of Health and Social Security (1986) *Promoting Better Health*. London: HMSO.

D'Houtaud, A. and Field, M. (1984) The image of health: variations by social class in a French population. *Sociology of Health and Illness*, 6(1): 30–60.

Dingwall, R. (1976) *Aspects of Illness*. London: Martin Robinson.

Dingwall, R., Rafferty, A.M. and Webster, C. (1988) *An Introduction to the Social History of Nursing*. London: Routledge.

Doyal, L. (1979) *The Political Economy of Health*. London: Pluto Press.

Doyal, L. (1987) Infertility – a life sentence? Women and the National Health Service. In M. Stanworth (ed.) *Reproduction Technologies: Gender, Motherhood and Medicine*. Cambridge: Polity Press.

Doyal, L. (1994) Changing medicine? Gender and the politics of health care. In J. Gabe, M. Calnan and M. Bury (eds) *The Sociology of the Health Service*. London: Routledge.

Doyal, L. (1996) *What Makes Women Sick*. Basingstoke: Macmillan.

Drever, F., Whitehead, M. and Roden, M. (1996) Current patterns and trends in male mortality by social class (based on occupation). *Social Trends*, 86: 15–20.

Dunnell, K. (1995) Population review: 2. Are we healthier?. *Population Trends*, 82: 12–18.

Durkheim, E. (1951, 1897) *Suicide*. London: Routledge and Kegan Paul.

Edgell, S. (1993) *Class*. London: Routledge.

Ehrenreich, B. (1990) *The Fear of Falling: The Inner Life of the Middle Class*. New York: Harper Perennial.

Ehrenreich, B. and English, D. (1979) *For Her Own Good: 150 years of the Expert's Advice to Women*. London: Pluto Press.

Eisenberg, L. (1977) Disease and illness: distinction between professional and popular ideas of sickness. *Culture, Medicine and Psychiatry*, 1: 9–23.

Elias, N. (1978, 1939) *The Civilising Process: The History of Manners*. Volume 1. New York: Pantheon Books.

Elias, N. (1991) On human beings and their emotions: a process – sociological essay. In M. Featherstone, M. Hepworth and B.S. Turner (eds) *The Body, Social Process and Cultural Theory*. London: Sage.

Elston, M. (1991) The politics of professional power; medicine a changing health service. In J. Gabe, M. Calnan and M. Bury (eds) *The Sociology of the Health Service*. London: Routledge.

Epstein, J. (1995) *Altered Conditions: Disease, Medicine and Storytelling*. London: Routledge.

Epstein, S. (1995) *Impure Science: AIDS Activism and the Politics of Knowledge*. Berkeley, CA: University of California Press.

Ettorre, E. (1992) *Women and Substance Use*. London: Macmillan Press.

Ettorre, E. and Riska, E. (1995) *Gendered Moods: Psychotropics and Society*. London: Routledge.

Etzioni, A. (1969) *The Semi-Professions and their Organisation*. New York: Free Press.

Fagin, L. and Little, P. (1984) *The Forsaken Families*. Harmondsworth: Penguin.

Farrant, W. (1991) Addressing the contradictions: health promotion and community health action in the United Kingdom. *International Journal of Health Services*, 21(3): 423–39.

Featherstone, M. (1991) The body in consumer culture. In M. Featherstone, M. Hepworth and B.S. Turner (eds) *The Body: Social Processes and Cultural Theory.* London: Sage.

Feminist Review (1988) Special Issue. Spring: 28.

Fenner, F. *et al.* (1988) *Smallpox and its Eradication.* Geneva: WHO.

Field, D., Hockey, J. and Small, N. (eds) (1997) *Death, Gender and Ethnicity.* London: Routledge.

Finch, J. (1989) *Family Obligations and Social Change.* Cambridge: Polity Press.

Finch, J. and Groves, D. (1983) *A Labour of Love: Women, Work and Caring.* London: Routledge and Kegan Paul.

Finch, J. and Mason, J. (1993) *Negotiating Family Responsibilities.* London: Routledge.

Flynn, N. (1989) The 'new Right' and social policy. *Policy and Politics*, 17: 97–109.

Flynn, R. (1992) *Structures of Control in Health Management.* London: Routledge.

Fossey, E., Loretto, W. and Plant, M. (1996) Alcohol and youth. In L. Harrison (ed.) *Alcohol Problems in the Community.* London: Routledge.

Foster, K. *et al.* (1995) *General Household Survey 1993.* London: HMSO.

Foster, P. (1989) Improving the doctor–patient relationship: a feminist perspective. *Journal of Social Policy*, 303: 22–6.

Foster, P. (1995) *Women and the Health Care Industry: An Unhealthy Relationship?* Buckingham: Open University Press.

Foucault, M. (1976) *The Birth of the Clinic: An Archaeology of Medical Perception.* London: Tavistock.

Foucault, M. (1979) *Discipline and Punish: The Birth of the Prisons.* Harmondsworth: Penguin.

Fox, J. and Goldblatt, R. (1982) *Longitudinal Study, Socio-demographic Mortality Differentials 1971–75.* OPCS LS Series. London: HMSO.

Fraser, S. (ed.) (1995) *The Bell Curve: Race Intelligence and the Future of the United States.* New York: Basic Books.

Freidson, E. (1970) *The Profession of Medicine: A Study of the Sociology of Applied Knowledge.* New York: Harper Row.

Freidson, E. (1975) Dilemmas in the doctor–patient relationship. In C. Cox and A. Mead (eds) *A Sociology of Medical Practice.* London: Macmillan.

Freidson, E. (1994) *Professionalism Reborn: Theory, Prospect and Policy.* Cambridge: Polity Press.

Furlong, A. and Cartmel, F. (1997) *Young People and Social Change: Individualization and Risk in Late Modernity.* Buckingham: Open University Press.

Furnham, A. and Radley, S. (1989) Sex differences in the perception of male and female body shapes. *Personality and Individual Differences*, 10: 653–62.

Fussell, S.W. (1991) *Muscle: Confessions of an Unlikely Bodybuilder.* New York: Poseidon Press.

Gabe, J. (ed.) (1991) *Understanding Tranquilliser Use.* London: Tavistock.

Gabe, J. and Thorogood, N. (1986) Prescribed drug use and the management of everyday life: the experiences of black and white working-class women. *Sociological Review*, 34: 737–72.

Gamarnikow, E. (1987) Sexual division of labour: the case of nursing. In A. Kuhn and A. Wolpe (eds) *Feminism and Materialism: Women and Modes of Production.* London: Routledge and Kegan Paul.

Garrett, L. (1994) *The Coming Plague: Newly Emerging Disease in a World Out of Balance.* Harmondsworth: Penguin.

Gerhardt, U. (1989) Ideas about illness: a review of research and prospect. *Sociology of Health and Illness*, 13(2): 451–68.

Giddens, A. (1990) *The Consequences of Modernity*. Cambridge: Polity Press.

Giddens, A. (1991) *Modernity and Self-Identity: Self in Society in the Late Modern Age*. Cambridge: Polity Press.

Giddens, A. (1992) *The Transformations of Intimacy*. Cambridge: Polity Press.

Giddens, G. (1997) *Sociology* (3rd edn). London: Polity Press.

Gilman, S. (1985) *Difference and Pathology: Stereotypes of Sexuality, Race and Madness*. Cornell: Cornell University Press.

Ginsberg, N. (1992) Racism and housing: concepts and reality. In P. Braham, A. Rattansi and R. Skellington (eds) *Racism and Anti-Racism: Inequalities, Opportunities and Policies*. London: Sage.

Glazer, P.M. and Slater, M. (1987) *Unequal Colleagues: The Entrance of Women into the Professions 1890–1940*. London: Rutgers University Press.

Glendinning, C. and Millar, J. (1992) *Women and Poverty in Britain in the 1990s*. Brighton: Harvester Wheatsheaf.

Glucklich, A. (1997) *The End of Magic*. Oxford: Oxford University Press.

Goffman, E. (1968) *Stigma: Notes on the Management of Spoiled Identity*. Harmondsworth: Penguin.

Goldstein, J.M. (1987) *Console and Classify: The Frecnch Psychiatric Profession in the Nineteenth Century*: Cambridge: Cambridge University Press.

Good, B.J. (1994) *Medicine, Rationality and Experience: An Anthropological Perspective*. Cambridge: Cambridge University Press.

Goode, W.J. (1960) Encroachment, charlatanism and the emerging profession: psychiatry, sociology and medicine. *American Social Review*, 25: 902–14.

Gove, W.R. (1984) Gender differences in mental health and physical illness: the effects of fixed roles and nurturing roles. *Social Science and Medicine*, 19(2): 77–91.

Government Statisticians' Collective (1993) How official statistics are produced: view from the inside. In M. Hammersley (ed.) *Social Research: Philosophy, Politics and Practice*. London: Sage.

Grace, V.M. (1991) The marketing of empowerment and the construction of the health consumer: a critique of health promotion. *International Journal of Health Services*, 21(2): 329–43.

Graham, H. (1984) *Women, Health and the Family*. Brighton: Harvester Wheatsheaf.

Graham, H. (1985) Providers, negotiators and mediators: women as the hidden carers. In E. Lewin and V. Oleson (eds) *Women, Health and Healing*. London: Tavistock.

Graham, H. (1987a) Being poor: perceptions and coping strategies of lone mothers. In J. Brannen and G. Wilson (eds) *Give and Take in Families*. London: Allen and Unwin.

Graham, H. (1987b) Women's smoking and family health. *Social Science and Medicine*, 25(1): 47–56.

Graham, H. (1993a) *Hardship and Health in Women's Lives*. Hemel Hempstead: Wheatsheaf.

Graham, H. (1993b) *When Life's a Drag: Women Smoking and Disadvantage*. London: HMSO.

Graham, H. (1996) Smoking prevalence among women in the European community 1950–1990. *Social Science and Medicine*, 43(2): 243–54.

Hakim, C. (1979) *Occupational Segregation: A Comparative Study of Degree and Patterns of Differentiation between Men's and Women's Work in Britain, the United States and Other Countries. Research Paper 9*. London: Department of Employment.

Ham, C. (1992) *Health Policy in Britain: The Politics and Organization of the National Health Service*. Basingstoke: Macmillan.

Hannay, D.R. (1979) *The Symptom Iceberg: A Study of Community Health*. London: Routledge and Kegan Paul.

Haralanbos, M. and Holborn, M. (1991) *Sociology: Themes and Perspectives*, 3rd edn.

Hardey, M. (1999) Doctor in the House: The Internet as a source of lay health knowledge and the challenge to expertise. *The Sociology of Health and Illness*, 21(6).

Hardey, M. and Crow, G. (1991) *Lone Parenthood: Coping with Constraints and Creating Opportunities*. Brighton: Wheatsheaf.

Hardey, M. and Mulhall, A. (eds) (1994) Nursing Research: *Theory and Practice*. London: Chapman and Hall.

Harding, F.L. (1996) *Family, State and Social Policy*. London: Macmillan.

Harding, S. (1995) Social class differences in mortality of men: recent evidence from the OPCS longitudinal study. *Population Trends*, 80: 31–7.

Harris, A. (1971) *Handicapped and Impaired in Great Britain*. London: HMSO.

Harris, A., Cox, E. and Smith, C. (1970) *Handicapped and Impaired in Great Britain*. Volume 1. London: HMSO.

Harrison, S., Hunter, D. and Pollit, C. (1990) *The Dynamics of British Health Policy*. London: Unwin.

Harrison, S., Hunter, D.J., Marnoch, G. and Pollitt, C. (1990) *Just Managing: Power and Culture in the NHS*. London: Macmillan.

Hart, J. (1971) The inverse care law. *Lancet* 27 February: 405–12.

Harvey, D. (1989) *The Condition of Postmodernity*. London: Basil Blackwell.

Harvey, J. (1995) Up-skilling and the intensification of work: the 'extended role' in intensive care nursing and midwifery. *Sociological Review*, 6: 765–81.

Haug, M. (1973) Deprofessionalisation: an alternative hypothesis for the future. In P. Holmos (ed.) *Professionalisation and Social Change*. Keele: University of Keele.

Haug, M. (1988) A re-examination of the hypothesis of physician deprofessionalization. *Milbank Quarterly*, 66 (suppl. 2): 117–24.

Heady, P. (1994) *1991 Census Validation Survey*. London: HMSO.

Hearn, J. (1987) *The Gender of Oppression: Men Masculinity and the Critique of Marxism*. Brighton: Wheatsheaf.

Hearn, J. (1992) *Men in the Public Eye*. London: Routledge.

Heath, C. (1984) Participation in the medical consultation: the coordination of verbal and non-verbal behaviour between the doctor and the patient. *Sociology of Health and Illness*, 2(3): 311–38.

Heaven, P.L.C. (1996) *Adolescent Health: The Role of Individual Differences*. London: Routledge.

Helman, C.G. (1978) Feed a cold, starve a fever: folk models of infection in an English suburban community and their relation to medical treatment. *Culture, Medicine and Psychiatry*, 2: 107–37.

Herrnstein, R.J. and Murray, C. (1994) *The Bell Curve: Intelligence and Class Structure in American Life*. New York: Free Press.

Herzlich, C. (1973) *Health and Illness*. London: Academic Press.

Herzlich, C. and Pierret, J. (1987) *Illness and Self in Society*, E. Foster (transl.). Baltimore, MA: Johns Hopkins.

Higgins, J. (1988) *The Business of Medicine*. London: Macmillan.

Higgins, J. (1992) Private sector health care. In E. Bek, S. Lonsdale, S. Newman and D. Patterson (eds) *In the Best of Health? The Status and Future of Health Care in the UK*. London: Chapman and Hall.

Hipgrove, T. (1982) The lone father. In L. McKee and M. O'Brien (eds) *The Father Figure*. London: Tavistock.

Hochschild, A. (1983) *The Managed Heart: The Commercialization of Feeling*. Berkeley, CA: University of California.

Hochschild, A. (1989*) The Second Shift: Working Parents and the Revolution at Home*. London: Piatkus.

Holman, B. (1991) It's no accident. *Poverty*, 80: 6–8.

Home Office (1993) *Information on the Criminal Justice System in England and Wales, Digest 2*. London: Home Office.

Howlett, B.C., Ahmad, W.I. and Murray, R. (1992) An exploration of White, Asian and Afro-Caribbean Peoples' concepts of health and illness causation. *New Community*, 18(2): 281–92.

Hunt, A.S. and Symonds, A. (1996) *The Midwife and Society: Perspectives, Policies and Practice*. Basingstoke: Macmillan.

Hunt, S.M. (1990) Emotional distress and bad housing. *Health and Hygiene*, 11: 72–9.

Hunt, S.M. (1993) The relationship between reassert and policy: translating knowledge into action. In J.K. Davies and M.P. Kelly (eds) *Healthy Cities: Research and Practice*. London: Routledge.

Illich, I. (1975) *Medical Nemesis*. London: Calder and Boyers.

Illich, I. (1976) *Limits to Medicine*. London: Martin Boyers.

Illsley, R. (1986) Occupational class, selection and the production of inequalities in health. *Quarterly Journal of Social Affairs*, 2(2): 151–42.

Impicciatore, P., Pandolfini, C., Casella, N. and Bonati, M. (1997) Information in practice. *British Medical Journal*, 314 (7098), http://www.bmj.com/archive/7098ip1.htm

Independent (1988) 30 January.

Independent Hospital Association (1989) *Survey of Acute Hospitals in the Private Sector*. London: Independent Hospital Association.

Ingelehart, R. (1990) *Culture Shift in Advanced Industrial Society*. Princeton, NJ: Princeton University Press.

Irvine, J. *et al*. (1979) *Demystifying Social Statistics*. London: Pluto Press.

Jackson, D. (1990) *Unmasking Masculinity: A Critical Autobiography*. London: Routledge.

James, N. (1992) Care = organisation + physical labour + emotional labour. *Sociology of Health and Illness*, 14(4): 488–509.

Jarman, B. (1983) Identification of underprivileged areas. *British Medical Journal*, 286: 1705–9.

Jarman, B. (1984) Underprivileged areas validation and distribution scores. *British Medical Journal*, 289: 1587–92.

Jefferys, M. (1991) Medical sociology and public health. *Public Health*, 105: 15–21.

Jewson, N. (1976) The disappearance of the sick man from medical cosmology. *Sociology of Health and Illness*, 1(2): 90–107.

Joffe, E. (1997) AIDS and the 'other'. In L. Yardley (ed.) *Material Discourses of Health and Illness*. London: Routledge.

Johnson, T. (1977) Professions and the class structure. In R. Scase (ed.) *Industrial Society: Class, Cleavage and Control*. London: Allen and Unwin.

Johnson, S., Ramsey, R., Thronicroft, G. *et al*. (1997) *London's Mental Health*. London: King's Fund.

Johnson, T. (1972) *Professions and Power*. London: Macmillan.

Jones, K. (1960) *Mental Health and Social Policy 1945–1959*. London: Routledge and Kegan Paul.

Kayawa-Singer, M. (1993) Redefining health: living with cancer. *Social Science and Medicine*, 37(3): 295–304.

Kelly, M.P. and Field, D. (1996) Medical sociology, chronic illness and the body project. *Sociology of Health and Illness*, 18: 241–57.

Kiernan, K. (1988) Who remains celibate? *Journal of Biosocial Science*, 289: 700–2.

King, D.S. (1989) *The New Right*. London: Macmillan.

Kitzinger, S. (1979) *The Good Birth Guide*. London: Croom Helm.

Klein, A.M. (1995) Life's too short to die small: steroid use among male body builders. In D. Sabo and F.D. Gordon. (eds) *Men's Health and Illness: Gender Power and the Body*. Berkeley, CA: Sage.

Klein, R. (1989) *The Politics of the National Health Service*, 2nd edn. London: Longman.

Kleinman, M. (1988) *The Illness Narrative: Suffering, Healing and the Human Condition*. New York: Basic Books.

Kleinman, M., Eisenberg, L. and Good, B.J. (1978) Culture illness and care. *Annals of Internal Medicine*, 88: 251–58.

Kramer, P. (1993) *Listening to Prozac*. New York: Penguin Books.

Kratz, C.R. (1979) *The Nursing Process*. London: Baillière Tindall.

Lacey, R.W. (1996) *Mad Cow Disease: The History of BSE in Britain*. London: Gypsela Publications.

Lader, D. and Matheson, J. (1992) *Smoking Among Secondary School Children in 1990*. London: OPCS.

Lancet (1989) Cerebral palsy, intrapartum care and a shot in the foot [Editorial]. *Lancet*, 8674: 1251–2.

Lancet (1992) Environmental pollution: it kills trees, but does it kill people? *Lancet*, 340: 821–2.

Laqueur, T. (1990) *Making Sex: Body and Gender from the Greeks to Freud*. London: Harvard University Press.

Larkin, G. (1983) *Occupation Monopoly and Modern Medicine*. London: Tavistock.

Lash, S. and Urry, J. (1987) *The End of Organised Capitalism*. Cambridge: Polity Press.

Lasker, J. and Borg, S. (1989) *In Search of Parenthood*. London: Pandora Press.

Latour, B. and Woolgar, S. (1979) *Laboratory Life: The Social Construction of Scientific Facts*. London: Sage.

Leap, N. and Hunter, B. (1993) *The Midwife's Tale*. London: Scarlett Press.

Leder, D. (ed.) (1992) *Medical Thought and Practice*. Dordrecht: Kluwer.

Lee, D. and Newby, H. (1983) *The Problem of Sociology*. London: Hutchinson.

Lee, D.J. and Turner, B.S. (eds) (1996) *Conflicts About Class: Debating Inequality in Late Industrialism*. London: Longman.

Leete, R. and Fox, J. (1977) Registrar General's social classes: origins and uses. *Population Trends*, 8: 1–7.

Leiss, W. (1983) The icons of the marketplace. *Theory, Culture and Society*, 1(3): 24–35.

Leslie, C. (ed.) (1976) *Asian Medical Systems: A Comparative Approach*. Los Angeles, CA: University of California Press.

Lewin, E. and Oleson, V. (1985) *Women Health and Healing*. London: Tavistock.

Lewis, C. (1986) *Becoming a Father*. Milton Keynes: Open University Press.

Locker, D. (1981) *Symptoms and Illness: The Cognitive Organisation of Disorder.* Tavistock: London.

Longino, C.F. and Murphy, J.W. (1995) *The Old Age Challenge to the Biomedical Model: Paradigm Strain and Health Policy.* New York: Baywood.

Longsdale, S. (1990) *Women and Disability: The Experiences of Physical Disability among Women.* London: Macmillan.

Longsdale, S. (1992) Support and care for people with physical disability. In E. Beck, S. Longsdale, S. Newman and D. Patterson (eds) *In the Best of Health?* London: Chapman and Hall.

Lowenberg, J.S. and Davis, F. (1994) Beyond medicalisation–demedicalisation: the case of holistic health. *Sociology of Health and Illness*, 16(5): 579–99.

Lowry, S. (1991) Housing and health. *British Medical Journal*, 365: 147–51.

Lundberg, O. (1991) Childhood living conditions, health status, and social mobility: a contribution to the health selection debate. *European Sociological Review*, 7: 149–62.

Lupton, D. (1994) *Medicine as Culture: Illness, Disease and the Body in Western Societies.* London: Sage.

Lupton, D. (1995) *The Imperative of Health: Public Health and the Regulated Body.* London: Sage.

Macfarlane, A. (1990) Official statistics: health and illness. In H. Roberts (ed.) *Women's Health Counts.* London: Routledge.

Macfarlane, A., Mugford, M., Johnson, A. and Garcia, J. (1995) *Counting Changes in Childbirth: Trends and Gaps in National Statistics.* Oxford: NPEU Radcliffe Infirmary.

Macintyre, S. (1977) *Single and Pregnant.* London: Croom Helm.

Macintyre, S. (1992) The effects of family position and status in health. *Social Science and Medicine*, 35(4): 453–64.

Macintyre, S., Hunt, K. and Sweeting, H. (1996) Gender differences in health: are things really as simple as they seem? *Social Science and Medicine*, 42(2): 617–24.

Mackay, L. (1989) *Nursing a Problem.* Milton Keynes: Open University Press.

Mackay, L. (1994) *Conflicts in Care: Medicine and Nursing.* London: Chapman and Hall.

Mant, A. and Darroch, D.B. (1975) Media images and medical images. *Social Science and Medicine*, 9(2): 613–18.

Marks, D.F. (1996) Health promotion in context. *Journal of Health Psychology*, 1(1): 7–21.

Marmot, M.G. and McDowall, M.E. (1986) Mortality decline and widening social inequalities. *Lancet*, ii: 274–6.

Marmot, M.G., Adelstein, A.M. and Bulusu, L. (1984) *Immigrant Mortality in England and Wales 1970–78, Studies on Medical and Population Subjects No. 47.* London: HMSO.

Marmot, M.G., Davey Smith, G., Stansfield, S. *et al.* (1991) Health inequalities among British civil servants: the Whitehall II study. *Lancet*, 337: 1387–93.

Marsh, A. and Matheson, J. (1983) *Smoking Attitudes and Behaviour.* London: HMSO.

Marshall, G., Rose, D., Newby, H. and Volgler, C. (1988) *Social Class in Modern Britain.* London: Unwin Hyman.

Marshall, G., Roberts, S., Burgoyne, J., Swift, A. and Routh, D. (1995) Class, gender and the asymmetry hypothesis. *European Sociological Review*, 11(1): 1–12.

Martin, J. (1984) *Hospitals in Trouble.* Oxford: Blackwell.

Martin, J., Meltzer, H. and Elliot, D. (1988) *The Prevalence of Disability Among Adults. OPCS Surveys of Disability in Great Britain. Report 1.* London: HMSO.

Maslow, A. (1954) *Motivation and Personality.* New York: Harper and Row.

Mauss, M. (1979) *Sociology and Psychology: Essays.* London: Routledge and Kegan Paul.

May, C., Dowrick, C. and Richardson, M. (1996) The confident patient: the social construction of therapeutic relationships in general medical practice. *Sociological Review,* 187–203.

McGuire, M.B. (1988) *Ritual Healing in Suburban United States.* New Brunswick: Rutgers University Press.

McKay, S. and Marsh, A. (1994) *Lone Parents and Work.* Department of Social Security Research Report 25. London: HMSO.

McKee, L. and O'Brien, M. (eds) (1982) *The Father Figure.* London: Tavistock.

McKeown, T. (1976) *The Role of Medicine: Dream, Mirage or Nemesis.* London: Nuffield Provincial Hospitals Trust.

McKinlay, J. (1972) Social networks, lay consultation and help-seeking behaviour. *Social Forces,* 51: 275–81.

McKinlay, J. and Stoeckle, J. (1988) Corporatization and the social transformation of physicians. *International Journal of Health Services,* 18: 191–205.

Mcleod, E. (1995) The strategic importance of social work. *Social Work and Social Sciences Review,* 6: 19–31.

McRae, S. (1986) *Cross-class Families.* Oxford: Clarendon Press.

Mechanic, D. (1962) *Students Under Stress.* New York: Free Press.

Mellor, P.A. and Shilling, C. (1997) *Re-forming the Body: Religion, Community and Modernity.* London: Sage.

Melville, J. (1984) *The Tranquilliser Trap and How to Get Out of It.* London: Fontana.

Miles, A. (1991) *Women, Health and Medicine.* Milton Keynes: Open University Press.

Miles, A. (1998) *Women and Mental Illness.* Brighton: Wheatsheaf.

Miles, R. (1989) *Racism.* London: Routledge.

Modood, T. (1997) Employment. In T. Modood, R. Berthoud, J. Lakey, *et al.* (eds) *Ethnic Minorities in Britain: Diversity and Disadvantage.* London: Policy Studies Institute.

Modood, T., Berthoud, R., Lakey, J. *et al.* (eds) (1997) *Ethnic Minorities in Britain: Diversity and Disadvantage.* London: Policy Studies Institute.

Mogan, M., Calnan, M. and Manning, N. (1985) *Sociological Approaches to Health and Medicine.* London: Routledge.

Morgan, D.H.J. (1985) *The Family, Politics and Social Theory.* London: Routledge.

Morgan, D.J.H. (1992) *Discovering Men.* London: Routledge.

Morgan, M. (1980) Marital status, health, illness and service use. *Social Science and Medicine,* 14(2): 633–9.

Morgan, M. (1989) Social ties, support and well-being. In D. Patrick and H. Peach (eds) *Disablement in the Community.* Oxford: Oxford Medical Publications.

Morris, J. (1979) Social inequalities undiminished. *Lancet,* 245: 87–90.

Morris, J. (1990) Social inequalities in health: ten years and a little further on. *Lancet,* 336: 303–4.

Moser, C.A. (1972) Statistics about immigrants: objectives, sources, methods and problems. *Social Trends,* 3: 20.

Moser, C.A., Foc, A.J. and Jones, D.R. (1984) Unemployment and mortality in the OPCS longitudinal study. *Lancet,* 8: 1324–9.

Moser, K., Pugh, H. and Goldblatt, P. (1988) Inequalities in women's health: looking at mortality differences using an alternative approach. *British Medical Journal*, 296: 1221–4.

Mount, F. (1982) *The Subversive Family*. London: Cape.

Muijen, M. (1995) Scare in the community. Part Five. Care of the mentally ill today. *Community Care*, 7–13 September: i–vii.

Mullen, K. (1993) *A Healthy Balance*. Aldershot: Avebury.

Murphy, M., Glaser, K. and Grundy, E. (1997) Marital status and long-term illness in Great Britain. *Journal of Marriage and the Family*, 59: 156–64.

Murray, C. (1984) *Losing Ground: American Social Policy 1950–80*. New York: Basic Books.

Nathanson, C. (1975) Illness and the female role: a theoretical review. *Social Science and Medicine*, 9: 57–62.

Nathanson, C. (1980) Social roles and health status among women: the significance of paid employment. *Social Science and Medicine*, 14a: 463–71.

Navarro, V. (1978) *Class Struggle, the State and Medicine*. London: Martin Robinson.

Nazroo, J.Y. (1997) Health and health services. In T. Modood, R. Berthoud, J. Lakey *et al.* (eds) (1997) *Ethnic Minorities in Britain: Diversity and Disadvantage*. London: Policy Studies Institute.

Nettleton, S. (1993) *How Do We Create a Healthy North? Consultation with the People in the Community Newcastle upon Tyne*. Newcastle upon Tyne: Northern Regional Health Authority.

Nettleton, S. (1995) *The Sociology of Health and Illness*. Cambridge: Polity Press.

Newman, E. (1985) Who controls birth control? In W. Faulkner and E. Arnold (eds) *Smothered by Technology in Women's Lives*. London: Pluto Press.

NHS Management Executive (1993) *The Quality Journey*. Leeds: NHS Management Executive.

Nissel, M. and Bonnerjea, L. (1982) *Family Care of the Handicapped Elderly: Who Pays?* London: PSI.

Nuland, S.B. (1988) *Doctors*. New York: Knopf.

Oakley, A. (1974) *The Sociology of Housework*. London: Martin Roberts.

Oakley, A. (1976) Wisewoman and medical men: changes in the management of childbirth. In J. Mitchell and A. Oakley (eds) *The Rights and Wrongs of Women*. Harmondsworth: Penguin

Oakley, A. (1983) Women and health policy. In J. Lewis (ed.) *Women's Welfare Women's Rights*, London: Croom Helm. pp. 103–30.

Oakley, A. (1985) *Sex, Gender and Society*. London: Temple Smith.

Oakley, A. (1986) *The Captured Womb*. Oxford: Blackwell.

Oakley, A. (1989) Smoking in pregnancy: Smokescreen or risk factor? *Sociology of Health and Illness*, 11(4): 311–35.

Oakley, A., Brannen, J. and Dodd, K. (1992) Young people, gender and smoking in the United Kingdom. *Health Promotion International*, 7(2): 75–88.

Oakley, A. (1993) *Essays on Women, Medicine and Health*. Edinburgh: Edinburgh University Press.

O'Brien, M. (1991) *The Politics of Reproduction*. London: Routledge and Kegan Paul.

O'Connell, M., Davidson, J. and Layder, D. (1994) *Methods: Sex and Madness*. London: Routledge.

O'Donnell, M. (1992) *A New Introduction to Sociology*. Walton-on-Thames: Nelson.

Offe, C. (1984) *Contradictions of the Welfare State*. London: Hutchinson.

Office of Population Consensus and Surveys (1970) *Classification of Occupations.* London: HMSO.

Office of Population Consensus and Surveys (1980) *Classification of Occupations.* London: HMSO.

Office of Population Consensus and Surveys (1990) *General Household Survey 1989.* London: HMSO.

Office of Population Consensus and Surveys (1991) *Mortality Statistics, Childhood, England and Wales.* Series DH6, No. 3. London: OPCS.

Oliver, M. (1990) *The Politics of Disablement.* London: Macmillan.

Oliver, M. (1996) *Understanding Disability: From Theory to Practice.* London: Macmillan.

Oppenheim, C. and Harker, L. (1996) *Poverty: The Facts.* CPAG: London.

Oppenheimer, M. (1973) The proletarianization of the professional. *Sociological Review Monograph*, 20: 213–37.

Orbach, S. (1988) *Fat is a Feminist Issue.* London: Arrow Books.

Owens, P. and Glennerster, H. (1990) *Nursing in Conflict.* London: Macmillan.

Pahl, R.E. (1990) *On Work: Historical, Comparative and Theoretical Approaches.* London: Basil Blackwell.

Parker, G. (1993) *With this Body: Caring and Disability in Marriage.* Buckingham: Open University Press.

Parker, R. (1981) Tending and social policy. In E. Goldberg and S. Hatch (eds) *A New Look at the Personal Social Services.* London: PSI.

Parkhouse, J. (1991) *Doctors' Careers: Aims and Experiences of Medical Graduates.* London: Routledge.

Parsons, T. (1951) *The Social System.* Glencoe: Free Press.

Parsons, T. (1957) The sick role and the role of the physician reconsidered. *Health and Society*, 53(3): 257–78.

Pascall, G. (1995) Women at the top? Women's careers in the 1990s. *Sociological Review*, February: 2–6.

Pearson, M. (1986) Racist notions of ethnicity and culture in health education. In S. Rodmell and A. Watt (eds) *The Politics of Health Education: Raising the Issues.* London: Routledge.

Peckham, S., Taylor, P. and Turnton, P. (forthcoming) *Public Health Approach and Primary Care.* London: Public Health Alliance.

Pellign, M. (1978) Medical practice in the early modern period: trade or profession? In W. Prest (ed.) *The Professions in Early Modern England.* London: Croom Helm.

Pembrey, S. and Punton, S. (1990) The lesson of nursing beds. *Nursing Times*, 86(14): 44–5.

Pescosolido, B.A. (1991) Illness careers and network ties: a conceptual model of utilization and compliance. In G. Albrect and J. Levy (eds) *Advances in Medical Sociology. Volume 2.* Greenwich, CT: JAI Press.

Pfeffer, M. (1987) Artificial insemination, in-vitro fertilization and the stigma of infertility. In M. Stanworth (ed.) *Reproduction Technologies: Gender, Motherhood and Medicine.* Cambridge: Polity Press.

Pfeffer, M. (1992) From private patients to privatisation. In M. Stacey (ed.) *Changing Human Reproduction: Social Science Perspectives.* London: Sage.

Phal, J. (1990) Household spending, personal spending and the control of money in marriage. *Sociology*, 24(1): 119–38.

Phillimore, P. and Moffatt, S. (1994) Discounted knowledge: local experience, environmental pollution and health. In J. Popay and G. Williams (eds) *Researching the People's Health*. London: Routledge.

Phillimore, P., Beattie, A. and Townsend, P. (1994) The widening gap. Inequality of health in northern England, 1981–91. *British Medical Journal*, 308: 1125–8.

Phillips, A. and Rakusen, J. (eds) (1989) *The New Bodies Ourselves*. London: Penguin.

Phillips, M.J. (1990) Damaged goods: oral narratives of experience of disability in American culture. *Social Science and Medicine*, 30(8): 849–57.

Pietroni, P. (1991) *The Greening of Medicine*. London: Gollancz.

Pilgrim, D. and Rogers, A. (1993) *A Sociology of Mental Health and Illness*. Buckingham: Open University Press.

Pill, R. and Stott, N.C.H. (1982) Concepts of illness causation and responsibility. *Social Science and Medicine*, 16: 43–52.

Pill, R. and Stott, N.C.H. (1985) Choice or chance: Further evidence on ideas of illness and responsibility for health. *Social Science and Medicine*, 20: 975–83.

Pilling, S. (1991) *Rehabilitation and Community Care*. London: Routledge.

Piore, M. and Sable, C. (1984) *The Second Industrial Divide*. New York: Basic Books.

Plant, M.A. and Plant, M. (1992) *Risk-takers, Alcohol, Drugs, Sex and Youth*. London: Routledge.

Plant, R. (1974) *Community and Ideology: An Essay in Applied Social Philosophy*. London: Routledge and Kegan Paul.

Platt, R. and Kreitman, N. (1984) Unemployment and parasuicide in Edinburgh 1968–1982. *British Medical Journal*, 19: 93–115.

Platt, S.D., Martin, C.J., Hunt, S.M. and Lewis, C.W. (1989) Damp housing, mould growth and symptomatic health state. *British Medical Journal*, 298: 1673–8.

Pleck, J. (1985) *Working Wives, Working Husbands*. Newbury Park, CA: Sage.

Plummer, K. (1995) *Telling Sexual Stories: Power, Change and Social Worlds*. London: Routledge.

Polednak, A. (1990) Mortality from diabetes mellitus, ischaemic heart disease and cerebrovascular disease among blacks in higher income areas. *Public Health Reports*, 105(4): 3939–99.

Popay, J., Bartley, M. and Owen, C. (1993) Gender differences in health: Social position, affective disorders and minor physical morbidity. *Social Science and Medicine*, 36(1): 21–32.

Porter, M. (1990) Professional–client relationships and women's reproductive health care. In S. Cunningham-Burly and N. McKeganey (eds) *Readings in Medical Sociology*. London: Routledge.

Preston, R. (1995) *The Hot Zone*. London: Corgi.

Prior, L. (1991) *The Social Organisation of Mental Illness*. London: Sage.

Privy Council Office (1981) *Government Statistical Services* (Report of the Rayner Review), Cmnd 8236. London: HMSO.

Pruchno, R.A. and Potashnik, S.L. (1989) Caregiving spouses: physical and mental health in perspective. *Journal of Geriatrics Society*, 37: 697–705.

Prusiner S.R. *et al.* (eds) (1996) *Prion Diseases of Humans and Animals*. Horwood: Anderton Ellis.

Pulkingham, J. (1992) Employment restructuring in the health service: efficiency initiative, working patterns and workforce composition. *Work Employment and Society*, 6(3): 397–421.

Radley, A. (1989) Style discourse and constraint in adjustment to chronic illness. *Sociology of Health and Illness*, 11(2): 230–46.

Radley, A. (1994) *Making Sense of Illness*. London: Sage.

Rajaram, S.S. (1997) Experience of hypoglycaemia among insulin dependent diabetics and its impact on the family. *Sociology of Health and Illness*, 19(2): 281–96.

Ranade, W. (1994) *A Future for the NHS? Health Care in the 1990s*. London: Longman.

Ray, L. (1991) The political economy of long-term minor tranquilliser use. In J. Gabe (ed.) *Understanding Tranquilliser Use*. London: Tavistock.

Reed, M. and Hughes, M. (1992) *Rethinking Organisation: New Directions in Theory and Analysis*. London: Sage.

Reid, S. (1987) *Working with Statistics*. Oxford: Polity Press.

Reiser, S. (1978) *Medicine and the Reign of Technology*. Cambridge: Cambridge University Press.

Rice, F. (1992) *The Adolescent: Development, Relationships and Culture*, 7th edn. Boston, MA: Allyn and Bacon.

Riska, E. and Wegar, K. (1995) The medical profession in the Nordic countries: medical uncertainty and gender-based work. In T. Johnson, G. Larkin and M. Saks (eds) *Health Professions in the State of Europe*. London: Routledge.

Roberts, H. (1985) *Women: The Patient Patients*. London: Pandora Press.

Roberts, S. (1993) *Sophi Jex-Blake: A Woman Pioneer in Nineteeth-Century Medical Reform*. London: Routledge.

Robins, J. (1995) *The Miasma: Epidemic and Panic in Nineteenth Century Ireland*. Dunlin: Criterion Press.

Robinson, S. (1989) Caring for child-bearing women: the interrelationship between midwifery and medical responsibilities. In S. Robinson and A.M. Thompson (eds) *Midwives, Research and Childbirth*. London: Chapman and Hall.

Roche, C. (1992) *Rethinking Citizenship: Welfare, Ideology and Change in Modern Society*. Cambridge: Polity Press.

Roper, A., Logan, W. and Tierney, A. (1980) *The Elements of Nursing*. Edinburgh: Edinburgh University Press.

Rose, D. (1995) *Official Social Classifications in the UK. Social Research Update 9*. Guildford: University of Surrey.

Rose, N. (1986) Psychiatry: the discipline and mental health. In P. Miller and N. Rose (eds) *The Power of Psychiatry*. Cambridge: Polity Press.

Rose, N. (1990) *Governing the Soul: The Shaping of the Private Self*. London: Routledge.

Rothman, D. (1991) *Strangers at the Bedside*. New York: Basic Books.

Rowntree, S. (1901) *Poverty: A Study of Town Life*. London: Macmillan.

Royal College of Obstetricians and Gynaecologists (1983) *Report of the Royal College of Obstetricians and Gynaecologists Ethics Committee on In Vitro Fertilisation and Embryo Replacement and Transfer*. London: Royal College of Obstetricians and Gynaecologists.

Russell, B. (1929) *Marriage and Morals*. London: George Allen and Unwin.

Ryan, F. (1996) *Virus X: Understanding the Real Threat of the New Pandemic Plagues*. New York: Harper Collins.

Saks, M. (1995) *Professions and the Public Interest*. London: Routledge.

Salvage, J. (1992) The new nursing: empowering patients or empowering nurses? In J. Robinson, A. Gray and R. Elkan (eds) *Policy Issues in Nursing*. Buckingham: Open University Press.

Samson, C. (1995) The fracturing of medical dominance in British psychiatry. *Sociology of Health and Illness*, 17(2): 244–68.

Savage, M., Barlow, J., Dickens, P. and Fielding, T. (1992) *Property, Bureaucracy and Culture: Middle Class Formation in Contemporary Britain*. London: Routledge.

Scambler, A., Scambler, G. and Craig, D. (1981) Kingship and friendship networks and women's demand for primary care. *Journal of the Royal College of General Practitioners*, 26: 746–50.

Schneider, J.W. and Conrad, P. (1983) *Having Epilepsy: The Experience and Control of Epilepsy*. Philadelphia, PA: Temple University Press.

Scruton, R. (1986) *Sexual Desire, a Philosophical Investigation*. London: Weidenfeld and Nicolson.

Scull, A. (1977) *Decarceration*. NJ: Prentice Hall.

Scull, A. (1993) *The Most Solitary of Afflictions. Madness and Society in Britain 1700–1900*. London: Yale University Press.

Seedhouse, D. (1986) *Health: The Foundations for Achievement*. Chichester: John Wiley.

Sen, A. (1994) *Inequality Re-examined*. Oxford: Clarendon Press.

Shakespeare, T. (1993) Disabled people's self organisation; a new social movement. *Disability and Society*, 8(3): 249–64.

Sharland, E., Seal, H., Croucher, M., Aldgate, J. and Jones, D. (1996) *Professional Intervention in Child Sexual Abuse*. London: HMSO.

Sharma, U. (1992) *Complementary Medicine Today: Practitioners and Patients*. London: Routledge.

Shilling, C. (1991) Educating the body: physical capital and the production of social inequalities. *Sociology*, 25: 653–72.

Shilling, C. (1993) *The Body and Social Theory*. London: Sage.

Sillitoe, K. (1978) *Ethnic Origins, 1, 2 and 3. OPCS Occasional Papers 8, 9 and 10*. London: HMSO.

Sillitoe, K. (1981) *Ethnic Origins, 4. OPCS Occasional Paper 24*. London: HMSO.

Singer, E. (1974) Premature social ageing: the social psychological consequences of a chronic illness. *Social Science and Medicine*, 8: 143–51.

Singer, L. (1993) *Erotic Welfare: Sexual Theory and Politics in the Age of Epidemic*. London: Routledge.

Slattery, M. (1986) *Official Statistics*. London: Tavistock.

Sly, F. (1995) Ethnic groups and the labour market: analysis from the 1994 Labour Force Survey. *Employment Gazette*, June. London: Department of Employment, HMSO.

Smart, C. (1997) Deconstructing motherhood. In E.B. Silva (ed.) *Good Enough Mothering? Feminists Perspectives on Lone Motherhood*. London: Routledge.

Smart, H.L., Mayberry, J.F. and Atkinson, M. (1986) Alternative medical consultation and remedies in patients with irritable bowel syndrome. *Gut*, 27: 826–8.

Smith, T. (1990) Poverty in the 1990s [Editorial]. *British Medical Journal*, 301: 349–50.

Sobel, M.E. (1981) *Lifestyle and Social Science: Concepts, Definitions, Analyses*. New York: Academic Press.

Sontag, S. (1977) *Illness as Metaphor*. New York: Allen Lane.

Sontag, S. (1988) *AIDS and its Metaphors*. Harmondsworth: Penguin.

Spensky, M. (1992) Producers of legitimacy: homes for unmarried mothers in the 1950s. In C. Smart (ed.) *Regulating Womenhood*. London: Routledge.

Stacey, M. (1988) *The Sociology of Health and Healing*. London: Unwin Hyman.

Stainton-Rogers, W. (1991) *Explaining Health and Illness: An Exploration of Diversity*. London: Harvester Wheatsheaf.

Stanworth, M. (ed.) (1987) *Reproduction Technologies: Gender, Motherhood and Medicine*. Cambridge: Polity Press.

Starr, P. (1982) *The Social Transformation of American Medicine*. New York: Basic Books.

Steinberg, D.L. (1990) The depersonalization of women through the administration of in vitro fertilization. In M. McNeil, I. Varco, I. and S. Yearly (eds) *The New Reproductive Technologies*. New York: St Martin's Press.

Stephan, N.L. (1982) *The Idea of Race in Science: Great Britain 1800–1960*. London: Macmillan.

Stephan, N.L. and Gilman, L. (1991) Appropriating the idioms of science: the rejection of scientific racism. In D. LaCapra (ed.) *The Bounds of Race: Perspective on Hegemony and Resistance*. Cornell: Cornell University Press.

Stern, J. (1983) Social Mobility and the interpretation of social class mortality differences. *Journal of Social Policy*, 12: 27–49.

Stevenson, H.M. and Burke, M. (1991) Bureaucratic logic in new social movement clothing: the limits of health promotion research. *Health Promotion International*, 6: 281–9.

Stewart, D.W. and Kamins, M.A. (1993) *Secondary Research: Information Sources and Methods*. London: Sage.

Stimson, G. (1974) Obeying doctors order: a view from the other side. *Social Science and Medicine*, 8(1): 97–104.

Stimson, G. and Webb, B. (1975) *Going to See the Doctor: The Consultation Process in General Practice*. London: Routledge and Kegan Paul.

Stroller, R. (1968) *Sex and Gender*. Chicago: Science House.

Strong, P. (1979) *The Ceremonial Order of the Clinic: Patients, Doctors and Medical Bureaucracies*. London: Routledge and Kegan Paul.

Strong, P. and Robinson, J. (1988) *New Model Management*. Warwick: University of Warwick, Nursing Policy Studies Centre.

Strong, P. and Robinson, J. (1990) *The NHS Under New Management*. Milton Keynes: Open University Press.

Symonds, A. and Hunt, S.C. (1996) *The Midwife and Society: Perspectives, Policies and Practice*. Basingstoke: Macmillan.

Tew, M. (1995) *Safer Childbirth: A Critical History of Maternity Care*. London: Chapman Hall.

The Boston Women's Health Collective (1984) *Our Bodies Ourselves*. New York: Simon Schuster.

The Daily Telegraph (1995) World News. 11 May.

Thompson, L. (1993) Conceptualising gender in marriage: the case of marital care. *Journal of Family and Marriage*, 55: 557–69.

Thompson, M.K. (1989) Hypothesis: old people would benefit from a patient-held standardized primary health record. *Age and Ageing*, 18: 64–6.

Thorogood, N. (1990) Caribbean home remedies and their importance for black women's health in Britain. In P. Abbott and G. Payne (eds) *New Directions in the Sociology of Health*. London: Falmer Press.

Thorogood, N. (1992) What is the relevance of sociology for health promotion. In R. Bunton and G. Macdonald (eds) *Health Promotion: Disciplines and Diversity*. London: Routledge.

Tickle, L. (1996) Mortality trends in the United Kingdom, 1982–1992. *Population Trends*, 86: 21–8.

Tonnies, F. (1957 (1887)) *Community and Association*. Ann Arbor, MI: Michigan University Press.

Tosh, J. (1991) Domesticity and manliness. In M. Roper and J. Tosh (eds) Manful Assertions. London: Routledge.

Townsend, P. (1979) *Poverty in the UK*. Harmondsworth: Penguin.

Townsend, P. (1987) Poor Health. In A. Walker and C. Walker (eds) *The Growing Divide: A Social Audit 1979–1987*. London: CPAG.

Townsend, P. and Davidson, N. (1982) *The Black Report on Inequalities in Health*. Harmondsworth: Penguin.

Townsend, P., Whitehead, M. and Davidson, N. (1992) Introduction. In P. Townsend, M. Whitehead and N. Davidson (eds) *Inequalities in Health: The Black Report*. Harmondsworth: Penguin.

Treacher, A. and Baruch, G. (1981) Towards critical history of the psychiatric profession. In D. Inglebly (ed.) *Critical Psychiatry*. Harmondsworth: Penguin.

Treichler, P.A. (1990) Feminism, medicine and the meaning of childbirth. In J. Jacobs, N. Fox, E. Keller and S. Shuttleworth (eds) *Body/Politic: Women and Discourse of Science*. London: Routledge.

Treweek, G.L. (1996) Emotional work in care assistant work. In V. James and J. Gabe (eds) *Health and the Sociology of the Emotions*. London: Blackwell.

Tuckett, D., Boulton. M., Olson, C. and Williams, A. (1985) *Meetings Between Experts*. London: Tavistock.

Turner, B. (1992) *Regulating Bodies: Essays in Medical Sociology*. London: Routledge.

Turner, B. (1996) *The Body and Society: Explanations in Social Theory*. London: Sage.

Turner, B.S. (1996) *The Body and Society* (2nd edn). London: Sage.

Umberson, D. (1992) Gender, marital status and the social control of health behaviour. *Social Science and Medicine*, 34(2): 907–17.

Umberson, D., Wortman, C.B. and Kessler, R.C. (1992) Widowhood and depression: explaining long-term gender difference in vulnerability. *Journal of Health and Social Behaviour*, 33(1): 10–21.

Ungerson, C. (1987) *Policy is Personal: Sex Gender and Informal Care*. London: Tavistock.

Urry, J. (1990) *The Tourist Gaze: Leisure and Travel in Contemporary Societies*. London: Sage.

Ussher, J. (1991) *Women's Madness: Misogyny or Mental Illness?* London: Harvester Wheatsheaf.

Vågerö, D. (1991) Inequality in health: some theoretical and empirical problems. *Social Science and Medicine*, 32(1): 367–72.

Vågerö, D. and Illsley, R. (1995) Explaining health inequalities: beyond Black and Baker. *European Sociological Review*, 11(3): 219–41.

Vågerö, D. and Leon, D. (1994) Ischaemic heart disease and low birth weight: a test of the fetal-origins hypothesis. *Social Science and Medicine*, 32: 367–72.

van't Hof, S. and Nicolson, M. (1996) The rise and fall of a fact: the increase of anorexia nervosa. *Sociology of Health and Illness*, 18(5): 581–608.

Verbrugge, L.M. (1976) Females and illness: recent trends in sex differences in the United States. *Journal of Health and Illness Behaviour*, 17: 387–403.

Verbrugge, L.M. (1984) How physicians treat mentally distressed men and women. *Social Science and Medicine*, 18(1): 23–8.

Verbrugge, L.M. (1989a) The twine meet: empirical explanations of sex differences in health and mortality. *Journal of Health and Social Behaviour*, 39: 282.

Verbrugge, L.M. (1989b) Multiple roles and physical health of women and men. *Journal of Health and Social Behaviour*, 20: 282–304.

Wadsworth, M.E.J. (1986) Serious illness in childhood and its association with later life achievement. In R.G. Wilkinson (ed.) *Class and Health: Research and Longitudinal Data*. London: Tavistock.

Wadsworth, M.E.J., Butterfield, W.J.H. and Blaney, R. (1971) *Health and Sickness: Research and Longitudinal Data*. London: Tavistock.

Waitzkin, H. (1979) Medicine, superstructure and micropolitics. *Social Science and Medicine*, 13A: 601–9.

Walby, S. (1986) *Patriarchy at Work*. Oxford: Polity Press.

Walby, S. (1990) *Patriarchy and Work*. Oxford: Polity Press.

Walby, S. (1990) *Theorising Patriarchy*. Oxford: Blackwell.

Walby, S., Greenhill, J. and Soothill, K. (1994) *Medicine and Nursing*. London: Sage.

Walker, A. (1989) Community care. In M. McCarthy (ed.) *The New Politics of Welfare*. Basingstoke: Macmillan.

Walkowitz, J. (1982) Male vice and feminist virtue: feminism and the politics of prostitution in nineteenth-century Britain. *History Workshop Journal*, 13: 77–93.

Watkins, S. (1987) *Medicine and Labour*. London: Lawrance and Wishart.

Watney, S. (1988) AIDS 'moral panic' theory and homophobia. In P.P. Aggleton and H. Homans (eds) *Social Aspects of AIDS*. London: Falmer.

Watt, A. and Rodmell, S. (1993) Community involvement in health promotion: progress or panacea? In A. Beattie *et al.* (eds) *Health and Wellbeing: A Reader*. London: Macmillan.

Weiss, M. and Fitzpatrick, R. (1997) Challenges to medicine. *Sociology of Health and Illness*, 19(3): 297–327.

Wellings, K. (1994) *Sexual Behaviour in Britain – The National Survey of Sexual Attitudes and Lifestyles*. Harmondsworth: Penguin.

West, P. (1991) Rethinking the health selection explanation for health inequalities. *Social Science and Medicine*, 32(2): 545–57.

Weston, A. (1992) On the medical self-care and holistic medicine. In D. Leder (ed.) *Medical Thought and Practice*. Dordrecht: Kluwer.

Which? (1989) Which? way to health. *Which*. April.

White, A., Nicolas, G., Foster, K., Browne, F. and Carey, S. (1993) *Health Survey for England*. London: HMSO.

White, P. (1990) A question on ethnic group for the census: findings from the 1989 census test post-enumeration survey. *Population Trends*, 59: 11–20.

Whitehead, M. (1992) *The Health Divide in Inequalities in Health: The Black Report*. Harmondsworth: Penguin.

WHO (1990) Environment and Health: The European Charter and Commentary. *WHO Regional Publications Series 35*. Copenhagen: WHO.

Wilkinson, R.G. (ed.) (1986) *Class and Health: Research and Longitudinal Data*. Tavistock: London.

Wilkinson, R.G. (1992) Income distribution and life. *British Medical Journal*, 304: 165–8.

Wilkinson, R.G. (1996) *Unhealthy Societies: The Afflictions of Inequality*. London: Routledge.

Wilkinson, S. and Kitzinger, C. (1994) Towards a feminist approach to breast cancer. In S. Wilkinson and C. Kitzinger (eds) *Women and Health: Feminist Perspectives*. London: Taylor Francis.

Willcocks, A. (1967) *The Creation of the National Health Service*. London: Routledge and Kegan Paul.

Williams, K. (1980) From Sarah Gamp to Florence Nightingale: a critical study of hospital nursing systems from 1840–1897. In C. Davies (ed.) *Rewriting Nursing History*. London: Croom Helm.

Williams, G. (1993) Chronic illness and the pursuit of virtue in everyday life. In A. Radley (ed.) *Worlds of Illness: Biographical and Cultural Perspectives on Health and Disease*. London: Routledge.

Williams, R. (1990) *A Protestant Legacy: Attitudes to Death and Illness among Older Aberdonians*. Oxford: Oxford University Press.

Williams, R.G.A. (1981) Logical analysis as qualitative method I and II. *Sociology of Health and Illness*, 3: 140–187.

Williams, R.G.A. (1983) Concepts of health: an analysis of lay logic. *Sociology*, 17: 185–205.

Williams, S. and Calnan, M. (1991) Key determinants of consumer satisfaction with general practice. *Family Practice*, 8(3): 237–42.

Wilson, E. (1975) *Sociobiology: The New Synthesis*. London: Tavistock.

Wing, J.K. (1962) Institutionalism in mental hospitals. *British Journal of Social and Clinical Psychology*, 1: 38–51.

Winkler, F. (1987) Consumerism in health care: beyond the supermarket model. *Policy and Politics*, 15: 1.

Winn, S. and Skelton, R. (1992) HIV in the UK: Problem of prevalence, sociological response and health education. *Social Science and Medicine*, 34(6): 697–702.

Winnicott, D. (1957, 1971) *The Child, the Family and the Outside World*. Harmondsworth: Penguin.

Witz, A. (1992) *Professions and Patriarchy*. London: Routledge.

Wood, R. (1997) Trends in multiple births. *Population Trends*, 87: 29–35.

World Health Organization (1948) *Constitution*. Geneva: WHO.

World Health Organization (1980) *International Classification of Impairments, Disabilities and Handicaps*. Geneva: WHO.

Wyke, S. and Ford, G. (1992) Competing explanations for associations between marital status and health. *Social Science and Health*, 34: 523–32.

Young, R. (1994) Egypt in America. In A. Rattansi and S. Westwood (eds) *Racism, Modernity and Identity on the Western Front*. Cambridge: Polity Press.

Zick, C.D. and Smith, K.R. (1991) Marital transitions, poverty and gender differences in mortality. *Journal of Marriage and the Family*, 53: 327–36.

Zola, I.K. (1972) Medicine as an institution of social control. *Sociological Review*, 20: 287–503.

Zola, I.K. (1973) Pathways to the doctor: from person to patient. *Social Science and Medicine*, 7: 677–89.

Zola, I.K. (1983) *Socio-Medical Inquiries: Reflections and Reconsiderations*. Philadelphia, PA: Temple University Press.

Index